Overview

Contents

Ellen Isaacs, Interaction Designer
Alan Walendowski, Software Engineer

DESIGNING

from both sides of the screen

New Riders

201 West 103rd Street,
Indianapolis, Indiana 46290

How Designers and Engineers
Can Collaborate to Build
Cooperative Technology

International Standard Book Number: 0-672-32151-3

Library of Congress Catalog Card Number: 2001089584

Printed in the United States of America

First Printing: December 2001

04   03   02   01   4   3   2   1

Trademarks

Warning and Disclaimer

Associate Publisher
Jeff Koch

Executive Editor
Steve Weiss

Acquisitions Editor
William E. Brown

Development Editor
Heather Goodell

Managing Editor
Matt Purcell

Project Editor
Christina Smith

Production Editor
Matt Wynalda

Indexer
Ken Johnson

Proofreader
Andrea Dugan
Linda Seifert

Technical Reviewers
Eric Berglund
Maxine Cohen
George Drapeau
Robin Jeffries
Robert Lockstone
Trevor Morris
Diane Schiano

Team Coordinator
Denni Bannister

Interior Designer
Gary Adair

Cover Designer
Aren Howell

Page Layout
Gloria Schurick

THE PROCESS

APPENDIXES

About the Authors

Ellen Isaacs is a technology design leader at AT&T Labs. She has been designing user interfaces for over 12 years at such companies as Sun Microsystems, Excite@Home, and Electric Communities, where she worked on systems for Palm PDAs, the Web, Windows, and OpenWindows. Active in the human-computer interaction community, Ellen has designed and studied the use of innovative applications that help people communicate, collaborate, and manage their information. She has a Ph.D. in cognitive psychology from Stanford University. Ellen can be reached at ellen@uidesigns.com.

Alan Walendowski is a software engineer at AT&T Labs. He has been writing software for 15 years, working for companies such as Sun Microsystems, 3dfx, IBM, and ComputerVision. A "general purpose" programmer, he has developed device drivers, graphics engines, distributed systems, and user interfaces on various platforms, including PalmOS, Solaris, Linux, and Windows. Alan has a bachelor's degree in computer science from Boston University. He can be reached at alan@uidesigns.com.

The authors have developed a Web site to continue the discussion started in this book. Please visit www.uidesigns.com to contribute your comments and questions.

Acknowledgments

Writing a book is almost as hard as designing cooperative technology. The process is quite similar: You need to understand your audience, develop a solid structure before you write, and iterate based on lots of feedback. We are very grateful to the following people for helping us with each of those stages.

It is quite a substantial task to review a book, and yet seven very busy people whose judgment we greatly respect were kind enough to read this book and give us their comments on everything from fine details to broad structural issues. Diane Schiano (human-computer interaction researcher) helped us with the big picture; her comments greatly improved the organization and tone of the book. Robin Jeffries (a leader in the UI design field) kept us honest with our claims about user interfaces and helped us refine our advice. Trevor Morris (senior software architect) validated our engineering claims and reminded us to be as frugal with words as we are with clicks. Robert Lockstone (software engineer) took our advice about flow to heart and told us when his flow was broken for any reason. As a Hubbub user, he also gave us lots of just-in-time feedback through IM as we revised the book. Eric Berglund (information technology director) paid special attention to the structure, tone, and validity of our claims, and couldn't keep himself from copyediting as well. George Drapeau (engineering manager) gave us astute comments, especially about project management issues. Maxine Cohen (associate professor teaching human-computer interaction) picked up on many confusing passages and helped us make the book accessible to a wider audience. We thank all of our reviewers for greatly improving the quality of this book. Thanks also to Leysia Palen for her expert input on calendar design.

We are also extremely grateful to those who helped us with the Hubbub project, which gave us so much of the material for this book. Thanks most of all to Dipti Ranganathan, the third member of our team who was not only gracious but also enthusiastic about iterating, polishing, and refining the user interface, even when it meant doing grunt work. She willingly allowed us to discuss her work on the project, and put up with comments such as, "What's a Dipti?" Robert Terek wrote the Hubbub Web site and was patient about making changes to improve its usability; he also taught us a great deal about database back ends. We received extensive help from Candace Kamm, with whom we became friends through Hubbub. She was not only an enthusiastic user, but she also actively promoted Hubbub, helped us debug problems, supported users on the East Coast, and acted as a thoughtful sounding board for our ideas—we consider her a member of the team. Ronald Brachman, our director, was also a stalwart Hubbub user and supporter, and we thank him for giving us the time and freedom to build it the way we believed was best. Thanks to Jonathan Helfman for giving especially insightful feedback and for writing a Palm-based sound design tool. We thank Melanie West and Mike Zalot for helping us design the sounds, and Dave Kormann for supporting the server in New Jersey for us. We are especially grateful to all those who participated in the Hubbub usage study for being willing to use very early software, allowing us to poke and prod them on a regular basis, and volunteering so much helpful feedback throughout the project. Hubbub would not be the same without them. A few people who started using Hubbub after it was released have also made some excellent suggestions and we thank them as well.

Over the years, there have been many people who have shaped our thinking about design, engineering, and how engineers and designers can work together. For sharing their wisdom, we thank Reuben Antman, Marney Beard, Eric Berglund, Eric Bergman, Maria Capucciati, Lynn Cherny, Joseph Dipol, George Drapeau, Tony Fang, Gordie Freedman, David Frohlich, Donald Gentner, Alan Greenblatt, Susan Gorbet, Anthony Grant, Sally Grisedale, Jonathan Grudin, Chet Haase, Robin Jeffries, Rick Levenson, Andrea Mankoski, Joanie McCollom, Mark Miller, Trevor Morris, Kevin Mullet, Bonnie Nardi, Russell Pflughaupt, Heidi Ramirez, Dipti Ranganathan, Thomas Rodriguez, Monica Rua, Patricia Russo, Darrell Sano, Diane Schiano, Michael Slominski, W. Dean Stanton, Noi Sukaviriya, John Sullivan, John Tang, Robert Terek, and Steve Whittaker.

This book took an unconventional route toward publication, and we're very grateful to the people at Sams and New Riders who shepherded us through. William Brown found us and was willing to take a chance on us and we appreciate his open and frequent communication throughout the process. Heather Goodell gave astute comments throughout the process, and we relied on her to "sanity check" our ideas. We especially thank William and Heather for being so patient and supportive whenever we asked to modify the process to suit our needs. Matt Wynalda's top-notch copyediting greatly smoothed the flow of the text, Gary Adair did a wonderful job with the interior design, and we're very pleased with the cover designed by Aren Howell. We appreciate the hard work of Christina Smith, who kept the process moving and made sure all the elements fell into place. And thanks to Steve Weiss and Kathy Malmloff for their help with naming, marketing, and promoting the book.

Being so concerned with design, collaboration, and iteration, we made many special requests to modify the established publishing process. To everyone at Sams and New Riders who worked on this book, we deeply appreciate how graciously you accommodated our requests.

Finally, we would like to thank our parents, Stan and Natalie Isaacs and Lillian Parisi, for supporting and encouraging us, and for teaching us to believe in ourselves. And thanks to Libby for being Libby.

A Message from New Riders

As the reader of this book, you are our most important critic and commentator. We value your opinion and want to know what we're doing right, what we could do better, in what areas you'd like to see us publish, and any other words of wisdom you're willing to pass our way.

As executive editor at New Riders, I welcome your comments. You can fax, e-mail, or write me directly to let me know what you did or didn't like about this book— as well as what we can do to make our books better. When you write, please be sure to include this book's title, ISBN, and author, as well as your name and phone or fax number. I will carefully review your comments and share them with the authors and editors who worked on the book.

Please note that I cannot help you with technical problems related to the topic of this book, and that due to the high volume of e-mail I receive, I might not be able to reply to every message. Thanks.

E-mail: steve.weiss@newriders.com

Mail: Steve Weiss
         Executive Editor
         New Riders Publishing
         201 West 103rd Street
         Indianapolis, IN 46290 USA

Visit Our Web Site: www.newriders.com

On our Web site, you'll find information about our other books, the authors we partner with, book updates and file downloads, promotions, discussion boards for online interaction with other users and with technology experts, and a calendar of trade shows and other professional events with which we'll be involved. We hope to see you around.

E-mail Us from Our Web Site

Go to www.newriders.com and click on the Contact Us link if you

- Have comments or questions about this book.
- Want to report errors that you have found in this book.
- Have a book proposal or are interested in writing for New Riders.
- Would like us to send you one of our author kits.
- Are an expert in a computer topic or technology and are interested in being a reviewer or technical editor.
- Want to find a distributor for our titles in your area.
- Are an educator/instructor who wants to preview New Riders books for classroom use. In the body/comments area, include your name, school, department, address, phone number, office days/hours, text currently in use, and enrollment in your department, along with your request for either desk/examination copies or additional information.

Preface

April 29, 1991: "I Can't Work This Thing," Bruce Nussbaum & Robert Neff, *Business Week*

Every day, across America, millions of managers, bankers, doctors, teachers, chief executives, and otherwise highly competent men and women are driven to helpless frustration by the products around them. In their offices, once-familiar telephones and copiers have suddenly turned silent saboteurs, while new systems that were supposed to make work more efficient—computers, faxes, electronic mail—often do just the reverse....

Enough! The great revolution in electronic products that promised so much—speed, efficiency, and, yes, fun—is not delivering. Office productivity isn't going up. Listening to music has been replaced by "programming." And VCRs? They're so painful to use that there are jokes about them: How do you know if a family has a teenager living at home? The clock on the VCR isn't flashing.

April, 1993: "Fighting Fatware," Ed Perratore, Tom Thompson, Jon Udell, & Rich Malloy, *BYTE Magazine*

Like the carnivorous plant in the movie *Little Shop of Horrors*, today's popular applications software cries out to users, "Feed me!" More RAM, more hard disk space, more CPU speed—it seems like you never have enough.... Many users have reported that flabware impairs usability, and vendors are beginning to agree. "If you just have a lot of features and you're not focused on usability," says Betsy Fortin, director of graphics-products marketing at Lotus, "you have what I call a 'bag of tools.' And the more tools you have, the harder it is to pick out which one to use."

December 29, 1997: "What Detroit Can Teach Silicon Valley," Patrick L. Anderson, *Wall Street Journal*

Almost any adult can step into any car sold today and competently drive it across the state. By contrast, most adults—even sophisticated, computer-literate folks—are frequently baffled by their PCs, and are made to feel stupid by the attendant technobabble. It's no coincidence that the most popular PC books go by names like, "Windows for Dummies." Detroit doesn't sell books like "Oldsmobiles for Idiots" or "A Foul-Up's Guide to Fords."

May 28, 1998: "Do Computers Have to Be Hard to Use?" Katie Hafner, *New York Times*

Bill Gates, the chairman of Microsoft, once said that if automobile manufacturers had kept up with technology as well as the computer industry had, people would all be driving $27 cars. E-mail boxes throughout cyberspace quickly filled with whimsy, including a statement attributed to an auto maker: "Yes, but would you want your car to crash twice a day?" And how would a car function if it were modeled after a computer? "Occasionally, executing a maneuver would cause your car to stop and fail and you would have to re-install the engine," and the airbag system would say, "Are you sure?" before going off.

September, 1998: "Opaque Transparency," Wendy M. Grossman, *Scientific American*

If the frustrations of all the world's computer users were brought together, the resulting explosion would make the big bang look like a Roman candle. This is true even though computers have come a long way in the decade since the industry pronounced "usability" a necessity.

October 28, 1999: "Using a PC Got Harder, but New Age Is Dawning," Walter Mossberg, *Wall Street Journal*

This personal column was launched in October 1991 with the intent of looking at personal computers and other consumer technologies from the point of view of the average, nontechnical user. These folks aren't afraid of computers. They're just frustrated with them. And they aren't dumb. They just have little interest in learning the technical details of the computer or the Internet just to use PCs and the Web or e-mail.

Every October since, I've tried to review the computer industry's progress—or lack thereof—in keeping its many promises to make its products easier, simpler and more reliable for these casual users. This year, I think things actually went backwards. Complications, in general, mounted. Few, if any, advances were made in reducing complexity, and reliability seems to have declined.

January 15, 2001: "High-Tech Overload," by James Lardner, David LaGesse, and Janet Rae-Dupree, *U.S. News and World Report*

Complex gizmos are driving Americans nuts. The message to manufacturers: Simplicity sells.... [W]ith the technology industry enduring its first bear market since gadgets became the hot new things, many companies are scrambling to find out why consumers aren't falling in love with the latest stuff. The answer? Most folks are still trying to figure out how to work the devices they already have.

Introduction

Suppose a friend were to ask if you would prefer chocolate or strawberry ice cream for dessert. You might say, "I'd like chocolate, thank you." Suppose your friend then said, "Sorry, we don't have any chocolate." That would be rude, right?

How about this: A friend walks by your desk at home, and you ask her to bring you a photo of your dog Sheba at the beach from the upper-right drawer of the desk. She brings it to you. A few minutes later, you point to your desk and say, "Would you mind getting me that other picture of Sheba?" She asks you, "Which drawer is it in?" She would seem a little slow, right?

Another one: Your administrative assistant puts some paperwork for you to sign on top of a pile of documents on your desk. You don't notice the paperwork until a few days later. You ask your assistant to please put time-sensitive documents on your chair so you'll see them. The next day, he leaves an important document on the pile of papers, and again it sits there for days. You remind your assistant. He does it a third time and then a fourth. You figure he's either incompetent or hostile, right?

Or what if you ask your daughter to grab you a soda from the fridge. She looks at you blankly for a few seconds and then leaves the room without acknowledging the request. Even if she later comes back with the soda, she would seem antagonistic, right?

These are all examples of uncooperative behavior. If a friend treated us this way on a regular basis, we would probably "forget" to return her calls. But computers commonly treat people this way, and most people accept it as normal behavior, sometimes even blaming themselves. On a regular basis, computers offer us options that they later tell us they can't provide. If we ask a computer to open a file, many applications ask if it's in a "default folder" of their choosing, rather than the folder where we opened the last file a minute ago. Every day, windows pop up on our computers and block our current work, so we move them to a better location, only to have to move them again next time, no matter how many times we've done it before. Frequently, computers give us no feedback about their activity after we ask them to do something, leaving us to wonder if they understood or if we should try again. There are hundreds of ways that computers treat us in ways we would consider uncooperative if they were people.

In this book we argue that those who are designing, building, or managing the development of technology should teach their products to follow the same basic rules of cooperation that people use with each other. We think technology should be much nicer to people. We describe some specific rules people follow when they're in a healthy, cooperative relationship, and we explain how technology can be designed to play by those same rules. But since building technology isn't just a matter of following a list of "do's" and "don'ts," we also walk through the process of building a real software application, illustrating what we did and why. Since there are two of us—a designer and an engineer—our goal was to build something that is usable and useful as well as robust, reliable, responsive, and easy to maintain. You even get to decide whether we succeeded. The software we built is available for you to use and evaluate from www.HubbubMe.com.

Who We Are

So who are we? One of us (Ellen) is an interaction designer and the other (Alan) a software engineer. Both of us have worked in the software industry for about 15 years, designing and building traditional installed software, Web-based applications, and applications for the Palm handheld device. Ellen has been building software using a user-centered design process and cares deeply about making technology easy to use. She does not write code (although she learned some Pascal in college and taught herself a little Web scripting), but she generally understands the architectures of the systems she designs and has a good sense of what's hard and easy to do in software. Alan is at heart a Unix hacker who tends to think of applications in terms of architecture and internal functionality, with the user interface merely providing access to those features. His main goal is to write software that doesn't break, performs well, and is easy to maintain, and he is always surprised and a little annoyed by how much time and effort it takes to build a good user interface.

We decided to write this book together because we wanted to demonstrate what it takes for people from these two perspectives to work together to create high quality technology that cooperates with people.

Who You Are

This book is likely to be of interest to several types of people who are involved in the processes of producing technology:

It is intended for *software engineers* who want to improve the usability of their work—or who are told they must—but are not sure how to go about it. We expect it to appeal especially to *application developers* and *user interface toolkit developers*. Some of these engineers may have to design the user interface of the software they will build, and want guidance. Others may work with a user interface designer and want to understand how designers work and what their concerns are.

This book is also for those involved or interested in the user interface design and testing process: *interaction designers* (also called user interface or UI designers) who want to improve their designs and learn to work more effectively with engineers; *graphic designers* (also called visual designers) who want to learn about the structure and behavior of user interfaces and how they relate to the visual design; and *usability testing specialists* (or usability engineers) who want to learn about the design process and how to conduct a usage study.

We expect that this book will be useful to *software engineering managers* and *design managers* who want to produce better products that people want to use and that don't require major overhauls from one release to the next because of customer complaints. We think this book may also be helpful to *marketing or product managers* who want to understand why the products they sell often are so difficult to use and how they might produce better products. *Technical writers* may also find this book of interest, especially if they would like to understand more about the design process and about collaborating with engineers.

What This Book Covers

There are many good software development books that explain best practices in engineering good software. We especially recommend *Rapid Development,* by Steve McConnell, and *Debugging the Development Process,* by Steve Maguire. But few software engineering books provide more than a cursory explanation of user interface design or show how to integrate it into the development process. There are also some excellent books on user interface design that provide hundreds of guidelines about what to do and not do in specific situations. We recommend Jeff Johnson's *GUI Bloopers* on software applications; Steve Krug's *Don't Make Me Think* and Jakob Nielsen's *Designing Web Usability* on Web design; and Eric Bergman's *Information Appliances and Beyond* on embedded devices. (See Appendix B, "Recommended Readings," for other books.) But few of these books address the implications of their design recommendations on engineering concerns. Both engineering and design books explain what's best to do from their own perspective, but few discuss the tradeoffs between them, which is where many hard decisions arise. Also, no other book that we know of brings to life the process by which a real interface was designed, built, studied, and repeatedly tested to create a usable piece of technology. This book is meant to supplement those other software engineering and user interface design books by describing that process and explaining how to make those tradeoffs.

This book assumes that you are willing to accept that technology should be easier to use. If you are looking for the argument for more usable software, we refer you to Alan Cooper's *The Inmates Are Running the Asylum* or Don Norman's *The Design of Everyday Things*. However, if you generally believe technology should be easier to use but you're not sure that you can justify the effort needed to make it easy to use, this book might change your mind. We do not have studies comparing the effort against the gain, but we do show how you can create more usable software without increasing effort. This is not magic. The tradeoff, you will see, is in doing fewer features but doing them well. We discuss why this is a better approach, and explain how you can choose which features to build.

Part I: The Goal

In the first section of this book, we describe the *goal* you're trying to achieve. We introduce the idea of technology that cooperates with people, laying out the guidelines of the Cooperative Principle for Technology. We illustrate the Cooperative Principle by showing examples of good and bad designs from many sources, including computer applications, Web sites, handheld computers, cameras, TVs, photocopiers, GPS devices, cell phones, phone menu systems, voice command systems, and more. We draw from many types of devices to show how our approach applies to the design of any type of technology, including new ones that haven't been invented yet. We want you to be able to recognize the attributes of a good, cooperative interface.

Part II: The Process

In the second section, we demonstrate the *process* of building technology that treats people well. As we walk through the process, we describe in detail how we built a real application called Hubbub, providing many examples that show how we applied the principles in the first section during each stage in the process. We've chosen to describe a real example from start to finish, rather than providing idealized examples, so that we can characterize the many complex decisions and subtle issues that arise in practice. We have found that the quality of technology is determined by how you handle those many complex tradeoffs along the way—tradeoffs between design rules as much as tradeoffs between design and engineering concerns. Even if you've read other interface design books describing the user experience you're trying to achieve, it isn't always clear how to create that experience when there are many other legitimate objectives in play. In this book, we try to show how to balance engineering and design tradeoffs in a realistic scenario. The danger in our approach is that we will be driven too much by the idiosyncrasies of this one application, so we try to start with the general principles that apply across projects and then use Hubbub to illustrate.

Before we begin showing how to build more cooperative technology, we define what we mean by cooperating…

THE GOAL

CHAPTER 1

On Being a Butler

Think about something you love to do, and think how you feel when you're very focused on it. Maybe you love to play tennis, take photographs, play the guitar, ride motorcycles—whatever it might be. When you're immersed in that activity, you get a sense of *flow* where each action comes naturally from the last, you're focused on your goal (or on nothing at all), and you're not aware of the mechanics of what you're doing. Then suddenly something goes wrong with one of your tools. Your shoelace comes untied, the camera starts taking half a second longer to autofocus, a guitar string goes out of tune, the throttle sticks for a fraction of a second just when you want to speed up, and so on. These are all small bumps and "bobbles," and they're easy enough to compensate for. But they're annoying because they get in the way of what you care about. They break your flow.[1]

If these small problems keep happening, you try to fix the cause, annoyed that you have to spend your time fixing your tools. And if these flaws keep breaking your flow, eventually you get another tool. It's as if you grant your tools a certain amount of points, or "tolerance capital," based on how much you value the features they provide. Each time your tool breaks your flow, its capital declines. If the difficulty of using something starts to outweigh its value, you stop using it (unless you're forced to use it, say for your job). Unfortunately for most people,

---

[1] Mihaly Csikszentmihalyi writes extensively about the concept of flow, for example in his 1991 book *Flow: The Psychology of Optimal Experience*.

much of the computer technology in our lives hovers just above the break-even point, leaving us in a love-hate relationship. Yes, technology lets us do things we couldn't do before, but we often don't enjoy using it and we usually end up feeling more frustrated than pleased with the result.

Why does this happen? Most people who build technology want to build quality products and they want people to enjoy using them. We believe the main problem is that the technology industry is set up to compete in terms of the number of features, not the usefulness of products. The development team makes a list of features, marketers list those features on the promotion materials, and product reviewers make matrices comparing the number of features across competing products. In this world, more features is better than fewer features. Sometimes, a product will list "Easy to Use" as a feature, but since there are no criteria for such a claim (having a graphical user interface or a Web interface is apparently enough to qualify), just saying it's true doesn't help you compete.

Meanwhile, the mass media and trade publications have been complaining for years that technology is so complicated that people can't use it. This book's Preface includes excerpts from such articles going back to 1991, when *Business Week* ran a cover story titled, "I Can't Work This Thing." Ten years later, with many similar articles in between, *U.S. News and World Report* took on the same problem in its cover story, "High-Tech Overload." All these articles complained about the same thing—too many features and not enough focus on usability. Reducing features may seem risky, but there is evidence that people will be loyal to and spread the word about usable technology, converting their friends who complain about their annoying technology. Alan Cooper makes this case about Apple, whose loyal fans ardently stuck by it, even as the company charged higher prices for a platform that had fewer applications. Prior to the debut of the Palm Pilot, there had been many attempts to market a handheld organizer device using handwriting recognition, all of which failed with great fanfare (for instance, Go, Apple's Newton). Now the Palm is widely recognized as one of the most useful and best-designed technology products available. Walter Mossberg, the influential and respected technology columnist for the *Wall Street Journal*, raves about the Palm, saying it has a "brilliant user interface."

"This is so cool! I'm flying this thing completely on my Palm pilot!"

Wouldn't it be nice if people using your technology said as many nice things about it as they say about the Palm? You can make this happen by paying attention to the user's flow and doing everything you can to remove those small bobbles along the way. Making a feature flow is just as important as implementing the feature itself. Since most projects are organized by listing features and checking them off when they are done, you can work within this system by creating a concept of "ease-of-use features," which are features that remove the bobbles in other features. A feature isn't done until its associated ease-of-use features are done. Before starting a project, the engineers, designers, marketers, and management have to decide whether they are willing to devote time and energy to ease-of-use features instead of "check off" features that most people won't use. You have to decide whether you want to build something people really want to use rather than something people will buy once and complain about.

It's the Relationship, Stupid

Okay, let's assume you're committed to building something useful and usable. Now what? The first thing to do is realize that when you're building technology, you're not just building a tool with features. You're building something that has a relationship with its users. Your tool reacts to people; it changes what it does depending on what they do. It offers to do things for people, and even asks how they would like them done. It asks people for information so it can do its job better. Sometimes it makes mistakes and tries to explain what went wrong. Meanwhile, people learn what your technology can do and how to ask for things. They change their behavior based on the responses they get. Sometimes they are delighted with it, sometimes they become frustrated with it. Sounds like a relationship.

Okay, it's not a deep relationship, and it's definitely not an equal one. Your technology is supposed to do things for people, not the other way around. But a relationship it is, and that means that people bring to it a rich set of expectations about appropriate behavior. The more you understand those expectations, the more pleasant you can make that relationship.

A good model for the type of relationship we're talking about is the one that exists between a butler and his employer. Not that either of us has any direct experience with butlers, but we've seen enough movies to form a healthy stereotype. A movie butler is always available, and when asked to do something, he is prepared to do it, with few questions and no complaints. If there is a problem, he finds a way to fix it or work around it without bothering the employer. (Also, he has an English accent.) Since he doesn't want to disturb his employer, he rarely interrupts to suggest ways he can be helpful. Instead, he pays attention to what his employer has done in the past so that he can better anticipate what she will want in the future. Still, he doesn't go overboard in anticipating her needs because he knows it is more costly to do something the employer did not want than it is to refrain from taking the initiative. Realizing his demeanor is as important as his competence, he makes a special effort to be courteous and respectful, even when she asks for things he cannot do.

In the meantime, the employer observes what the butler can do and what he does well. She doesn't ask the butler to tell her how to make requests; that would be awkward. Picking up on his feedback, she gradually learns that she gets better results if she asks one way rather than another. Over time, if they have a good relationship, they learn to work together without noticing the interaction. They learn to collaborate.

Your goal in building technology is to teach it how to behave like a movie butler. To do that, you have to teach it how to collaborate.

How to Collaborate

All social activities have certain conventions for appropriate behavior. When we have a conversation, dance, play in a band, drive, build a house, share a meal, and so on, we follow conventions. Usually they are unspoken, and sometimes they are arbitrary, but they let you know what you can expect of others so you can work together more effectively. You can think of them as rules of polite behavior: While driving, signal when you want to change lanes. Applaud at the end of a play. Raise your hand when you want to speak. Collaborating is all about adopting these conventions so you can focus on the more interesting aspects of the activity.

For decades, social scientists have been studying collaborative behavior, particularly as it relates to conversation. We use some of their observations in drawing up our own rules about how technology should cooperate with people. There are two types of politeness: negative politeness and positive politeness. To be negatively polite one should do no harm; don't ask too much of people, don't impose, don't offend. How does technology impose? It asks people to put in lots of effort for a small benefit. It overwhelms people with too many options so they can't find what they want. It asks people to keep track of too many things. At a minimum, you want your technology to be negatively polite so it's not seen as rude. This in itself is a challenge and most technology doesn't accomplish it, so just getting that far can make your technology stand out from your competition.

If you want to delight your users, you can design it to be "positively polite" by actively cooperating. It's difficult to list all the ways you can cooperate, but back in 1967, a linguist named Paul Grice came up with what he called the Cooperative Principle for Conversation, which we use as our guide. It consists of four rules, called Quantity, Quality, Relevance, and Manner. The Quantity Rule says you should offer just the right information for the circumstances, not too much and not too little. For example, suppose you ask a shop clerk, "Do you take personal checks?" It is more polite to respond, "I'm sorry, no, but we take credit cards, debit cards, and cash" than it is to say just, "I'm sorry, no." The first answer is better because it addresses your goal of paying for something, probably using something other than cash, and offers reasonable alternatives. But you also don't want to offer too much information. If you stopped to ask someone directions, and that person told you every street you would cross and every landmark you would pass along your way, they would make it too hard for you to remember the important information and you would consider them uncooperative.

The Quality Rule basically says, "Don't lie or blatantly mislead." Enough said. The Relevance Rule addresses expectations that are raised by choosing to give certain pieces of information over others. If I mentioned that my printer is out of paper and you said, "There's a supply cabinet around the corner," by the Relevance Rule, I would take you to believe that paper is stored in that cabinet. If I found out that you knew there was no paper in the cabinet, I would figure you were playing a joke on me or just being mean. Finally, the Manner Rule says to be clear, that is, to say things in a way that the other person can understand.

We've taken these ideas and converted them into a set of rules for building cooperative technology:

The Cooperative Principle for Technology

- **Don't impose** (negative politeness)
  - Respect the user's physical effort
  - Respect the user's mental effort

- **Be helpful** (positive politeness)
  - Offer sufficient information early and in context; prevent errors (Quantity)
  - Solve problems; don't complain or pass the buck (Quantity)
  - Be predictable (Quality)
  - Request and offer only relevant information; don't mislead (Relevance)
  - Explain in plain language (Manner)

We do not offer these rules just for the sake of politeness. The rules are useful because they allow you to forget about the mechanics of the interaction and instead focus on the interesting stuff—the activity you came for. If your technology enables people to rotate complex figures in 3D, you want them thinking about how their object looks from the top, not how to get it to rotate. If you enable people to send messages through a small, handheld device, you want them thinking about the conversation, not how to enter text. If your technology enables people to see where they are on a map, they should be focusing on the destination, not how to get the map to zoom out. By following rules of cooperation, you help people focus on their task.

In the next three chapters, we show how to apply the Cooperative Principle for Technology. We break down the rules into further guidelines, giving positive and negative examples from a broad range of technologies. We hope to help you develop the mindset needed to build cooperative technology, regardless of whether it's traditional PC software or the latest "information appliance." Then we'll move on to show you how to apply that mentality in the day-to-day process of building technology.

CHAPTER 2

Don't Impose: Respect Physical Effort

You may wonder why we would start out by worrying about physical effort. How hard is it to click a mouse, press a key, push a button, or tap a screen? For most people, not very. But we're not worried about wearing out people's muscles. Instead, we're asking you to think of physical effort as a measure of the effort required to use your technology. The more you ask people to click, type, or tap to accomplish the same task, the more you're imposing on them. Each click represents another step in the process, and after a short while, those steps add up so that using your technology feels burdensome rather than pleasant. It's best to think of your customers' physical effort as a limited commodity to be carefully conserved.

Unfortunately, much of our technology requires so much clicking, you'd think technology developers were getting paid by the number of clicks per session. The positive side of this is that it's relatively easy for you to distinguish your product by removing clicks. The single best thing you can do to distinguish your technology from the rest is to completely shift your attitude about making the user click. In other words, treat clicks as sacred.

Treat Clicks as Sacred

We use the term "click" as a shortcut to refer to any type of user input, including keyboard presses, taps on a touch screen, button presses on a physical device, and voice commands in a speech system. Every one of these is precious and should be asked for cautiously.

Earlier, we raved about the Palm Personal Digital Assistant (PDA) as one of the easiest to use devices on the market. What makes it so good? Consider this quote from Rob Haitani, a product manager who worked on the design of the original Palm applications, from an interview in Eric Bergman's *Information Appliances and Beyond*:

> Well, someone would say, "That's just one more tap," or "That would only take another second." I would respond that it is analogous to the way you organize your desk in your office, your physical desk, in that you have some things on top of your desk and you have some things in drawers or file cabinets. Why is that? Well, if you look at the things on top of your desk, those are the things you use very frequently and they need to be easily within your grasp; whereas things in your drawer you don't use as frequently. So I would say, imagine taking something you use all the time like your mouse or the phone and put it in a drawer. It's just one extra step to pull it out. It just takes a second. But if you use it that frequently, the cumulative effect of that one extra step is excruciatingly annoying. On the other hand, one more tap does not matter for features you use infrequently.

Later in the interview he said

> I say if you only read one book to understand handheld user interface, it should be Strunk and White's *Elements of Style*. It's a classic college reference book that...talks about how to edit extraneous words. The gist is that the fewer words you can communicate the same sentence in, the more powerful your writing is. For example, if you clean up a sentence that's in passive voice and it's 14 words, and restate it in 9 words, it's a much stronger sentence. It's very easy to be verbose, as I'm doing now just babbling on. It's easier to write a 20-page paper than it is to write a 5-page paper because it doesn't require any discipline. UI design is like an editing process—you start with a screen and one by one start ripping things out. But the key is you still have to communicate that point—you don't want to throw that out.

This is a powerful concept. The more you eliminate while keeping the essence of a feature, the better your design. Every click you remove improves the feature, saves people time and effort, and makes your technology more pleasant to use. (Haitani also talks about making tradeoffs in favor of frequently used features, which we discuss later.)

This conservative philosophy shows in the Palm software. For example, to start the Address Book you tap one button—the hardware Address Book button that also turns on the device. There's no booting up or waiting for the application to load. On the main screen, there is a single button: New. That's all you need to get started creating contacts (see Figure 2.1). To view an existing contact, you tap it. That's it: two taps to view a contact—one to turn on the Palm and one to tap the name. Even if that contact is scrolled below the screen, you can write the first letter of the name and the display scrolls down to the first person with that name. (You don't have to tap the Look Up field first; it's the only field that accepts text entry so any text is assumed to apply to that field, saving a tap.) Also, the main screen shows the phone number for each person, so if you're looking up someone's phone number, you don't even need to tap their name, you just look at their entry. So really, looking up a phone number requires just one or two clicks, one to turn on the Palm and possibly one more to enter a letter.

2.1

Palm's Address Book main screen. The user has typed a T and the screen has scrolled down to the first entry beginning with T.

In most PC-based address book applications, looking up a person's phone number takes far more clicks, even assuming the computer is already on. Here are the steps it would take:

Action	Clicks
Double-click to start up the application (which usually takes several seconds)	1
One click to open a menu and another to choose Find	2

Action	Clicks
One click to enter the name of the person, after switching from the mouse to the keyboard (which we count as a half-click)	1.5
One click to press the Enter key to initiate the Find, plus a half-click to go back to the mouse	1.5
Double-click to open that person's entry, where we'll assume their phone number is easily visible, although that may be a generous assumption	1
Total	**7**

Seven clicks versus two. Clearly, Palm cares about clicks.

Even technology critics worry about clicks. Walter Mossberg frequently dings products for requiring extra steps. In his February 22, 2001 *Wall Street Journal* column evaluating Personal Video Recorders (PVRs), for example, he praised UltimateTV's remote because it "has a button that takes you right to a list of your recorded shows. With TiVo, you have to first go through a menu." On TiVo, it takes two clicks to get to the list of recorded shows; on UltimateTV it takes one, but since this is such a common task, Mossberg noted it in his column.

Design Guideline

Agonize over every click you ask of your user. Every click you remove improves the feature, saves your user time and effort, and makes your technology more pleasant to use. Be especially sparing with "complex clicks," such as menus, drag-and-drop, scrolling, and keyboard-mouse combinations.

To get a little more sophisticated about clicks, you might notice that not all clicks are the same. For example, clicking a button or check box requires aiming and clicking, but choosing a menu item on a PC or a Web page requires aiming and clicking, holding the mouse button while dragging, and then releasing the mouse. That's more physical effort, so you might consider menu items to be two clicks (as we did in the preceding table). Submenus are worse, because they require holding the mouse longer and controlling its motion that much more. Think of those as three clicks. Scrolling takes effort to hold and release at just the right point, so think of it as 1.5 clicks. Drag-and-drop can be challenging to accomplish and should also be considered two clicks (plus the clicking involved in getting the source and destination in view at the same time, if necessary). Keyboard-mouse combinations require coordinating two hands, so should be considered at least 1.5 clicks. Again, these motions are not *that* difficult, but they take effort. Keep in mind, not everyone is in the ideal situation when using a computer. People using laptops usually don't have a mouse, and it's harder to click and hold while moving the cursor with a trackball, touch pad, or joystick. Those with a physical impairment also have a hard time with complex motions, and at one time or another we all have impairments (for example, when you cut your index finger, when you're borrowing your lefty/righty friend's computer, when you're using a cheap mouse, when your fingers are cold). On mobile devices, people are often distracted or in motion, which makes it harder for them to click.

Some Examples

Here are some examples of conservative and extravagant uses of clicks in real products. They will help you start to get a sense of "what a difference a click makes."

 On Delta Airlines' flight status Web page (www.delta.com), if you enter a flight that doesn't exist, it presents a page that politely explains that it has no information on that flight, along with a set of alternatives for finding the flight (see Figure 2.2). Under the explanation is a New Search button, indicating that Delta expects you to try again. But to do so, Delta asks you to waste an extra click and extra time as the browser makes another trip to the server to reload the flight entry page. Instead, it would have been more polite to repeat the flight form on this page, including the data you already entered, so you can try again from here. (We checked a number of international airlines' sites, and all of them require you to click to try again.)

2.2

On Delta's Web site, if you enter a nonexistent flight, you see this page, which forces you to click again to go back to the flight entry page. Delta could have allowed you to retype your flight number on this page and try again to save a click. This page should also tell you what flight number you entered so you can better diagnose the problem.

On Barnes and Noble's Web site (www.barnesandnoble.com), if you search for something that results in a single match, it presents you with a results page indicating that it found a single match. You have to click on that option to see that page, costing you an extra click and page load. This happens because the software is designed to respond to every search by showing a page of results, since most searches find many matches. On the other hand, Amazon.com and IMDB.com (a movie database site) behave more like a butler. If you search for an item that has a single match, it goes directly to the page for that match. With this small amount of extra work, Amazon and IMDB have probably saved their customers millions of clicks.

The Xerox copier in our office is a high-end machine that serves as both a printer and a copier, a nice enhancement. It has a touch screen display in addition to its hardware buttons (see Figure 2.3). If you press the green hardware Start button when the copier hasn't finished copying the previous page, a window pops up on the touch screen telling you it's busy. Once it finishes, the Busy pop-up stays there. If you press Start again (as the pop-up suggests), nothing happens. You *have* to tap the Close button on the touch screen and then go back to the hardware button to request the next copy. Less fancy machines queue the copy request and start as soon as the machine is ready (one click), but this enhanced machine requires three clicks and two shifts in hand position (click to request the copy, shift and tap Close to the busy message, wait until it is really done, shift back and click to request the copy again). We usually walk to a different machine.

2.3

The Xerox Document Centre 200ST. The software display is not well integrated with the hardware buttons. You must tap Close on the touch display before pressing the green Start button. Instead, the machine should automatically dismiss the pop-up and start copying as soon as it has finished the last job.

The Corvette key remote has the ultimate in Clicks Are Sacred features: no clicks. When you approach the car with the remote, the car automatically unlocks. When you leave, it automatically locks and gives a short beep to let you know it locked. You don't even have to have the key out—it can be in a purse, pocket, or fanny pack. This is our favorite feature in this car (well, okay, next to its performance). When approaching the car with a load of packages, you don't have to shift the bags awkwardly to get your keys out and press a button; you just open the door. It's almost as good as having your butler open the door for you.

 Quicken, Netscape Navigator, Eudora, and Outlook, among others, have a "name suggestion" feature, one of our favorite ideas for reducing clicks. As you start typing a Web address in Netscape, for example, the text field automatically fills in the first previously visited Web address that matches those letters, updating with each character typed. As soon as the name you want appears in the field, you can stop typing and press Enter. If you're typing a new address, the name suggestion feature causes no harm. You just finish typing the full address, just as you would if there had been no such feature. This is a wonderful idea, often more helpful than browsers' bookmark feature, which requires several clicks to save a Web site and several more clicks to retrieve (if you can find it in your mess of bookmarks). In e-mail programs, name suggestion reduces the number of addresses you need to save in the address list, since the names of all your correspondents are remembered for you. In Quicken, once you enter a payee, all the other details associated with that entry are filled in (as in Figure 2.4). So if you're paying your cable TV bill, you type the first few letters of the cable provider's name and press enter, since the amount and category information will be the same (unless, of course, they raised the rates again).

 Pacific Bell's customer service number greets you and asks you to enter your phone number. Already you have to wonder: The company sells caller ID but doesn't know your number when you call? After you enter your number, you're given some options. If you choose to speak to a person, the first thing that person asks is your phone number. If you tell them you already entered it, they explain that their system doesn't transfer that information to the customer support people, it's used only for automated information. However, the menu doesn't give the option to speak to a person until *after* you've entered your phone number. Pacific Bell spends tolerance capital each time you call for assistance. On the other hand, if you call Schwab, you enter your account number and the person who picks up the phone has your information available. They confirm your name and you're on your way.

2.4

As you type, Quicken pops up a menu of previous transactions and fills in the first one that matches (step 1). When you press Tab, the rest of the information is filled in to the checkbook entry (step 2). To enter the transaction, you press Enter.

2/28/01	DEP	Ebay				12 00		1,371 43
		Reimbursement						
2/28/01	EFT	AT&T Cable				37 93		1,333 50
		--Split--						
3/1/01	EFT	Pacific Bell				28 33		1,305 17
		--Split--						
3/1/01	EFT	Armadillo Willy's Ba...	-18.37 Dining			56 21		1,248 96
		Armadillos St Helen...	-23.00 Dining					
3/5/01	EFT	Aroza Bergb/weiss...	-26.22 Recreation			395 46		853 50
		Aspen Rent-a-car J...	-60.50 Travel					
		AT&T @HOME 30...	-42.09 Computer:ISP	2479262...				
3/9/01	EFT	AT&T Cable	-37.93 --Split--			73 73		779 77
		AT&T Dividend	-5.35 Interest earned					
3/27/01	EFT	AT&T Cable				*Payment*	*Deposit*	
		Category		*Memo*			Enter	Edit ▼	Split
		[Ellen checking]						
3/23/01	EFT	Pacific Bell				38 49		
		--Split--						
3/27/01	EFT	AT&T Cable				37.93	*Deposit*	
		--Split--	✓✗ *Memo*				Enter	Edit ▼
3/11/01								

Design Guideline
If the effort required to implement a feature is significantly lower than the cumulative effort saved by your customers, build it. Apply extra implementation effort to smoothing out flow breaks in features that many customers encounter frequently.

In most of these examples, the programming effort to reduce clicks is low, relative to the customer effort saved. It would be trivial for the Delta Airlines Web site programmer to repeat the flight entry form on the response page, and this effort would likely pay off in just one day of customers typing incorrect flight numbers. We're guessing it took a few extra lines of code for Amazon and IMDB to skip the search results page when only one match was found. Most likely it would not be hard for Xerox to queue copy requests or at least automatically remove the pop-up when a job is done. It would be trivial for Pacific Bell to offer the customer support option before asking for your telephone number. However, if the company wants to discourage people from talking to agents because that costs more money, it should at least be able to transfer the phone number to customer support. (If not, the phone company that sells such equipment has bigger problems to solve.) The name completion feature and the Corvette auto-unlock feature probably require more effort to implement. But at least both of those can be treated as real *features* that can be promoted in marketing materials, whereas the others remove annoyances.

"Do You Really Mean It?" Pop-Ups

One of the most flagrant violators of the Clicks Are Sacred rule in all of software is what we call the "Do you really mean it?" pop-up. These annoying pop-ups appear in nearly every software technology we know of, including desktop computer software, Web sites, PDAs, digital cameras, interactive TV, and more. They come in many forms, including "Do you really want to delete that?", "Do you want to save your changes?", "Do you really want to print that?", "Do you really want to shut down?", or the worst offender, "How can you possibly want to leave my precious application?" (see an example from AOL in Figure 2.5). Every time one of these appears—and they appear frequently—it breaks your flow. You ask the computer to do something, and instead of doing it, it asks you a question and insists that you click once more to get what you asked for. Sometimes to answer the question you have to switch to a different input device or shift your hand position. Imagine if every time the doorbell rang the butler said, "Madam, are you sure you want me to answer the door?" He probably wouldn't keep his job for long.

2.5

AOL's Instant Messenger (AIM) asks if you really mean it when you close the application, adding another step to the process. Since you can't lose any data and it's easy to restart the application in the rare case that you closed it by mistake, there's no need to put this roadblock in the way of everyone who closes it on purpose. At least it lets you tell it never to appear again.

Most engineers offer "Do you really mean it?" pop-ups to be helpful, to protect users from making a mistake. They might be concerned that people will make more unrecoverable errors if they remove these pop-ups. Unfortunately, these pop-ups have become so common that they often appear in cases where little damage would be done. Since they're so common, and because most of the time people *do* really mean it, they get used to saying "Yes" to any "Do you really mean it?" pop-up without thinking about the question. So even if they did issue the command in error, they're likely to realize it after they've already clicked "Yes" to the pop-up.

"Do you really mean it?" pop-ups are really a way for the program to pass the buck to the user. In effect, they say, "I can't undo this, so if you make a mistake, it's your responsibility—I gave you another chance." The only good time to offer a "Do you really mean it?" pop-up is when

1. The user could lose a lot of data
2. The data cannot be recovered or reconstructed without a lot of effort, if at all

This situation should happen rarely. Imagine if every time you used the backspace key, you were asked, "Do you really want to remove that character?" There's no need to ask because even if you backspaced in error, the most you would lose is a single character and it's easy to retype it. The AIM example in Figure 2.5 is similar because you lose no data and it's easy to restart the application if you closed it by mistake. (If it takes a long time, work on speeding up the startup process rather than punishing people for exiting.) In most cases, you should be able to avoid the need for the pop-up altogether.

Design Guideline

If you have an Undo feature, there is no need to break the users' flow to ask them whether they really want the program to do what they just asked it to do.

One good way to avoid "Do you really mean it?" pop-ups is to implement an Undo feature. Undo not only removes the need to check whether users meant what they said, but it also gives people room to explore and helps them flow with their tasks without worrying about losing their work. Amazingly, some systems have gone to the trouble of implementing an Undo feature and yet they still ask you to confirm minor commands. For example, Windows has the Recycle Bin, whose sole purpose is to let you retrieve files you didn't mean to delete. Still, every time you delete a file, Windows asks you "Are you sure you want to send <filename> to the Recycle Bin?" (You can configure it not to do so, but as we'll discuss later, few people ever customize this type of behavior.) Adobe Photoshop 6.0 has an elaborate history feature that allows you to get back to *any* prior state, and yet it asks if you really mean it when you ask to remove a layer (a particular set of data). Since it's easy to recover the data, why ask for a confirmation?

Even if you don't have Undo—it can be complicated and work-intensive to implement—you usually can find a way to get around the "Do you really mean it?" pop-up. Let's look at Eudora, Qualcomm's e-mail program. If you start a new e-mail message to jane@doe.com and then change your mind, when you close the window, it asks, "Save changes to jane@doe.com, No Subject?" (see Figure 2.6). The pop-up isn't needed because the amount of data potentially lost is minimal. If you close the window in error, it's easy to start a new message and retype the address. So the pop-up breaks your flow to save you from a potential minor loss. Here's a case where "it's just one click" really snowballs: Many Web pages include a "mailto" link, which brings up a pre-addressed e-mail message. Mailto links look the same as regular links in Web browsers (someday they'll fix that), so it's not uncommon for people to click on a mailto link expecting to go to another Web page, and be surprised when their e-mail program opens. Already their flow has been broken. Now they have to close that e-mail message, but when they do, they're asked if they want to save their changes. But they haven't made any changes. What started as a simple task—going to a Web page—cascaded into a series of surprises and extra clicks just to get back to where they started.

2.6

Eudora asks if you really meant to close an e-mail message even when it contains very little data. Because you won't lose much data and it's easy to retype the address, there's no need to break the flow of everyone who closed it on purpose. In this case, auto-saving before closing is a way to avoid the "Do you really mean it?" pop-up.

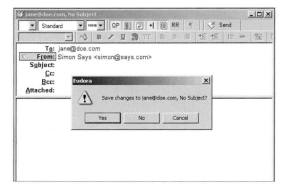

So how do you remove this pop-up safely? One approach is to remove the pop-up if an unsaved message has only header information. But maybe the user has entered only one word of a message without filling out header information. This message would also be easy to recon-struct. How do you decide what's too much information to lose? In this case as in many others, we suggest that you avoid the problem altogether by including an auto-save feature. Quicken's money management software is a great example. Every so often, without bothering you, Quicken saves whatever you've done. You never have to remember to save, and when you close the program, you're not bothered with questions. Instead, you can focus on your task. In general, we recommend auto-saving the users' work by default so that you take the responsibility of keeping their data rather than forcing them to decide each time they close a window. It's easy to implement, and it greatly reduces breaks in flow, so the usability value greatly outweighs the implementation cost.

Design Guideline
Engineers are trained to think of edge cases, while interaction designers think of common cases. When designing an interface, make the features that most people encounter most of the time as smooth to use as possible, even if it means requiring more effort for infrequent tasks. It is much better to bother few people rarely with a big effort than to bother most people frequently with a medium effort.

Design Guideline
Sometimes to reduce clicks, you have to revise related features to make those clicks unnecessary. Determine the underlying need for a click and be creative about removing the click while supporting the need.

Some people might be concerned that auto-saving occasionally saves something they didn't want to keep. This is a legitimate concern, but it is *far* more common and devastating for people to lose data because they forgot to save than it is for people to back out of a change by quitting and not saving. This brings up an important principle that underlies good interaction design and conflicts with the engineer's mindset. Engineers are rightly trained to think of *edge cases*, those rare but possible events the program has to handle. Since there are more edge cases than common cases, and since unaddressed edge cases can break the system, engineers spend more of their energy thinking about them. Interaction designers are trained to think of the *common case*, since that's what most people encounter most of the time. Interaction designers spend most of their time polishing the common case, because the usability bang for the buck is much greater. Each of these approaches is correct for its discipline. The problem comes when engineers apply edge case mentality to interaction design. When designing an interface, make sure the common case is handled elegantly and the rare cases are handled adequately. (Designers, too, can cause problems by ignoring edge cases and not specifying how the engineers should handle them. Rare or not, they have to be designed.)

To get back to the Eudora example, we're surprised to note that Eudora already has an auto-save feature. Every few minutes it saves any message being composed. If you close a partially composed message of any length, you can get it back by opening the Out folder. Even if you close Eudora without sending the message, the next time you start the program, the partially composed message window appears just as you left it. That's a thoughtful feature. To remove the "Do you really mean it?" pop-up, all the Eudora team has to do is auto-save any non-empty messages before closing the window. If you didn't want the message, you'll never need to care about it, but in the rare case when you needed the e-mail address you'd entered, you can find it again in the Out folder. Some unsent messages will accumulate in the Out folder, but this tiny amount of disk space is worth the saved effort. (If it is an issue, you can easily clear the Out folder of unsent messages every so often.)

The Eudora example is typical of the type of thinking you want to adopt to avoid clicks. Instead of thinking about why you need each click, think about what you're trying to let people do and find a way to do it without bothering them.

We spent a lot of time on the "Do you really mean it?" pop-up because it is a common and glaring example of being disrespectful of people's effort. But there are many other ways that computers don't treat clicks as sacred. Here are some straightforward ways you can reduce clicks on many devices.

Remember Where They Put Things

Many applications have a notion of *Preferences* that let you customize some aspect of the user interface. It takes a reasonable amount of effort to implement these preferences, and yet most people never use them. On the other hand, users *do* specify their preferences all the time in ways that most applications ignore. In desktop applications, every time you move or resize a window, you are saying, "I'd like that window here, please, and I'd like it to be this size." But as soon as you close that window, many applications immediately forget your preference. The next time you request that window, you have to specify the size and location again.

Design Guideline
Remember everything users do to adjust the application. The next time they come back, it should be just as they left it. This includes moving or resizing windows, choosing tabs, scrolling, moving toolbars, sorting data, reordering items, and so on.

Some applications use a tabs metaphor as a way of cramming more information into a space. When you choose a tab, you're saying, "I'd like to see that tab, please." But many applications forget which tab you were looking at the next time you go back to that window/screen/Web page. Other times you scroll down a page and then leave (close the window, go to another Web page, go to another screen), but when you come back, most applications return you to the top of the page. Other applications let you move task bars, swap columns around, or sort columns of data, only to forget your settings the next time you ask to see that information.

  Web browsers do a good job of remembering where you are scrolled on a page. If you're looking at the bottom of a page, click on a link, and then go back, usually you're returned to the bottom of the page, not the top. TiVo (the Personal Video Recorder) is another good example. Its interface mainly consists of menus, and each time you return to one, not only is it scrolled to the place where you left it, but the item you had selected is still selected, even if you've shut off the TV and returned a day later. By remembering where you are, TiVo reduces the effort required to continue a task. It acts like a butler who remembers what you asked for even if you interrupt him with another task.

Web sites don't do as well with tabs. Nearly every Web site that uses the tab metaphor treats it as just another type of link instead of as a real tab that saves its own context. Say you go to 800.com's Web site and click on the Electronics tab, and then choose the Video/TV subcategory, shown in Figure 2.7. Then you pop over to Music, where you poke around for a while, and then you go back to Electronics. If this worked like a real tab, Electronics would still be "open" to Video/TV, not the main Electronics page. But it's not. To get back to Video/TV, you have to click again. People don't shop on a linear path. They often look at multiple items before deciding what to buy. By making people retrace their paths on every tab, most Web sites with tabs cost their customers millions of clicks. (Some Web sites deliberately force users to click multiple times so that they can show more ad banners, but it's unlikely they are making up in ad revenue the amount of tolerance capital they are spending.)

2.7

The Web uses a false notion of tabs that forces you to click more. This is 800.com's Video/TV page within the Electronics tab. If you click on the Music tab and then return to the Electronics tab, you will go to the main Electronics page, not this one (the last one you were visiting within this tab).

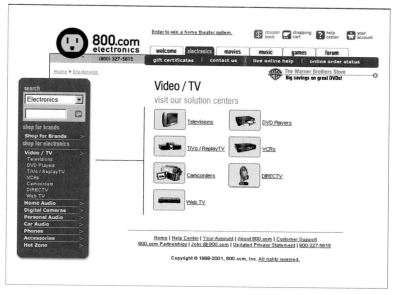

www.800.com

There is an implementation cost of remembering the state of each user's session between page loads (possibly a longer URL or some database overhead), which may be unacceptable in some cases.

However, in a PC software application, there's no good reason not to remember which tab was last open. People often open the same window several times in a row as they try to figure out a task. It's impolite to revert to the first tab each time they open the window, forcing them to click to get back where they were.

  Remembering the user's position is especially important on cell phones, cameras, and other menu-intensive devices with limited input mechanisms. Because there is no way to go directly to a menu item, you must cycle through menu choices. Once you select an item, you're usually presented with another menu of choices, and so on, sometimes five or six levels deep. Often you're looking for something and you discover that your choice was wrong, so you pop back up, ready to try the next choice. Some cameras we've tried, like the one in Figure 2.8, bounce you back to the first option on that screen, rather than showing your last selection. You're forced to click many times to cycle your way through the options again just to get to the next item in that list. In this type of limited-access interface, it's important to remember where the user left off each screen, as TiVo does.

2.8

This display appears on the Casio QV3000EX camera when you press Menu. Zoom is selected (highlighted in green) every time this menu appears. To move to Delete, for example, you press Next four times to tab from Zoom to 9Multi to Slide Show to DPOF and finally to Delete. It would be more cooperative if the menu remembered the last item you had selected when you left it.

 Another way that many applications disregard what you told them is by forgetting where you saved or opened a document. For example, in Windows, suppose you open a Microsoft Excel document located in your Data folder. While in that document, you start another spreadsheet, so you use the New command in the File menu. When you save that new spreadsheet, it doesn't assume you also want to keep it in your Data folder. Instead, it offers the default My Documents folder. A butler would understand that the current folder is a much better guess.

A similar example comes from Adobe Photoshop. It is common to work on a document in PSD format and then save multiple versions of it in another format, say JPG or GIF if you're creating images for the Web. Each time you ask Photoshop to Save As, it assumes you want to save the document in your current folder as a PSD file. That's not a bad default, but if you've just saved the last copy in a different folder and in a different format, it makes more sense to offer that option instead. (Many applications allow you to change your "default save location" in the preferences, but again, most people never change preferences, and even if they do, their save location depends on the document. It's more effective to remember what someone just did when deciding what to offer next time.)

Remember What They Told You

If you ask your customers to take the effort of providing personal information, by all means remember it. Think about how embarrassing it is when you realize you've just asked someone a question they've answered before. If you've asked several times before, it's disrespectful. You should feel just as impolite if your software commits the same blunder.

 We've already mentioned a common violation of this: telephone systems that require you to enter information that you have to repeat when you speak to a person. Many Web sites violate this rule when they ask you to register and then later ask you to fill out forms that request some of the same data you've already provided. Other times Web sites don't update their records with the latest information you gave them. A good example of this is the book review feature of Amazon's Web site. If you click "Write an online review" of any item, you see a page that lets you rate the item and enter a review. Before submitting your review, you're asked, "Where in the world are you?" Ellen has submitted over 30 reviews, and yet that field is always filled in with the town she lived in when she first registered for Amazon years ago (see Figure 2.9).[1] With each new review, she changes it, and yet it

---

[1] Recently Amazon updated the field with Ellen's current address, but that's not the location she enters into book reviews. She prefers to indicate the metropolitan area rather than her town, which few would have heard of. This field should remember what each user entered the last time they filled it in.

always reverts back to the incorrect location. Not only does this cost extra effort, it erodes our confidence in Amazon and its personalization features (for example, its recommendations). Remembering the last location entered into this form would help restore that trust.

2.9

Amazon's book review feature tries to be helpful by providing "Sunnyvale, CA USA" in field 5 as the location, but that is an old address. Instead, it should remember the location from the last book review entered.

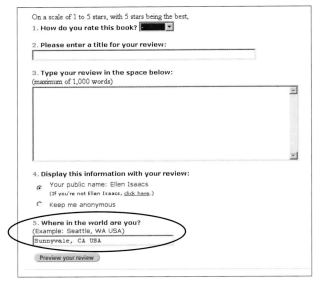

On a scale of 1 to 5 stars, with 5 stars being the best,
1. **How do you rate this book?**

2. **Please enter a title for your review:**

3. **Type your review in the space below:**
(maximum of 1,000 words)

4. **Display this information with your review:**
   ◉ Your public name: Ellen Isaacs
      (If you're not Ellen Isaacs, <u>click here</u>.)
   ○ Keep me anonymous

5. **Where in the world are you?**
   (Example: Seattle, WA USA)
   Sunnyvale, CA USA

   Preview your review

www.amazon.com

Design Guideline

If you ask people to give you information, remember it. If they update their information, remember it. If you ask them to fill out forms that include information they've previously given you, fill in those fields with the information you have.

Many cell phones do a good job of remembering what you've told them. Once you go through the considerable effort of entering the names and phone numbers you want to remember, that information is used effectively. When a phone call arrives from someone in your address book, the screen shows you the name of the person calling rather than a phone number you may not recognize. This is a nice touch that improves your experience and makes you feel as though your personal cell phone knows something about you. Also, if someone calls who is not in your address book, you can save the number and add a name, which helps you build up your address book with a minimum of clicks.

These last two guidelines ("Remember Where They Put Things" and "Remember What They Told You") are often overlooked when engineers estimate schedules. If these kinds of ease-of-use features aren't spelled out early and clearly, the team will focus on the core functionality and not on the supporting code to make them enjoyable to use. It's not hard to remember where a window was moved, but it takes time. The earlier these features are incorporated into an application's architecture, the easier it will be to apply them to new functionality later on.

Stick with a Mode

We have already mentioned how disruptive it is to switch your hands from one position to another. Moving from the mouse to the keyboard is especially burdensome. Even those who touch type usually have to look at the keyboard to get their hands back in position, and those with limited hand control have an even harder time.

 A good way to minimize switching modes is to provide multiple ways to enter the same data. For example, most desktop software has the concept of a "default" button that is pressed when you press the Enter key, saving the user from moving to the mouse. This is a basic concept, and Microsoft has incorporated it into its Internet Explorer browser, allowing the user to press the Enter key to submit a Web form. As useful as this feature is, Netscape still has not made this possible, even in its most recent 6.0 Navigator release. Every time you sign in to a Web site on Netscape, you *have* to move your hand to the mouse to click a button, even if the page has only one button on it. (Netscape treats Enter as a button press only if there is just a single text field and button on a page.) Think of the hundreds of millions of mode switches Netscape has inflicted on its users.

 Another trivial but useful way to save the user from switching is to automatically put the insertion point in the first text field in a window or on a Web site. If you're going to ask your customers to type, you know they're going to have to go to the keyboard. So don't make them grab the mouse and select the first field and then go back to the keyboard to type. Of all the major Web search engines, only Google.com automatically sets the cursor in the search field so you can just start typing. We couldn't find any shopping sites that did so, even though the main thing people do at such sites is search for products and there are often no other text fields on the page. Also, allow users to tab through fields in a meaningful order.

Devices that don't use the standard keyboard and mouse input mechanisms should also be carefully designed. For example, the recently discontinued Psion series of PDAs had both a keyboard and a stylus, and switching between them was especially awkward if you were trying to hold the device in midair (see Figure 2.10). Even if you rested it on a desk, you either had to type with the stylus in your hand or pick it up and put it down each time you switched. For any task that requires typing, make sure people can stick with the keyboard.

2.10

This Psion PDA has two input mechanisms, a stylus and a keyboard. It's awkward to switch between them, so it's important to allow people to stick with one input mechanism for any given task.

Design Guideline
Avoid asking the user to shift hand position. If you have more than one input device, make it possible to do each task without switching between input mechanisms.

 Cell phones require you to switch between putting the phone to your ear to listen and looking at the phone to enter numbers. AT&T Wireless's voice mail system does a nice job of eliminating some needless mode switches. When you call for voice mail, it tells you how many messages you have and then, knowing most people want to listen to them, immediately plays the first message. You don't have to press a key to play each message, as many office voice mail systems require. A further improvement would be to allow you to speak your password or say "delete" to remove a message, rather than having to enter numbers for those commands.

The guidelines we mention here are a few of the many ways you can reduce your customers' physical effort. The goal is to internalize the principle that physical effort matters, and to minimize the effort you ask of your users.

CHAPTER 3

Don't Impose: Respect Mental Effort

Let's assume you agree that clicks are a precious commodity and you're trying to remove them from your technology. It may have crossed your mind that one way to do so is to make a button for every possible variation on every task, and then make all those buttons visible from the main screen. Then every task is one click away! We'd give you an *A* for effort, but it won't work. It's true that an interface like that would reduce physical effort, but the cost would be mental effort. Even if your technology lets people do only 100 things, it would be far too difficult to pick the one right button. Just as you should reduce your customers' physical effort, you should also reduce their mental effort. You want to leave them as much mental energy as possible so they can flow with their task and forget about the technology entirely.

Every now and then, a product comes along that greatly reduces mental effort. PVRs such as TiVo, Replay, and UltimateTV are such an example. Among other things, PVRs allow you to record television shows and replay them later. Instead of asking what time and channel you want to record, PVRs ask you what *television show* you want to record. That's just how you would ask a butler: "Please record *East Enders* for me," not "Please record Mondays and Tuesdays at 7:30 p.m." You can ask a PVR to record a particular episode or all episodes. If you do the latter and the show is moved to a new time or station, you don't even have to know about it. The PVR continues to record it. If the show is cancelled one week, it won't record that week. PVRs minimize mental effort by allowing you to focus on the thing you care about (which show to watch), and not irrelevant aspects of the technology (the channel and schedule).

With most technology, you won't be able to reduce mental effort that much, but you can do so in many small ways on many tasks. In his book *Don't Make Me Think!*, Steve Krug calls it "thinking" any time you have to stop for a split second to figure out the interface rather than focus on your task. Here we discuss several ways you can minimize "thinking."

Use Visual Elements Sparingly

Think of user interface controls and other visual elements as you think of clicks. Use them sparingly. Again, this might seem strange. What's one more menu or button or graphic? But just as clicks add up, so does visual clutter. The fewer things there are, the more easily you can find the one you need. Look at the two sets of "menus" in Figure 3.1. See how quickly you can find these items in each menu: Orange, Edinburgh, Cherry, and Gold.

3.1

Find the following items in Set A and Set B: **Orange, Edinburgh, Cherry,** *and* **Gold**. *It's much easier to find them in Set B because there are fewer choices.*

Set A

Colors	Cities	Fruits	Schools	Metals	Capitals	Trees
Red	Bangkok	Apple	Yale	Nickel	Paris	Eucalyptis
Blue	Washington	Kiwi	Cambridge	Copper	Beijing	Cherry
Yellow	Santiago	Pineapple	Sorbonne	Silver	Canberra	Cedar
Purple	Interlaken	Orange	Stanford	Platinum	Ottawa	Maple
Magenta	Siena	Pear	Tokyo	Iron	Istanbul	Willow
Gold	Auckland	Banana	Edinburgh	Steel	Tripoli	Lemon
Green	London	Plum	Technion	Bronze	Montivideo	Aspen
Pink	Rabat	Mango	Brown	Aluminum	Amman	Birch
	Kabul	Nectarine	Delft		Caracas	Bamboo
			McGill		Cairo	
					Tel Aviv	
					Stockholm	

Set B

Colors	Cities	Fruits	Schools
Red	Bankok	Apple	Cambridge
Blue	Santiago	Pineapple	Sorbonne
Yellow	Auckland	Banana	Stanford
Orange	London	Mango	Tokyo
Purple	Rabat	Cherry	Delft
Gold	Kabul		McGill
Green			Edinburgh

It was much easier to find the words in the second set than in the first, right? We made the task hard by choosing items that could have been in either of two or sometimes three categories in Set A. When searching for menu items in software, the situation is often worse because the categories are more arbitrary, so you may be able to rule out only one or two menus. The same principle holds true for buttons and other UI elements: Fewer items are better. Although scanning the screen doesn't take *that* much effort, once you start focusing on finding an item rather than doing a task, your flow is broken.

You might think that the more powerful your application is, the more widgets you need (buttons, menus, check boxes, and so on). Perhaps, but the fewer widgets you have for the same functionality, the more powerful your product. People can more easily find what they need, and since they can see what you're offering, they're more likely to use the functionality you worked so hard to provide.

 Maybe you think we were exaggerating by showing such a strong contrast in the number of menus and menu items. Consider Figure 3.2. Out of the box, Microsoft Outlook 2000 Calendar has seven main menus, 69 menu items (16 of which are submenus), and 68 submenu items (not including your Web bookmarks, which are for some reason available in the Calendar), far more than our Set A has. Behind these 137 menu items are 42 pop-up windows, many of which launch yet more pop-ups. On the main screen are 12 task buttons across the top, access to six applications on the left, a column for folders, a view of today's appointments, an overview of this and next month, and a task pad.

3.2

Microsoft Outlook 2000 Calendar has far too many menus and user interface elements on its main screen, making it difficult to find the one thing you want.

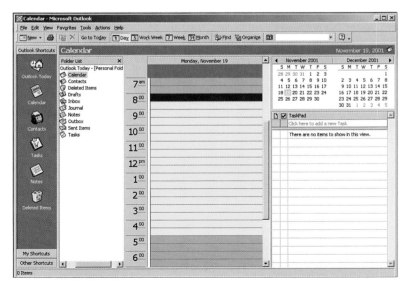

 In contrast, the Palm Date Book (shown in Figure 3.3) has three main menus with 18 menu items, no submenus, and 6 pop-up windows, fewer than our Set B. The main screen has three buttons at the bottom, two sets of choice boxes (lower left and upper right), and a view of today's appointments.

3.3

Palm's Date Book has a much simpler main screen that makes it easy to find what you want.

We have used both calendar applications, and although Microsoft's lets you do more things, we find Palm's far more effective. It's also less intimidating. You can find the things you most want to do quickly and carry them out easily, and even the things you do a little less often are easy to find.

Many Web sites struggle with this principle, especially on the home page. Everyone wants to have a link to the part of the site they're working on so that people are more likely to use their feature. The problem is that the more links there are, the less likely it is that people will find any one of them.

Design Guideline

Agonize over every visual element on the screen. The more there are, the fewer that get noticed. Make sure every visual element on the main screen is worthy of prime real estate. Even hidden elements must pull their weight because each one adds complexity.

Once you start to think of every element on the screen as a scarce resource, you begin to feel cautious about adding features. Features almost always require extra visual elements. Even if you add just one more menu item, that item makes it harder to find the other items already in the menu. When you start to think about the UI cost of adding features (even ones that are easy to implement), you're beginning to think like a good interaction designer.

Make Common Tasks Visible; Hide Infrequent Tasks

How do you reduce visual clutter? Second to eliminating unnecessary features, the best way is to hide infrequently used features. You'd like your main screen/window to offer people quick access to the things most people do most often, while giving newcomers an easy way to get started (as mentioned earlier by Palm's Rob Haitani). If you overwhelm people with choices, you'll intimidate new users and annoy frequent users who have to wade through the clutter to get to what they want. At the same time, most people don't look hard for features unless they're very motivated to find them. So the challenge is to present the frequent tasks cleanly while *suggesting* further functionality without cluttering the screen. Easy, huh?

Here's a good example of making common tasks visible and hiding infrequent tasks. What are the most common things people do when contacting an airline? You'd probably agree that they plan trips (find out about flight schedules and rates, possibly booking them) and check flight status (current departure and arrival times of today's flights). Of course, there are many other things people might do: look for discount promotions, find out about lost luggage, look for a job, sign up for the frequent flyer program, and so on. But those happen far less often. So if you're building a Web site for an airline, you want to make the two main functions very easy to find, and then get people started in the right direction if they want anything else.

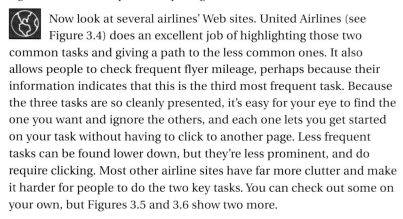 Now look at several airlines' Web sites. United Airlines (see Figure 3.4) does an excellent job of highlighting those two common tasks and giving a path to the less common ones. It also allows people to check frequent flyer mileage, perhaps because their information indicates that this is the third most frequent task. Because the three tasks are so cleanly presented, it's easy for your eye to find the one you want and ignore the others, and each one lets you get started on your task without having to click to another page. Less frequent tasks can be found lower down, but they're less prominent, and do require clicking. Most other airline sites have far more clutter and make it harder for people to do the two key tasks. You can check out some on your own, but Figures 3.5 and 3.6 show two more.

3.4

United Airlines' home page makes it easy to find the most common tasks, and it lets you get started on any of those tasks from the main page. Less frequently visited pages are visually separated but easily accessible from categories below.

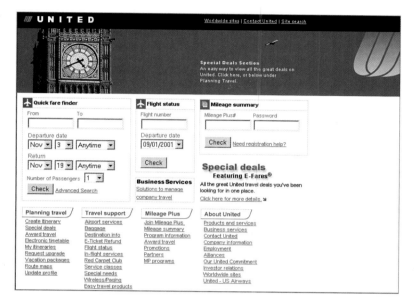

www.ual.com

American Airlines' page (see Figure 3.5) is a mishmash of information. It assumes that the two most frequent tasks are to check today's news on American (high on everyone's list, no doubt) and to plan a trip, and those two tasks are not cleanly delineated. See if you can find the place to check flight status. It is buried between the two prominent tasks ("Click Here for Gates and Times Information"). The rest of the page is a clutter of pulldowns broadly named, so it's hard to know where to look for a less common task. For example, what would you click to check your frequent flyer mileage? (Answer: It's under the AAdvantage pulldown menu.)

3.5

American Airlines' home page makes it hard to find the two most common tasks: planning a trip and checking the status of today's flights. The main screen is cluttered with less frequently used information (Today's News, for instance), and different tasks are not cleanly separated.

www.aa.com

On Lufthansa's site (see Figure 3.6), the orange border helps you find the flight planning section on the right, but the top center section features a collection of unrelated features (highlighted in gray), followed by a set of specials. Again, it's hard to find the flight status. (Arrivals/Departures is the fourth link in the left-side navigation menu.)

3.6

Lufthansa's home page is also visually cluttered and makes it difficult to find trip planning and today's flight status information (under Arrivals/Departures in the Cockpit section). Again, less commonly requested information is featured.

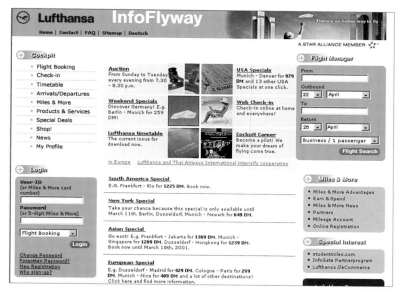

cms.lufthansa.com/de/fly/en/homepage

The importance of making common tasks more accessible than rare ones applies just as much to desktop software and especially to smaller devices. People frequently use handheld devices when they are mobile and focused on other activities. In such situations, it's especially important to help people find what they need quickly. For example, when the phone rings, the only thing you want to do (and can do) is answer it. This should be trivial to do, and on some cell phones, it is. Instead of hunting for the Talk button, you can press any button at all to answer a ringing phone. How nice! To hang up, however, you do have to find a particular button because other buttons could be used for other purposes while on a call. We like the Nokia 6162 model, which has a flap, shown in Figure 3.7. To answer the phone, you open the flap, and to hang up, you close it. At the end of the call, it's much easier to close the flap without looking than it is to find a certain button. And since you would close the flap anyway, it feels like no effort to hang up.

3.7
*The Nokia 6162 phone
makes it easy to end a
phone call without hunting
for the End button—you
just close the flap.*

 Here's another way that Nokia does a nice job of making common tasks accessible. Many cell phones have a "soft key" whose label is presented in software, so it can be modified depending on the context. Some cell phones include a Short Messaging Service (SMS), which displays text messages on the phone. Nokia does an excellent job of offering just the right option as the default. Figure 3.8 shows the process of reading new SMS messages when you already have one saved. When a message arrives, the main (left) soft key changes to Read, which takes you to a screen with a list of message headers. The first *new* message is already selected (not the first one in the list of saved messages) so you can press Read again to view the new message. When you're done reading it, that soft key becomes Options, and when you press it you see a list of things you might want to do, in order of likelihood. If you want to read the next message, you press OK, again the default button, and it appears. So reading new messages is a matter of pressing the same button multiple times, keeping mental and physical effort to a minimum.

3.8

To read a series of text messages on this phone, you repeatedly press the left soft key as it keeps changing to the most likely next command.

Soft keys

Design Guideline
Determine the most common user tasks and make sure they are visible and easily accessible. Hide less common tasks that clutter the screen and make it hard to find the common tasks.

We have a friend who has complained about the controls in car dashboards. He believes you should be able to find any of the frequently used controls without taking your eyes off the road. He suggested a good idea: Provide an anchor position for the hand on the dashboard that is easily found by feel. From there, put buttons for the frequently used controls beneath each finger. Figure 3.9 is an artist's rendering of this feature. With this design, you would be able to reach out and, for example, cycle through your preset radio stations or adjust the temperature, keeping your eyes on the road all the while. (Audio feedback would be useful here, as we'll discuss later.)

3.9

A design sketch for a dashboard that lets you locate frequently used controls without looking. The pinky stop and grooves help your hand find the right position, and the buttons give tactile and auditory feedback when pressed.

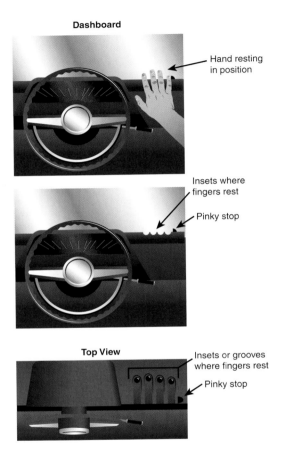

Dashboard

Hand resting in position

Insets where fingers rest

Pinky stop

Top View

Insets or grooves where fingers rest

Pinky stop

Give Feedback; Show Signs of Progress

In conversation, people give each other many verbal and nonverbal cues about their level of attention and understanding of each other's comments. People rely on these cues to adjust their contributions to the conversation, and if the cues are not there, people start focusing on the mechanics of the conversation rather than its content. In the same way, your program should tell people immediately whether it understood their request and provide its status in responding to it. Usually it does so by complying with the request. For example, when the user enters text, each character is displayed on the screen; when the user deletes an item, it disappears. But if the program can't carry out the task instantly or the results are not clearly visible, then it should do something to indicate that it "heard" them, just as a butler would. If it doesn't, they'll ask again, which will only bog down the program further.

One common way to provide "I heard you and here's what I'm up to" feedback is to display a progress bar when a task is going to take a long time. This technique is used frequently for such tasks as copying or transferring information. However, there are more subtle ways to stay in sync with the user. Sometimes people ask your program to draw something that takes a little time. Suppose it's a fancy CAD package drawing the internals of a car. Rather than waiting until the entire drawing is ready before presenting it, you can show the car being drawn. It turns out that people perceive the entire process as faster if they can watch it as it occurs rather than seeing the final result all at once, even if it takes the same amount of time. Since Web pages are slow to appear, it's better to show the text first, since it can be downloaded faster, and then have the images fill in. (The way you design your HTML determines how the browser displays the data, so it's worth learning the optimal approaches.) Another nice example is the way browsers show a low-resolution version of certain pictures first and then gradually increase the resolution as more information arrives.

Any time you know it will take a long time to complete a task, consider allowing users to interrupt. Nothing takes longer than waiting for something you didn't want in the first place! The Stop button on Web browsers feels like a godsend when you're waiting for a long download on a page that you didn't want (or decided isn't worth the time). More sophisticated speech-based systems allow you to interrupt the system's voice instructions with a command, which helps the system seem more human and less clumsy.

Sometimes the program can comply immediately, but there is no inherent feedback to let you know it did. In this case, the program should offer feedback to reassure you that it did what you asked. For example, when you end a call on a cell phone, there is no obvious way to tell that the call has been disconnected.[1] Most phones handle this by beeping and changing the display back to the main screen to show you that they are ready for another call. Some volume controls give feedback not just by moving the level indicator but also by playing a sound at the new volume.

 Another good time to give feedback is when you ask people to walk through a multistep process, say going through a checkout procedure or filling out a survey. People need to pace themselves and it's helpful to know how long the process will take and how far along they are. Provide a visual indication of the number of steps and which step they're on. 800.com does this nicely by showing you where you are in the checkout process (see Figure 3.10). From this page, it's clear that you will be asked about payment options next, then you'll have a chance to review the information, and finally you'll get a receipt. Harris Poll does this with a continuous meter (see Figure 3.11), which is less effective because it's hard to tell how much the meter moves with each step. Still, it is better than nothing.

3.10

800.com shows you the steps of the buying process, indicating where you are in that process. This feedback helps keep people oriented.

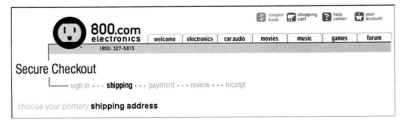

Secure Checkout

— sign in · · · **shipping** · · · payment · · · review · · · receipt

choose your primary **shipping address**

www.800.com

---

[1] In movies, when the other person hangs up, you immediately hear a dial tone, even though this does not happen in real life. Apparently, movie directors realize that the audience needs immediate feedback. (Of course, in movies, people never seem to say "bye," they just hang up. We've never understood why.)

3.11

Harris Poll indicates your progress in a Web-based survey with a continuous progress meter in the upper-right corner. This is helpful, but because it's not clear how much the meter moves with each question, it would be more effective to indicate on each page which question you're on and how many questions there are altogether.

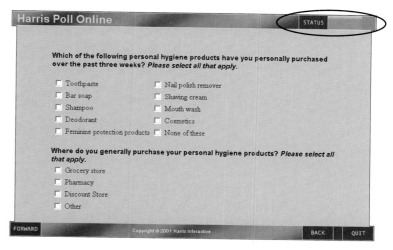

www.harrispollonline.com

Design Guideline

Always acknowledge the user's request and, if you can't comply immediately, let them know what you're up to and how much longer it will take.

Design Guideline

If a command can't be carried out quickly, allow users to interrupt.

 With a speech interface, you can't give visual feedback, but you can use conversational techniques to show your level of understanding. For example, Schwab has a speech recognition system that lets you get stock quotes over the phone. If you ask for the stock price of *Sun*, it says, "There are seven items that match that name. Either speak the full name of the security at any time, or listen to the following list to help narrow down the security you want," followed by a list of the companies that begin with *Sun*. (It appears to present them in order of frequency of request, rather than alphabetically, which is a nice touch.) Schwab handles ambiguous references well. Rather than offering the user no help by saying, "Please say the full name of the security," it presents the possible matches, while still letting you interrupt *at any time* with the full name, either as soon as you hear it or right away if you know what it is. A slight improvement would be to confirm the name it heard, perhaps with, "There are seven items that match *Sun*."

 At a different level, it's helpful to let people know they've successfully pressed a button, especially when you're providing software buttons on a small screen. For example, when you're viewing photos, the Canon Digital Elph camera makes a quick, soft click sound each time it scrolls to the next image, subtly reassuring you that it did move, which is useful if two images in a row are similar.

The Palm, too, plays a click sound each time you tap a button. Researchers have found that buttons with audio feedback can be smaller than those without, since the sound lets people know when they've successfully tapped the button.

  Sounds can also be used to give other kinds of feedback. We have a Panasonic portable phone that flashes a light *and* beeps when you place it in the cradle to let you know it made a solid connection for recharging. We mentioned earlier how the Corvette beeps as you walk away from the car to let you know that it locked itself. Sounds are useful because they don't require you to look to get the information. And without realizing it, you quickly get used to hearing these sounds, so when they're missing you notice that there's a problem. It's especially good to combine sounds with visual cues, as the Panasonic phone does, partially to reinforce the information and partially to support users who have either hearing or visual impairments. (Even people with perfect hearing or vision may be in a noisy environment or have their line of sight blocked.)

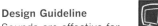

Design Guideline
Sounds are effective for letting people know when something has occurred or that a task is in progress. It is good to combine sounds with visual cues to reinforce the information and to support those with visual or hearing impairments.

TiVo makes strong use of sound in its interface. Different buttons make different sounds, and the sounds are quite expressive, giving TiVo a personality. The sounds were chosen to correlate with their meaning. For example, if you try to scroll past the bottom of a list, a low-pitched tympani sound plays, as if you've hit bottom. To fast forward, you can press once to move slowly, twice to move a little faster, and a third time to move quickly. With each press, two rising notes play (ba-boop), and as the speed of fast fowarding increases, so does the pitch of the second note (ba-boop, ba-BOOP, ba-**BOOP**!), so it *sounds* as if it's going faster. To reinforce the sounds, the display shows one, two, or three right-facing triangles, and the cursor moves faster each time.

Keep Preferences to a Minimum; Give Smart Defaults

Many programs offer Preferences or Options that allow people to specify how they want the user interface to operate. Usually, applications offer Preferences because the development team disagrees on what "most people" will want (usually because the team members want different things), so they decide to allow each user to choose. The

Preference is offered as a gift, giving people the freedom to choose how they want the application to behave. While the sentiment is laudable, Preferences are about as heavyweight as you can get in terms of imposing mental effort on the user. Remember, most people just want to focus on their task. When you ask them to pop out of their task to focus on how the program operates, you're asking them to do some serious mental work.

You're also working against people's expectations. Most technology can't be molded to each person's needs, so people don't think they can change the way something works. (You can't just flip a switch to make a can opener left-handed; you have to buy a left-handed can opener.) Also, most people aren't aware that the user interface is distinct somehow from the application and can be changed to suit their needs. Yes, people will change the *appearance* of an application, perhaps by modifying the color scheme or applying a "skin," but rarely do they modify the *behavior.* If they keep bumping their heads against the same problem over and over again, their tolerance capital declines each time. Even experts who realize that they can modify a program usually struggle and complain about a problem until it gets so painful that it dawns on them to check the Preferences to change it. (Ellen confesses that it was two years after she got a new Windows PC that it occurred to her to see whether she could set the default folder where Office applications save or open documents. She had been annoyed each time it offered to save a document in My Documents, which she'd never used. Even though she was aware that she could modify Preferences, it took a lot of effort to "pop out" of the task and think about looking for a remedy in the Preferences.)

You should assume that almost no one will change Preferences that modify the system's behavior. So be careful about choosing the default behavior because for most people, it *is* the program's behavior. Some tech-savvy users do make use of Preferences, but unless the product is primarily for them, take care of most users' needs before offering them options. Here we return to the idea that you should focus on the common case for most people, not what *some* people *might* want to do in *some* situations (that is, edge cases).

Figure 3.12 shows just one of dozens of Preference sheets from ICQ, an instant messenger. Rarely would it occur to someone to change an item. Consider "Display Email notification on Contact List if Email is assigned to user." Most likely, if someone weren't noticing their e-mail, they wouldn't think to look in the Preferences to find the problem. This window has a scrolling list of categories on the left that change the display on the right. Some categories have subcategories, displayed in tabs. It's hard to believe that the amount of work that went into offering these hundreds of Preferences could be justified by their usage.

3.12

This is just one of dozens of pages of Preferences for ICQ's instant messenger. Each item in the list on the left displays a set of Preferences on the right, some of which have multiple tabs. Most people stick with default behaviors and never look at the Preferences, so much of this is wasted effort. Usually, the presence of a lot of Preferences in a program indicates that the development team couldn't decide on the right behavior.

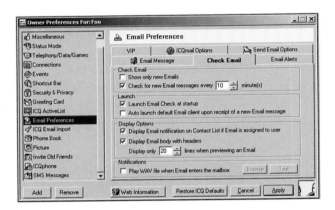

Design Guideline

Treat "We'll make it a Preference" as a copout. The default behavior *is* the application's behavior, since few people ever modify Preferences that affect the *behavior* of the application. Use Preferences mainly to allow people to customize the application's *appearance*.

Your goal should be to have no behavioral Preferences. You may not achieve it, but it might help you think harder about whether "We'll make it a Preference" is really a good solution.

Follow Conventions (Even If They're Not Your Ideal Design)

Usually, you build technology on a platform that supports other applications. Most platforms have a set of conventions for interacting with the user. There is always a tension between the conventional method and the method best suited to your program. Most of the time, it's best to go with the convention. As painful as it might be from your standpoint, think about it from the users' view. As they use applications, they gradually learn the conventions. They aren't necessarily aware of them as conventions, but they come to expect certain behavior. For example, Web users learn to look across the top or left side of the page to find the categories of items available at a Web site. Cell phone users expect to use the left soft-key button to select an item and the right to go back. Palm users expect that most things they want to do will be available on the screen and so they rarely look in menus. It helps users if your program behaves in the same way as other programs.

Design Guideline
Use platform conventions. Violating a convention confuses people about when the convention applies, so they stop using it across all applications, including yours.

Also, many people aren't clear about the distinction between a platform and applications that run on the platform. From their standpoint, they have a computer or phone or PDA, and it lets them do things. If your application operates differently from all the others, people are not likely to correlate that difference with your application, but instead think the device is inconsistent. For example, in Windows, there is a convention to use Ctrl+C for Copy, Ctrl+X for Cut, and Ctrl+V for paste. Suppose you decide to use Ctrl+X to place a mark in the data because it's a common action in your application and X is good way to convey "mark the spot." People won't think "Usually, Ctrl+X means Cut, but in this application it means Mark the Spot." Instead, they'll say "Sometimes when I use Ctrl+X it cuts the text, and other times it places a mark. I can never remember when it does which, and since I got tired of being surprised, I stopped using the shortcut."

Look for "Widgetless Features"

The ideal features you can build are what we call "widgetless features." Widgets are user interface controls, such as buttons, scrollbars, and menus. Usually, widgets are necessary because there's no way to access a feature (or know about it) without them. But there are some cases when functionality can become available just when you need it, without a widget to request it. One example of a widgetless feature is name suggestion, which we discussed earlier. As you type a Web address, the name is expanded to the first match of your previously viewed Web addresses, allowing you to stop typing as soon as you see what you want. Automatically setting the insertion point in the first text field on a page is another widgetless feature. There's nothing to press; the interface is ready for you to type. Widgetless features minimize mental effort by not cluttering the screen, and they minimize physical effort by reducing clicks. If we had a butler, we'd call him Widgetless.

 Another example of a widgetless feature is the auto-scroll feature on some desktop software. If you're dragging an item from one place inside a window to another, once you move it to the border of the window, the data pane automatically starts scrolling so you can see the rest of the contents of the window. If you didn't have this feature, you'd have to either increase the size of the window to get the source and the destination in view, or you'd have to keep dragging and dropping in increments, scrolling the window between each one until the destination is in view. What an effort! Auto-scrolling the window makes dragging and dropping feasible. There is no widget—it just "does the right thing."

 The Garmin eMap Global Positioning System (GPS) device has a nice widgetless feature. It has no keyboard, so to enter text, you have to cycle through the alphabet, which is tedious. But when you search for a street address, it helps you by presenting only letters that are possible given the addresses it knows about. In Figure 3.13A, your cursor is placed at the top after *WELLE*. From the streets listed below, you can see that the first possible next letter is *R*, so when you press the hardware down arrow, an *R* appears in that slot and the display scrolls you to the first match, Weller Ct., as shown in Figure 3.13B. There's no need to make you scroll from *A* to *Q* if no such streets exist. If you press down again, the letter will change to *S* because there are streets that begin with *WELLES*.

3.13

The eMap GPS helps you search by skipping letters that don't have any matches. In this example, the first possible next letter after WELLE is R, so pressing the down arrow displays an R, skipping A–Q.

A

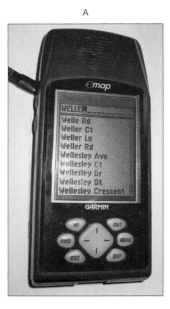

B

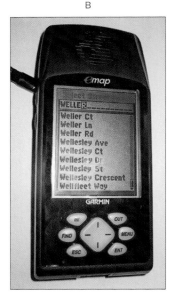

Netscape Navigator and Internet Explorer have implemented widgetless features to make it easier to download and install applications. It used to be that you downloaded the application to a file, then you had to find that file and double-click on it to start the installation. Now you no longer have to find and click on the application file; you can just click to download and then agree to install it without extra steps. Similarly, Yahoo! Messenger, an instant messenger program, makes it trivial to download an upgrade by doing all the work for you. A window pops up when you run the program asking if you want the new version, and if you say Yes, it closes the current version, downloads the new one, installs it, and starts it, putting it in the same screen location as the last one. How thoughtful!

 A different kind of widgetless feature is the spell-checking feature in Microsoft Word. Before this feature came along, you would write your document and then pass it through a spell checker when you were done. Spell checkers are complex features, usually involving a separate window that shows you the incorrect word along with options such as Replace It, Ignore the Problem, Add the Word to the Dictionary, and so on. With the Word feature, as you type, a wavy red line appears under any word it doesn't recognize, as shown in Figure 3.14. If you want to correct it, you can replace it manually, or if you want suggestions on how to spell it, you right-click on the word to see possible replacements. If you select one, the word is replaced with the one you chose. If the word is correct, you can ignore the wavy line or you can right-click to add the word to the dictionary. This is a nice feature because it takes so little effort to use and you can choose to correct as you write or fix errors later.

3.14

Word offers a spell checker that lets you correct words in place, rather than running a separate spell-checking feature after finishing a document. A wavy red line indicates that the word may be misspelled, and you can right-click on it to get spelling suggestions or to add the word to the dictionary. Choosing a word from the menu replaces the incorrect word with the one you selected.

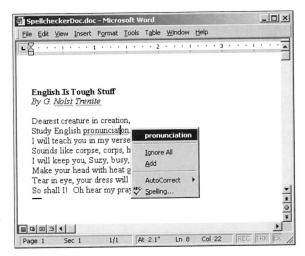

Word also has a nice spelling correction feature. If you type "hte," Word automatically changes it to "the." Perfect. It takes no effort and just "does the right thing." Word has a table of common typos that it automatically replaces with the correct words. You can add your own common typos to the list, although most people probably never do. Of course, it's important not to be overzealous in correcting too many "typos," and Word could do a better job of allowing you to insist on a typo if you really meant what you typed. (Backspacing and retyping it should be enough.) Still, this is a good effort, and is based on an understanding of how people write documents.

 The Canon Digital Elph camera, among others, has a neat feature to help you take a series of pictures for a panorama. After you take a photo and move the camera to the right, the display shows you the right-most third of the previous picture so you can line up the next shot to overlap it. Seeing part of the last image is just what you need to make sure you don't wind up with gaps in your panorama. The camera also remembers the exposure settings of the first shot so that subsequent pictures have the same lighting. What a helpful feature!

Design Guideline
Look for widgetless features—features that do just what you need when you need it, without any visible representation on the screen. But beware of becoming *too* helpful. It's worse to offer help that people don't want than it is to not offer a pleasant surprise.

A word of caution: Don't get carried away with widgetless features. Remember the butler mentality. It is worse to incorrectly anticipate the user's need than it is to not offer an unexpected treat. You want to look for features that do no harm if the user doesn't want them, but are likely to save effort for most people most of the time. The Microsoft Office Assistant paper clip help system is a good example of going overboard. You started a document with the word "Dear" and it popped up with a manic gleam in its eye, demanding to help you write a letter. That system was so widely disliked that you could even buy T-shirts of the paper clip in the crosshairs of a rifle. Finally, after the paper clip taunted its users for years, Microsoft decided to remove it. Try to be subtler. Find cases where the program can do the right thing itself rather than breaking the user's flow with an explicit offer of help.

CHAPTER 4

Be Helpful

In the last two chapters, we talked about ways you can avoid imposing on your users. Now we get to talk about helping them. Our goal is not to provide a complete list of all the ways you can be helpful. Instead, we present five approaches, each building on ways that people cooperate in conversation. Our hope is that you will find other ways to make your technology cooperative.

Offer Sufficient Information Early and in Context; Prevent Errors

It often takes a few steps to complete a task. The more you can give people useful information up front, the more you can help them avoid errors or unpleasant surprises. This guideline comes into play in a wide range of situations, so we provide many examples.

Many Web sites include forms to collect information about their users. Usually, some information is required and some is optional. Some information is expected in a certain format (for instance, dates and account numbers). It's helpful to see these requirements up front rather than finding out only after making "errors." Buy.com does a nice job of indicating its expectations on its registration form (see Figure 4.1). All required fields are marked with asterisks. The width of each field suggests how many characters it expects and each field stops accepting input once you've hit its limit (for example, you can only type two characters for the

State), thus preventing errors. The password field indicates the number of characters allowed, and the explanation appears immediately above the entry area so you'll see it. If you still submit the form with a mistake, the next page points out the error and lets you correct it on that page, rather than making you go back to fix it. Buy.com makes you feel as if it's helping you provide the information rather than demanding it.

4.1

Buy.com's registration page indicates up front which fields are required and what types of passwords are acceptable. The size of each text field suggests the length of its expected input, and the fields stop accepting characters when the maximum is reached. All of these features help prevent errors.

My Account Log In
Enter your eMail address and a password so you can securely access all your account information. Please type in a few key words for your "hint" in case you forget your password. For your security, avoid an obvious hint, such as "My dog's name."
NOTE: Items with a "*" are required.

*Enter Your eMail Address

Hint

*Choose A Password
(must be between 5 & 20 characters)

*Account Type
Select Account Type

*Verify Your Password

☑ Newsletter (To receive buy.com news)
○ I'm a Business Customer
○ I'm a Home Customer

Billing Information

Please note that paying by check or money order requires extra processing time.
More information on payment options

Payment Method
Choose Payment Method

Credit Card Number

Expiration Date
01   2000

Your billing address must be entered exactly as it appears on your credit card statement. Please check your statement for accuracy to avoid delays in processing your order.

*First Name   *Last Name

*Home Phone Number
(   )   -

Company Name

Company Phone Number
(   )   -   Ext:

Fax Number
(   )   -

*Address – Line 1

Zero Liability VISA THE ONLINE CURRENCY

Address – Line 2

*City   *State *Zip Code

www.buy.com

Design Guideline

If you have expectations of the user, let them know up front rather than surprising them later. Indicate which information is required, what format you're expecting, and so on. Try to prevent errors wherever possible.

Symantec provides system utilities that include a feature that offers to download updates when they're available (see Figure 4.2A). If you accept the offer, the program first shows you what it will update and, if you agree, automatically downloads what it needs and installs it. Very nice. However, only after the update is done does the program inform you that you must reboot (see Figure 4.2B). You're not given the option to reboot later, you must reboot immediately. Rebooting is the mother of all clicks. Think of it as 100 clicks, since it takes so long and wipes out your context. If this program needs you to reboot, it should tell you *before* you decide whether to initiate an update or allow you to reboot later. By not warning you, it squanders a lot of tolerance capital.

4.2

Symantec offers a LiveUpdate service that appears when updates are available (A). The window allows you to choose which products to update, but it gives no indication that you will be forced to reboot. After updating, you are told you must reboot your machine now (B), and are given no option to reboot later. For such a major break in flow, Symantec should either inform you before you decide whether you want to update or allow you to reboot later.

A

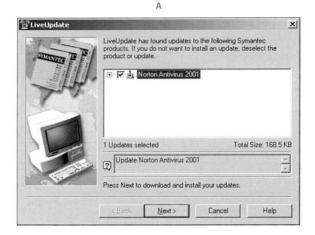

B

Here's a way to be especially helpful. Most shopping Web sites charge for shipping and some charge sales tax depending on where you live, so it makes sense to compare final prices. However, most shopping Web sites don't tell you how much shipping and/or tax will cost until you've gone through a multistep buying process, providing your credit card along the way. AbesOfMaine.com does. From your shopping cart, you can enter your zip code and it will calculate the final charges on your order (see Figure 4.3). An even better butler would remember your zip code once you've provided it and then always indicate final prices in the shopping cart.

4.3

AbesOfMaine.com's shopping cart allows you to provide your zip code (A) to find out tax and shipping charges for your order (B).

A

SHOPPING CART

Item	Price	Qty		Total	
Canon Powershot S-100 Digital Elph Camera Kit	$ 609.99	1	Change Quantities	$ 609.99	Remove Item
Order SubTotal				$ 609.99	

Select the desired Shipping Method   UPS Ground ▼

Please enter the shipping address' zip code: 94025

    Final Charges / Checkout   Empty Cart   Shop More!

B

FINAL CHARGES

These are your final calculated charges. If these charges are acceptable press "Check Out" to complete your order. If you want to shop more or change the shipping method, press "Change Order" to return to the previous page.

Item	Price	Qty	Total
Canon Powershot S-100 Digital Elph Camera Kit	$ 609.99	1	$ 609.99
Order SubTotal			$ 609.99
Shipping			$ 30.50
Sales Tax			$ 0.00
Order Total			$ 640.49

    Change Order   Secure Check Out

www.abesofmaine.com

Design Guideline

If you have a multistep process, give users relevant information about the procedure before they start.

Some phone-based customer support systems tell you the expected hold time before you speak to a person. While you may not be happy to learn of a 20-minute wait, at least you can make an informed decision up front, rather than waiting 10 minutes before giving up in frustration. Another way to offer helpful information up front is simply to tell people how many menu choices will be offered. For example, Schwab's customer service line asks you to "Please select from the following five choices." Knowing that there are five choices helps you choose the best category as you hear the options.

A nice example of providing useful information early comes from Casio's QV3000EX digital camera. When you ask to delete an image, it displays a "Do you really mean it?" pop-up (which is not good), but it *does* place that pop-up over the bottom of the image you're about to delete rather than replacing the screen with the pop-up, so you're sure which image you're deleting.[1]

These examples vary in many ways. Your goal should be to think about the type of information people need when doing a task and provide it where they need it most.

Solve Problems; Don't Complain or Pass the Buck

The flip side of providing too little information is being too verbose, giving people information they can't interpret, or passing off responsibility. Just as a butler does, it's best to figure out the right thing to do and not bother people. Doing so also reduces clicks. There are many ways to do this. Here we provide a range of good and bad examples.

 AOL's Instant Messenger (AIM) is a great example of bothering the user with unnecessary information. You typically run instant messengers in the background all the time, not paying attention to them unless you're interacting with someone. Yet if AIM loses contact with the Internet, it immediately blasts a pop-up in your face telling you so, asking if you want it to try to reconnect (see Figure 4.4). First, if you're not using AIM right now, there's no need to interrupt you. And second, if it can try to reconnect, it should. The pop-up stays up for several seconds, telling you how long until it goes away. Probably this countdown was provided as a helpful gesture. Unfortunately, the result is that you have to choose between waiting for the pop-up to disappear or dismissing it by answering OK and then immediately clicking OK again on the subsequent pop-up informing you that it still cannot reconnect. After that, it doesn't try any more.

---

[1] You could argue that removing a picture by mistake is damaging enough that the "Do you really mean it?" pop-up is justified. We would prefer that the last deleted image be saved to a buffer, allowing people to undo the last delete.

A

4.4

If AOL's Instant Messenger loses contact with the Internet, it immediately disrupts you by popping up a window (A). If you click OK, it immediately pops up another window (B) to tell you that it still can't connect. If you wait for the first window to go away, it pops up again when it can't reconnect. If you click Cancel, it won't keep trying to connect. A better approach is to silently keep trying to reconnect without bothering you at all.

B

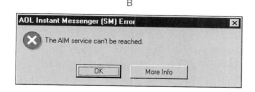

Yahoo! Messenger, on the other hand, does this right. If it loses its connection, the connection light in the footer changes from green to yellow and the message says "Connecting" (see Figure 4.5). It keeps trying, and once it reconnects, the status light goes back to green. In most cases, you're not even aware that the application temporarily lost connection.

4.5

Yahoo! Messenger is much more subtle about handling disconnections. When it loses its connection to the Internet, the status light changes from green to yellow and the message changes from "Connected" to "Connecting." It keeps trying to reconnect, and when it does, the light goes back to green. This feedback is enough to let you know of the problem without disrupting your flow.

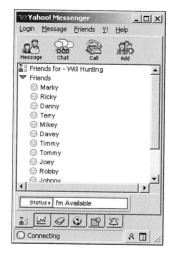

 Here's an example of bothering the user with a problem and not explaining the consequences or offering advice. The pop-up window in Figure 4.6 appeared when Alan was installing an application. InstallShield seems to be complaining that the version of Windows Installer it found is old. Not only is the message unclear, it gives no indication of what you're supposed to do about it or what problems will result if you continue. All you can do is click OK and hope nothing goes wrong. This pop-up appears because the application's install function encountered an old version of the Windows Installer. Normally, the Windows Installer would be silently updated (which is the right thing to do), but Windows 2000's security model does not allow this. By default, InstallShield pops up this message, but the application programmer could have suppressed it. That would have been the right thing to do.

4.6

This pop-up complains about a problem without explaining the consequences or giving advice about what to do. In this case, since there is nothing the user can do and there are no negative consequences, the pop-up should not appear.

Design Guideline
Beware pop-ups with a single option (usually an OK button), especially those the user did not request. If there's a problem, handle it yourself or offer some help—don't just inform people. If you want to provide status information, don't use a single-option pop-up unless it's urgent; instead, put a message in the status area.

In general, an alarm should go off in your head whenever you create a pop-up that has a single option (usually an OK button). It may mean you're giving the user bad news without offering to fix the problem, or you're bothering them with problems you can solve on your own. There are some exceptions, especially in cases where the user has asked for information (for instance, an About box, a calendar appointment reminder), or when a problem is so critical that you must get the user's attention immediately. But generally, if you have the urge to notify the user, try to solve the problem yourself, possibly informing people of the system's status in the footer (or the standard area for status information on your platform). Don't pop up a window that users have to waste a click to dismiss.

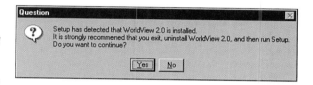

Sometimes a program tries to be helpful by explaining why it couldn't do what you asked it to do and how to ask properly. If the program can recognize what the user is asking well enough to explain what to do, it's much better if it can just do it. For example, while installing a later version of an application called WorldView, we saw the message in Figure 4.7.

4.7

WorldView knows that a previous version is installed and that you need to uninstall it before installing the new version. WorldView could be more cooperative by doing the uninstall itself as part of its own installation.

Since the system seems to know exactly what to do, wouldn't it be nice if it just did it? We mentioned earlier that Yahoo! Messenger does this for you, uninstalling the old one and downloading and installing the new one. On the other hand, Messenger doesn't get everything right. Even when you're not logged on, the interface still shows you the names of your buddies, implying you can click on them to start a message. But if you do, it pops up an error message telling you to log in first. Since it knows you want to start a message and it already has your login information, Messenger should automatically log you in and display the message window. If you're not connected to the Internet, it shouldn't display your buddies' names at all, so you can't try to send them a message.

Here's a blatant example of not solving a problem. Yahoo! Real Estate lets you find the current value of a home given the purchase price and date. Although you're not told so up front, you're not allowed to include a comma in the purchase price. If you do, you see the page in Figure 4.8. Instead of complaining about the comma, Yahoo! could remove the comma and show the results—and probably reduce the amount of code to boot. A butler would have known what you meant. (At least this page allows you to fix the "error" here rather than making you go back to remove the original comma.)

4.8

Yahoo! Real Estate could easily strip out the comma itself rather than telling you to remove it and resubmit your request. Removing the comma would be more cooperative and it would probably take fewer lines of code as well.

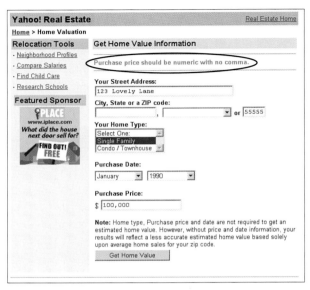

realestate.yahoo.com

Design Guideline
Don't bother the user with problems you can solve yourself. If you can figure out the problem well enough to tell the user how to solve it, try to solve it yourself.

Of course, some problems take much more work than this one to fix, so you need to decide whether the amount of user time and effort saved is worth the implementation cost.

Occasionally, when you ask for a feature offered by a program, the program asks you to specify a lot of options. Sometimes that can't be avoided, but often it's obvious what most people want most of the time. If you have convinced yourself it's worth supporting other things that *some* people *might* do *sometimes*, at least provide the standard feature with one click and then offer another way to specify something else.

 A simple example of this is the Shut Down menu in Windows. Instead of shutting down when you choose this menu item, the system displays a pop-up asking which command you want that is related to shutting down (for example, Stand By, Log Out, Restart, Hibernate, Shut Down). Here's what frequently happens: You pack up for the day, shut down your computer, and leave. The next day, you come back to find that your computer hasn't shut down; it's been patiently waiting for you to clarify what you meant by "shut down." You want to ask, "Which part of shut down didn't you understand?" A similar thing happens with the Print pop-up—you select Print from the menu and go get a cup of coffee, only to come back to find the pop-up asking you how you'd like it to print. Instead, it's best to have a single menu item that does what it says with no questions asked, and then have a separate item that allows you to specify something other than the usual (for instance, Print and Print Setup). In the Shut Down case, we would offer all the relevant shut down options directly from the menu. However, since it would be a fairly time-consuming error to shut down by mistake, we might show a pop-up with a five-second countdown that lets you cancel the shutdown (or explicitly confirm it to skip the countdown). This way, shutting down is still a one-click command, but you can change your mind if you made a mistake.

Design Guideline
If you find yourself wanting to ask the user what they meant (that is, if you're tempted to put up options before you complete the task), redesign the feature to provide an unambiguous command. Decide what most people want most of the time, and let them do that with few clicks. Then let the few choose a different command if they want something else.

 If the program has to ask what you meant, it should ask in a way you can answer. For example, Photoshop allows you to save images in GIF format. After you've indicated where to save it, you're presented with two pop-ups in sequence offering a number of technical options (see Figure 4.9). There are several problems here. First, there's no indication of what those options mean or what the consequences will be. Perhaps Adobe thinks that anyone saving in GIF format knows what they're doing, but we suspect not. It would help to have some explanation of the options. A second problem is that Photoshop waits until after you've specified where to save the file before asking these complex questions. Third, it interrupts your flow with not one but two pop-ups. A solution to all those problems would be to save with default settings, and then let the few who want to do so change them from a property sheet.

A   B

4.9
When you save an image in GIF format, Photoshop pops up first one window (A), then another one (B). The consequence of each of these choices is not clear. Also, presenting them in separate pop-ups breaks your flow twice. The better solution is to save the file with the defaults, and then allow you to modify them later from within the file.

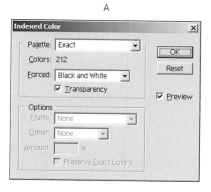

Be Predictable

Another way to be cooperative is to behave consistently so that people can learn to anticipate your actions. Your goal is to enable people to predict how to use an unfamiliar feature based on other features' behavior. At least their instincts about how to get started should be on target. We talked earlier about using platform conventions, and the same sentiment applies here. If you learn something in an application, it helps if you can apply it to other applications, or to other functions in the same application.

 Here's an example of an inconsistency that has boggled many a Photoshop user. In version 5.0, when you choose to Save As, the only format you are offered is PSD (Photoshop format). To save in another format, you have to choose Save a Copy, which offers all possible formats. This method is inconsistent with all other applications, which have a single Save As that lets you save in all available formats. Worse, even in earlier versions of Photoshop there was an inconsistency. If you wanted to save a file in GIF format, you didn't choose a Save option, you chose Export. So Photoshop taught you to Save a Copy if you want another format, but then fooled you if you happened to want GIF. When you finally figured it out, you could almost hear Photoshop saying, "Gotcha! Good one, eh?" Finally, in Photoshop 6.0, you choose Save As and all formats are available. Ahh!

 The computer game Diablo II has two nice examples, one of a visual consistency and one of a behavioral inconsistency. First the consistency. Throughout the game, any time you open up any inventory window, objects that are not accessible to you have a red background (see Figure 4.10). When you roll your cursor over such an item, a menu appears that indicates in red text why you cannot have the object (for example, your character is not advanced enough or isn't strong enough). This use of red is a consistent cue you can rely on in any part of the game.

4.10

Shopkeeper's inventory in Diablo II. The items with a red background (the two war hammers and the claws) are not available because the character does not have the required attributes. If you roll your cursor over a red item as shown, the background turns green (always the selection color) and a menu appears, indicating in red text the reason the item is inaccessible (in this case because the character is a barbarian, not an assassin). This use of red is a consistent visual cue throughout the game.

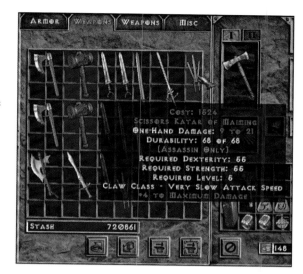

On the other hand, there is a behavioral inconsistency. In the game, to pick things up from the floor, you click on them and your character walks over and picks them up (see Figure 4.11A). If your inventory window is closed, the item automatically goes into the inventory in any available slot. But if it is open, it does not. The item goes into your character's hand and you have to drag it and place it into a slot in the inventory, which is much slower (see Figure 4.11B). If there are multiple items on the floor, it is especially cumbersome to have to pick each one up and put it in the inventory. Probably the reason for the inconsistency is that you might want to rearrange the items in your inventory when you pick things up. However, the game would be more consistent if it added the items in any available slot and then let you rearrange them if you wish.

4.11

To pick up the potions on the floor, you click on them and they automatically go into any available slot in your inventory (A). However, if your inventory window is open, the items go into your character's hand and you have to manually place them in inventory slots (B). This is a behavioral inconsistency, and it is especially annoying if you're trying to pick up multiple items with the inventory window open.

A

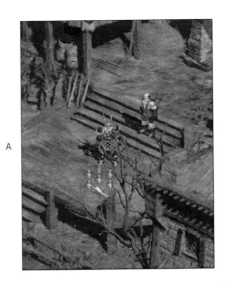

B

Design Guideline
Develop a set of conventions and use them throughout the application. You've succeeded if your users can predict how to use a new feature based on other features' behavior.

It's worth making the distinction between being consistent and being predictable. Consistency means behaving the same way every time, whereas predictability means behaving the way people expect you to behave (that is, the way that you've taught them to believe you will). We prefer to think in terms of predictability. Remember the Nokia Short Message Service example from Chapter 3? In that case, the left soft key didn't show you the same command every time. Instead, it always presented the most likely command based on the situation.

Request and Offer Only Relevant Information; Don't Mislead

We started this book with the example of a friend offering chocolate or strawberry ice cream, only to reveal that they don't have any chocolate ice cream. Here's a computer equivalent: You ask to print something, a pop-up asks how you would like it printed, and then when you tell it, it says the printer is out of ink. While the printer software is being helpful by telling you about the ink, it would be more cooperative if it told you *before* asking you about irrelevant options. (Although, as we mentioned earlier, it shouldn't be asking about those options at all.)

 Here's another example of offering an option that is not really available. Netflix.com offers a service by which you can rent DVDs by mail. You create a list of movies you want to see on the Web site, and as you watch them, you mail them back and they send you the next movie on your list. It's a nice service. However, they have a "gotcha" on their Web site. Suppose you go to their site to search for a movie to add to your list. Once you find it, you click the Rent button. If you are not already signed in, Netflix brings up the sign in or register page, since it needs to know whose list to add the movie to. The problem is that once you sign in, it loses track of the task you were doing and takes you to the main screen for signed-in members without adding the movie to your list. You have to find the movie all over again and add it. If you can't add movies to your list without being signed in, the Rent button shouldn't appear at that point. Better yet, of course, the system should remember your request and add it once you've signed in.

Another common Web error is to present a link for the current page. For example, Drugstore.com's main page offers a set of links on the left under the label "shortcuts." If you click on "your account," you see the page shown in Figure 4.12A. Even though you're on the "your account" page, that item is still a link, making you think "your account" is a different page. But of course, if you click on it, it takes you back to the same page. It's like offering chocolate ice cream to someone who's already eating some. A better design is to make "your account" a label, not a link, which we show in Figure 4.12B.

A

4.12

The Drugstore.com site presents "your account" as a clickable link (A), even when it is the current page. A simple redesign (B) presents "your account" as a label and not a link, so it's more obvious that you're on that page and you won't try to click to go there.

B

www.drugstore.com

On desktop software, the convention is to gray out options that are not possible in a certain context (for example, options that modify an object are grayed out when no object is selected). This is useful because it lets you know the feature is offered, but it tells you up front that it is not available right now for some reason. (We've often wished a ToolTip were available over grayed-out items to tell you what to do to make them available.) Other devices may have other conventions, but in general, it's good to gray out unavailable items on platforms that can update dynamically, and not offer unavailable options at all on platforms that have static offerings.

 Interestingly, the Palm's style guide recommends not offering options that are not available rather than graying them out. Sometimes this can be difficult to accomplish because it means some

Design Guideline
Don't offer options that are not available. Instead of surprising people with a "That's not available" message, gray out the option or don't present it. Don't mislead people.

buttons would have to appear and disappear frequently. Palm even violates its own rule. For example, even if you don't have an appointment selected in the Date Book, you can still tap the Details button, at which point the program pops up a message saying you need to select an appointment first (Figure 4.13A). Here we think it would be better to gray out Details when no appointment is selected, but since the platform's convention says not to gray things out, we would go with the convention. Or we would find a different way to offer Details. You might have an icon that appears next to any appointment (similar to the alarm icon) that opens the Details page. We've mocked up an example of this approach, shown on the right (though a graphic designer could no doubt create a better icon for Details).

4.13

If you tap Details in the Palm Date Book without selecting an appointment, an error pop-up appears (A). It would be better to prevent the error, perhaps by offering a Details icon that appears next to each appointment (B).

A

B

 It's also rude to ask for information that you aren't going to use. For example, Ellen once called to sign up for a NextCard credit card. It had an automated system that, among other things, asked for a social security number—one of the most private things you can ask because so much other sensitive, personal information is tied to it. After she overcame her misgivings and entered the number, the automated system finished its questions and tried to switch her to a human to finish the process. However, it then explained that the office was closed. Couldn't it have checked whether the office was open before sending people through the automated process? You can bet that we'll never request a credit card from them again.

Design Guideline
Ask for information only if and when you will use it (and then remember it). Never collect and then ignore sensitive information.

Here's an example of egregious behavior from an embedded device at Safeway's grocery store checkout (see Figure 4.14). We have a card that can be used as either a credit card or a debit card. The payment device starts by asking whether we're paying with a credit card or a debit card, which is perfect—except that it accepts only one answer, DB/CR, presumably meaning "either debit or credit" (step 1).[2] Then it asks to us slide the card through (step 2). For some reason, it then assumes we want to use the debit card and asks for our Personal Identification Number (step 3). But we want to pay with the credit card, so the *required response* is to press the red Cancel button. Then we're asked again whether we're paying with a debit or credit card (step 4). We press Credit, and the transaction goes through. This system saps tolerance capital. If it showed step 4 first, we could press Credit and swipe our card, finishing in two steps. Instead, it asks for information it doesn't use (DB/CR), then asks an irrelevant question it could have avoided (PIN), taking four steps to do what could have been done in two (indicate whether paying by debit or credit, then slide card).

4.14

Paying by credit card with Safeway's payment mechanism is a confusing process. First it asks whether you're paying by debit/credit card (step 1), offering only one possible response. After you slide your card (step 2), it asks for your PIN (step 3), which is relevant only if you're paying by debit. To pay by credit card, you press the red Cancel button, after which you're asked again whether you're paying by debit or credit card (step 4). After you press Credit, the transaction finally goes through.

Another common example of asking for irrelevant information is another form of the "Do you really mean it?" pop-up: the "Do you want to save changes?" pop-up. Some programs ask this question even when you open a file and close it, without making any changes. Usually this happens because the program sets a "dirty bit" when a file is opened, which triggers this pop-up when you close the file. Of

---

[2] We've tried pressing the second button on the theory that the labels are misaligned, but we get the same result.

course, this wouldn't happen if programs always auto-saved data, but even without auto-save, programs should never confuse you by asking whether you want to save something you didn't change. In contrast, Adobe Photoshop does an especially good job avoiding this pop-up. If you open a document and make a change but then undo it, it notices that the document hasn't really changed and doesn't bother you by asking whether you want to save your changes. Given that Adobe went to such trouble to develop a rich Undo model, it's nice that they use it to understand your context that well.

 A good example of asking information only when it's relevant comes from Eudora. If you delete an entire mail folder, it asks if you really mean it. This isn't too bad, since you could lose a lot of data that would be hard to recover, and you rarely delete folders. But if you delete an empty mail folder, it removes it without bothering you. Nicely done.

Explain in Plain Language

All applications "speak" to their users both by offering options (in menus, buttons, pop-ups, or speech prompts) and by providing explanations (in help or error messages). Whenever your technology uses words, use plain language that your audience will understand.

Here are some of the ways to speak plainly:

- Avoid jargon.
- Don't blame the user.
- Indicate the consequences of options.
- Use common sense.

Avoid Jargon

 When you spend a lot of time building something, you forget how much you adopt terminology specific to your application. Technical terms are useful for communicating within the team, but those terms should never appear in your user interface. Expert users may even know some of your technical terms, but it's best not to exclude everyone else. Here's an example from Windows. Apparently, Microsoft has a notion of an "Active Desktop," which we gather is the screen background.

We discovered this concept when the desktop crashed and the entire screen was filled with the image shown in Figure 4.15.

4.15

This Microsoft error message refers to "the Active Desktop," which is not a concept conveyed through the interface. Stick with terminology that is clear to the user.

Active Desktop Recovery

Internet Explorer has experienced a problem or error. As a precaution, your Active Desktop has temporarily been turned off. To start the Active Desktop again, use the following troubleshooting tips:

Did your browser stop working or did you restart your computer without shutting down? If so, click Restore my Active Desktop.

Did you recently add a new item to your Active Desktop? If so, try the following:

●   1. Click on the **Start** button, point to **Settings**, point to **Active Desktop**, and then click **Customize my Desktop**.
●   2. Clear the check box for the item you added most recently.

Do you want to turn off your Active Desktop and restore your wallpaper? If so, click the **Start** button, point to **Settings**, point to **Active Desktop**, then click **View as Webpage** to remove the check mark.

●

It turned out that clicking "Restore my Active Desktop" returned the background to normal (although the system remained unstable and we soon had to reboot). We had no idea that the background was "active" or that it was even an entity that could be restored. The last paragraph of the error message gives instructions on turning off the Active Desktop, which violates several of the guidelines presented here. First, if it can explain what to do, it could offer to do it for you. And it doesn't explain the consequences of turning off the "Active Desktop," other than restoring your "wallpaper," another unexplained term. (If turning it off would make it stop crashing, it's probably worth choosing.)

It's also important to avoid jargon in menus and labels, not just in error messages. These short labels are an important means of communication, so make them as clear as possible. Consider the pop-up from Netscape Navigator in Figure 4.16. The lower part of the window starts out well, explaining briefly that this property has to do with documents that provide their own fonts. The first option is clear, but the second and third refer to something called "Dynamic Fonts." Since it's capitalized it seems to mean something special, but this concept is never defined. (Incidentally, notice how the top part of this pop-up *shows* the fonts selected—Western, Times New Roman, and Courier New—so you can see what you're choosing. That's a nice example of providing information up front. However, we do wonder what percentage of people ever set these options.)

4.16

This Netscape Navigator Preferences window refers to "Dynamic Fonts," as if this were a commonly understood term. However, it does a nice job of previewing the fonts right in the place where you choose them so you can see what you're getting up front.

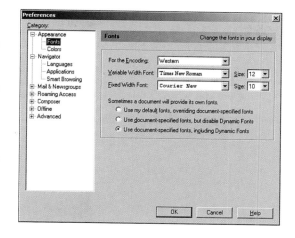

Design Guideline

Use everyday language. Don't assume people know the jargon of your industry or the terminology specific to your application.

Telephone handsets and cell phones often have unclear labels, partly because they must be short, but partly for less understandable reasons. Our Panasonic 900MHz cordless phone has a Flash button. Any idea what that means? The first time we met anyone who knew what "Flash" meant was when we both started working at a phone company. Most people use it to put someone on hold to switch to another call, although you can also use it for things such as initiating a second call on the same calling card. The term reflects the quick electrical "flash" on the line that causes the quick disconnect and connect. From a user's perspective, "Hold" or even "Switch" would be more helpful. Even though they don't capture all possible uses, they do a better job of suggesting the meaning so you might try it if you were looking for a way to switch to another call.

Don't Blame the User

When something goes wrong, a lot of technology presents messages that blame the user. It's better to adopt the mentality that if there's a problem, your technology wasn't clear enough, so it's your fault, not your user's. Even if the person is being a dolt, simple politeness tells you that there's no need to insult them. Sometimes error messages make problems seem more severe than they are. Terms such as "illegal" are extreme for providing information in the wrong format. "Fatal Error" is an overreaction, especially since it implies it was the user's error. Our all-time favorite was a Unix message that asked, "Abort child process?" Talk about extreme!

Consider the Web page from Schwab's BillPay service in Figure 4.17.

4.17

*This message from Schwab's BillPay service treats you as if you typed the wrong password on purpose by emphasizing what you **MUST** do to log in.*

www.mybills.com/Schwab/

"Invalid" is another term that implies blame. Also, is there really a need to scold you that you **MUST** (bold and in caps) provide the correct user name and password? It implies that you typed it incorrectly on purpose, just to see whether you could get away with it. A nicer way to say this is "That user name or password is incorrect. Please try again." If the number of times you can try again is limited, you should be told when you're on your last chance, and what you can do if you've forgotten your password.

Design Guideline

If something goes wrong, assume it's your design or implementation error and take responsibility. Write your error messages with humility, not blame.

 Perhaps the most infuriating of all "blame the user" messages is the one Windows presents all too often when the entire operating system crashes. If requiring a reboot is 100 clicks, an operating system crash is 1,000 clicks. You can't get much more uncooperative. Upon restart, it says, "Windows was not properly shut down," as if it had nothing to do with it. In earlier versions, this message explicitly blamed the user, saying "You did not properly shut down," but then Microsoft changed it, probably in response to negative feedback. Of course, the current message still implies it's your fault, especially since it goes on to provide "helpful" information about the proper procedure for shutting down. You think, "Let's see, first you crash and lose my data, and then you blame me for not properly shutting down? Why, I oughta…" If your technology crashes, your message should say something more like "We're terribly sorry, but we've done something horribly wrong. We hope you will please find it in your heart to forgive us and give us another chance." Maybe the button could say "Strike 1" after the first crash and add a strike each time it crashes. Okay, maybe that's going overboard, but if you can't avoid a crash, at least show that you understand the gravity of your error.

Indicate the Consequences of Options

Sometimes programs present you with options without explaining what will happen if you choose them. We frequently encounter one example in Microsoft Word. Say you are working on a document, which you save occasionally as you work. After a break you return to your work, and you click on that document in the file browser, forgetting that you already have it open. You see the pop-up in Figure 4.18A.

4.18

An error message from Microsoft Word appears when you try to open a document that is already open (A). The message takes real effort to work out. Which one is the saved one? It also offers no way out because you can't cancel, and the pop-up blocks you from looking at the open document to see whether you saved it. Pick the wrong button and you've lost some of your changes. A possible revision of this message (B) makes the result of each choice clearer.

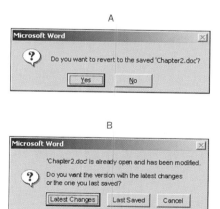

Design Guideline
If you give options or ask questions, explain the consequences of the choices.

Which one is the "saved" document? The one you've been editing and saving? Or the one that was saved on disk before you opened it in the first place? You start to wonder—did you save the last changes you made? There are two problems here. First, if you *have* saved the open version, Word shouldn't ask which document you want, since they're both the same. It should bring the open one to the front. If you haven't saved it (and Word hasn't auto-saved for you), Word should ask you which you want in terms that are meaningful to you. What you care about is which one has the most recent changes. Figure 4.18B is our suggestion for a revision.

This pop-up has two other serious problems. First, it does not have a Cancel button. You *have* to make a choice, even though you have no way of knowing which is the saved version. Second, it is a "blocking pop-up"—it prevents you from using any other feature in the application. (Blocking pop-ups, also known as modal dialog boxes, are one of the most hostile user interface elements because they take control away from the user while forcing them to take an action.) If forced to answer the question, you want to look at the one that's open and figure out if it is saved. But you can't. So you're stuck having to make a decision that could cause you to lose data, without a way out and without a way to find the right answer. As you reluctantly click one of the buttons, your tolerance capital for Word drops a few notches.

You may have noticed that when we rewrote the pop-up, we did not use the labels "Yes" and "No." Instead, we used "Latest Changes" and "Last Saved." In general, button labels should indicate what will happen if you click them. People don't like to read explanations in pop-up windows, they want to make decisions quickly and move on. If you use labels such as "OK," "Yes," and "No," you force people to read the message carefully so they know what "Yes" will do, even if they've seen this message many times before. You're also likely to wind up with error messages like the WorldView message back in Figure 4.7. It tells you that "It is strongly recommended that you exit, uninstall WorldView 2.0, and then run Setup," and then it asks, "Do you want to continue?" Your choices are "Yes" and "No." What does "Yes" do? It's unclear whether "continuing" means doing what they strongly recommend or installing anyway.

If you label buttons by the command, the outcome is clear and people can skip the explanation and pick the action they want. For example, if you ask "Do you want to print?", instead of using "Yes" and "No," offer a choice between "Print" and "Cancel." Buttons should have command labels such as Save, Print, Apply, Add, Remove, Convert, Search, and so on. Sometimes you have to work harder to clarify what action will take place, but it's worth spending time finding a descriptive label.

Design Guideline

Avoid at all costs blocking pop-ups that prevent people from using the rest of the application before handling a dialog box or responding to an error message. Often people need to look at something else in the application to make their choice. Even if you can't imagine why they would need to look elsewhere, don't prevent them from doing so.

Design Guideline

Avoid labeling buttons with generic terms such as "Yes," "No," or "OK," which force people to read the text carefully every time. Instead, label them with the action that will take place, such as "Search," "Add," or "Print."

 On small devices such as cell phones, you often need to keep labels short. Even so, try to use verbs rather than the generic "OK." Nokia uses "Select" rather than "OK" whenever possible, and also makes clear what you are selecting by keeping the screen uncluttered and highlighting the selected command (see Figure 4.19).

4.19

Cell phones and other small devices need to keep labels short, but Nokia makes it easier to understand what will happen by using the label Select rather than the generic OK, and by keeping the screen uncluttered and clearly identifying the selected item.

Use Common Sense

Finally, don't forget to use plain old common sense. This sounds obvious, but you'd be surprised how easy it is to find messages that don't make sense. Consider the message from Mozilla's e-mail program shown in Figure 4.20.

4.20

Mozilla's e-mail program pops up this message when you exit the program while mail is being sent. If you press OK, what happens?

What do you suppose OK will do? (If the button labels were commands, this problem would not have occurred.) There was a similar error back in Figure 4.15. The second paragraph of the Active Desktop Recovery error message offers two possibilities, "Did your browser stop working or did you restart you computer without shutting down?" and then says "If so, click." Which one is "so?" After reading this many times, we realized that it is offering two possible problems that would be fixed by clicking, but it reads as an either-or decision.

 Figure 4.21 shows another good one from an old version of Yahoo! Messenger.

4.21

Yahoo! Messenger's error message, while technically accurate, is almost comical.

Can you imagine a butler saying this with a straight face?

 You also won't make sense if you don't understand your user's context. @Home is a cable Internet service provider. When the service goes out, you call the main customer service line, which has a 45-second greeting telling you to go to a certain Web address to get customer support, followed by some menu options. If you don't have access to the Internet because the service is out, how can you go to a Web page? A butler would never waste your time making you listen to instructions that seem to rub your problem in your face. @Home could easily offer a different phone number to report service outages.

 Here's a message so painful it's amusing. If you have Developer Studio installed on Windows and a program crashes, you see the message in Figure 4.22.

4.22

In this painful error message, OK means Cancel and Cancel means Debug. If you make the mistake of choosing Cancel to cancel, your woes are compounded. First, you wait for a debugger to come up, and then when you close it, it asks whether you want to save your changes. Doh!

In other words, OK is Cancel and Cancel is Debug. What's worse, if you click Cancel intending to cancel, you wait a long time for the debugger to come up (remember, there's nothing slower than waiting for something you don't want), and when you close it, the program commits another blunder by asking, "Do you want to save this project?" There goes a major chunk of tolerance capital.

Design Guideline
Do a sanity check on all the language in your application. Get someone else to look over all the text and tell you when you're not making sense.

It's not hard to avoid these obvious bloopers. Ideally, get a technical writer or other skilled writer to write every word that appears in your application. If that's not an option, at least show all your error messages, pop-ups, menu labels, and so on to someone not on your project who is familiar with the area but not an expert. Ask them to point out anything they don't immediately understand. Then talk to them to make sure you understand what's confusing them and revise the language until they know what you're trying to say. (Don't just explain it until they get it, unless you want to do that for all your customers.) Once you revise the wording, show the new version to someone else to see whether you've done any better.

These are just some of the ways your technology can be helpful. Try to internalize the notion of being helpful and consider how it applies to your situation. Think about the metaphor of a butler—how would a competent, unobtrusive butler behave in this situation? In the next part of the book, we show how we applied these principles as we built a real application.

THE PROCESS

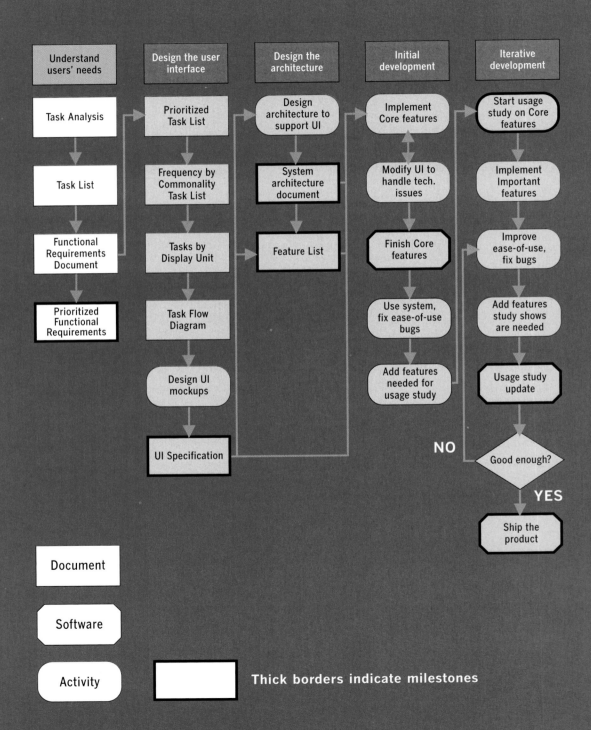

CHAPTER 5
Setting Up: Understanding Users' Needs

So far, we've explained some underlying principles for interaction design and some guidelines that should help you make better design decisions. But those don't tell you *how* to design a user interface. You also need to understand the steps involved in going from a description of features to a set of screens with controls laid out in a certain way. The rest of this book explains how that process works. We explain by showing how we built a real application called Hubbub, walking through the process of iteratively designing, implementing, testing, and deploying it. In addition to the basic steps, we focus on how we made decisions when faced with tradeoffs—sometimes between engineering and design goals and sometimes between design principles. We believe that well-designed technology depends on how you make those many small tradeoffs.

The Components of User-Centered Design

Before we begin, we'll lay out our beliefs about how design and implementation should be carried out to produce cooperative technology. This approach is called "user-centered design." That term can be applied to any development process that makes the users' needs a central priority, and here we briefly describe our approach. We spend the rest of the book illustrating how we carry it out in practice.

1. **Understand users' needs:** Build a product that meets real, observed needs rather than building something because it can be built. Spend time observing people who have this need so you can understand what tasks they carry out to meet it and what problems you could solve with your technology. If you understand how people carry out the activities you want to support, you'll be in a good position to focus on the features people really need and to design your technology to cooperate with them. We discuss the process of gaining an understanding of users' needs and tasks later in this chapter.

2. **Design the UI first:** Design the user interface first, and then design the architecture to support that UI before implementation begins. Some people think of the user interface as the surface characteristics of the application (the menus, buttons, and so on), but the UI refers to everything affecting the user's experience, which has implications all the way through the system. If you design the UI up front, the engineering architect can build in mechanisms to handle the desired interface rather than force-fitting it after the fact. It's a matter of knowing *all* the constraints on the engineering before implementation, rather than focusing on the machine constraints first and later worrying about user constraints. The design will change quite a bit as you accommodate implementation issues and usage feedback, but building the architecture to support a well-defined user interface greatly improves your chances of building cooperative technology. We discuss this concept later in this chapter, and then we describe how to design a UI in Chapters 6 and 7 and how to design an architecture to fit the UI in Chapter 8.

3. **Iterate:** The best interaction designer in the world will produce only a decent sketch of a user interface design on the first try. Their experience may enable them to design a solid structure and avoid some of the more straightforward interaction problems, but it is impossible to anticipate all the ways to smooth out the flow. A great design requires iteration. Plan to make iteration a part of the development process, building in time to make changes at each stage in the process. Start iterating right away by showing your designs to others as you lay them out to get as much feedback as possible. Then iterate during development as you learn more about implementation constraints. Continue to iterate as you try out the technology yourself. Iterate most of all as you observe the technology being used in context by real users during development. We demonstrate iteration at these different levels in Chapters 7–10.

4. **Use it yourself:** As soon as you've developed the technology to the point where you can carry out the core tasks, start using it yourself to do those tasks if at all possible. Not all systems lend themselves to being used by the development team, but where possible, using the system yourself can help you start to polish it. As you use it, observe all the ways your flow is broken when you do the tasks. You'll find obvious problems that you hadn't anticipated, and you can fix them while it's still relatively cheap to do so. You certainly won't find all the ease-of-use problems, but you will discover some of the obvious bobbles

to fix. However, using your own technology can help you find only certain types of problems. It does not tell you whether the system is easy for your customers to use. Chapter 10 illustrates the types of problems you can find by using your own technology.

5. **Observe others using it:** It is absolutely critical to observe other people using your technology in as realistic a way as possible *very early* in the development cycle. By very early we mean about halfway through development, when you have just the core set of functionality working with little supporting functionality. This is much earlier than most teams are used to. There are two main ways to get usage feedback from users: usability testing and usage studies. *Usability testing* is a technique for putting technology in front of users in a lab and asking them to carry out a set of predefined tasks. Usually, you test an overview of the most important tasks, but you might also zero in on a particular set of features of special interest. *Usage studies* are conducted by giving a preliminary working version with minimal features to a group of people who agree to use it as part of their ongoing activities in their own environment. This gives you feedback on a wide range of features as they will be used in a realistic setting, and it lets you know which features people naturally use. With both methods, you collect data on the problems people have when using the technology and incorporate changes to address those issues. Then you test the new version, either by running another usability test or giving the usage study participants an updated version. You keep doing this until you have a version in which all the features necessary to ship have been tested with users.

Although both techniques are effective, we are big proponents of usage studies because we believe they give a broader and deeper understanding of how people will use your technology, and they more explicitly build in an iterative process of studying use, modifying, and then studying again. The time you spend observing people and iterating the design saves you much more time in the long run. Not only will you discover that you don't need to implement some of the features you planned, but you'll be able to release a first version that is as polished as your competitors' third release, and is more focused on the features people really use—some of which you hadn't initially thought of as requirements. And you have the great advantage of making changes without worrying about backward compatibility, which saves time and gives you freedom to produce the best design. However, the development team must be willing to shift the process to accommodate the emphasis on iteration based on observation of use. This approach *won't* take more time; it *will* reallocate how the time is spent—on fewer features that are implemented well. We spend the bulk of Chapter 10 walking through the details of conducting a usage study.

As you'll see, we try to take a practical approach to user-centered design. You can certainly do more to understand or accommodate users at many stages in the process, but you're always working to find a balance between the ideal and the practical. After all, the most usable technology in the world won't help anyone if it never gets out the door. In this book, we show you when we believe it pays to be thorough, and when we're willing to take a more informal approach.

The Role of Hubbub

We hope to persuade you that our approach to user-centered design is feasible by spending the rest of this book illustrating how we used it to build Hubbub (described in the next section). Of course, the point is not to teach you how to build Hubbub, but we think it's easier to learn by studying concrete examples. So much of good design (and engineering for that matter) is about handling many small decisions that crop up along the way, which are hard to simulate with the idealized examples often used for instruction. Still, we don't want to bore you with too much Hubbub-specific information, so we try to provide just enough detail to explain the principles behind our decisions, hoping that we've struck the right balance—and that you'll bear with us when we haven't. As we go through the process, we each explain things from our point of view so we can show how we worked together to build Hubbub and resolve issues as they arose. We hope that by walking through this specific example, you'll gain a richer understanding of the day-to-day activities and decisions that enable you to build cooperative technology.

Let's start with some background about Hubbub. We built it while at AT&T Labs as an advanced development prototype for a product. During development, we conducted a usage study for just over five months among a group of people associated with AT&T, iterating the design five times during that period. We released the first version of

Hubbub in early 2001. It has been downloaded and used by people around the world, and we have since released a second version. You can download Hubbub free from www.HubbubMe.com. Since we use Hubbub as our example throughout this book, we encourage you to try it so you can get a better understanding of the application and make your own judgments about how usable it is.

Since Hubbub was not built in a product environment, there are some differences between our process and that used in a product division. The biggest difference is that we built Hubbub with just the two of us plus a second engineer named Dipti, who didn't start until over four months into what became a 15-month project (November 1999–January 2001). We also got a few months of support from another contract engineer, Bob. Many projects have a much bigger team, which may include more engineers, product managers, project managers, graphic designers, functionality testers, usability testers, documentation writers, managers, and business development and sales representatives. Some teams even include representative users, which is a wonderful resource to have.

In our case, since we had such a small team, we all played multiple roles. We all did functionality testing, and Ellen played the role of project manager, tech writer, and graphic designer. We had minimal business support and we borrowed a little help from a real graphic designer (though we could have used more). All of these limitations slowed us down or made it harder to get the information we needed. On the other hand, we did not have to integrate with any existing back-end systems (say for billing or operations), we did not have strong pressure to ship, and our management put fewer constraints on us than is typical. So we also had a little more freedom than we would have had in a product environment. While all of these differences are important, we believe the essential design and development process was not greatly affected by them. We've been able to apply this approach in product settings to various degrees with both small and large teams. (We describe those experiences briefly in the last chapter.) The main obstacle has always been the team's willingness to adjust its approach, not schedule or business concerns.

What Is Hubbub?

So what is Hubbub? Hubbub is an instant messenger that runs on wireless Palms and Windows PCs. For those not familiar with instant messengers, they allow you to send someone a short text message that pops up in a window on their screen as soon as you send it. If that person sends a response, you immediately see it in your window, and you can continue the conversation indefinitely. Instant messengers are similar to chat programs such as IRC and MUDs, except that conversations are between two people instead of among a group. You can have as many conversations going as you want, but each one is in its own window with just one other person. Instant messengers include a "buddy list" that shows the list of people you've decided to add, typically colleagues, friends, and family. You can initiate messages only to those on your list, and usually only when they are online. There are many instant messengers (often called "IMs") on the market, including ICQ, AOL Instant Messenger, Yahoo! Messenger, and Microsoft Messenger. You can download all of them free from those companies' Web sites.

While Hubbub is similar to the existing instant messengers, it has a number of differences. The biggest difference comes from our desire to transform an instant messenger from a message exchange application into a "presence awareness" application. In other words, we wanted people to be able to stay aware of remote colleagues, friends, and family even when they weren't interacting with them. (We explain the reasons for this later.) So Hubbub makes extensive use of sounds, which are effective in notifying people of information even when they're attending to other things. Hubbub has the notion of a *Sound ID*, a string of notes from a song that represents a person, just as their name represents them in other contexts. You choose the song that represents you to others. Each time you start using your computer, the people who have you in their buddy list (we call them *bubs* in Hubbub) hear your Sound ID, so they know you're around. Hearing your sound might trigger them to contact you, or they might just note your arrival and feel more connected to you even if you're thousands of miles away. Hubbub also has the concept of a *sound instant message*, a string of notes that have meaning (for example, "Hi," "Bye," "Thanks," or "Cool"). You can send someone a sound message just as you would send a text message, and they hear it as well as see it on their screen. So even if they're not looking at their computer, they can hear a set of sounds and know that you have sent a "hi" message, for example.

Hubbub also focuses on supporting people who are mobile. It runs on a wireless Palm so you can instant message (or IM) someone while on the road. It also allows you to stay logged in to multiple locations (home, work, school, Palm, and so on) at the same time so you can easily move from one place to another and stay connected without having to remember to log in at each place.

Hubbub is a networked client-server application with a server written in Java running on Unix, a Palm client written in C, and a Windows client written in C++. Alan worked on the server and the Palm client, and Dipti wrote the PC client and contributed to the design of the server. All setup and administration features are made available through a Web interface, written in PHP (a Web scripting language). This was written by our contractor, Bob. You don't need to know any of these computer languages to understand the rest of this book, but it helps to have a basic understanding of software architecture so you can follow the examples. We also assume you have used a PC, the Web, and to some extent a Palm, and can recognize the user interface conventions on each. Because Hubbub has both a PC and a Palm client and a Web interface, you will see how we designed the same application differently for different platforms, addressing each platform's interaction style and engineering constraints while making them consistent enough so that people can transfer their understanding of one to the other.

Understanding Users' Needs

Now that we've explained what Hubbub is, we need to take a step back and explain the first step in the user-centered design process: understanding users' needs. This process is sometimes known as a *task analysis* or *user analysis.* You could write a separate book on the subject of deriving ideas for technology based on understanding people's needs, and translating those needs into features. In fact, some people have done just that, and we recommend *Contextual Design* by Hugh Beyer and Karen Holtzblatt, *User and Task Analysis for Interface Design* by JoAnn Hackos and Janice Redish, and *The Art of Innovation* by Tom Kelley. Here we give a general description of the process and focus on the important aspects of how we came up with the idea for Hubbub. The diagram at the beginning of the chapter (see page 86) shows the set of steps involved, highlighting the ones covered in this chapter.

A lot of technology has been developed because it became technically feasible. Someone realizes they can make something, so they do it. They may decide to try it for the technical challenge, or maybe they realize they can use it to fill a personal need. Undeniably, a lot of good technology has been conceived of in this way, but developing such technology is a high-risk undertaking. You have to hope that enough other people have the need that the technology fills, and that they'll be willing to pay for it.

Requirements Guideline

When conceiving of a new technology, it is better to build something that supports an observed unmet need than it is to build something because you can and then hope people have the need it fills.

Another way to conceive of a technology is to learn what unmet needs people have and then try to develop technology to address those needs. Usually you have some idea of the type of need you're interested in. You may know you'd like to build something that helps people share pictures, or design buildings, or navigate in cars, so you focus your efforts on studying those activities. With this approach, though, you do not start with a piece of technology and then look for a need. Instead, you start with an activity you'd like to support and let that determine what technology to build. This is the approach we took because we believe it increases the chances of building something people will want.

Requirements Guideline

To understand the requirements for your technology, observe people doing the activity you want to support and talk with them about their experiences. Stay open to what you see; don't simply look for confirmation of your initial ideas.

This approach requires you to spend time observing people doing the activity you want to support so you can understand what works about their current method as well as the problems you could address with technology. You want to understand how people think about the activity (that is, their internal model of how to achieve their goals). Even though people may have many problems doing the task today, it's important to notice the advantages of their current methods so you don't forget to address those in your solution. You can conduct these observations formally or informally. In a formal study, you find a group of people who are representative of the target users and, with their permission, systematically observe them under a range of circumstances, preferably recording your observations in some way and carefully analyzing your records using specific methods for handling qualitative data. (Typically, you would work with an anthropologist, psychologist, or other social scientist who specializes in studying the use of technology.) Or you could do informal studies in which you watch people doing the activity in natural settings and talk to them about it, making notes about what you learn. Either way, the important thing is to stay open to what you see. Don't look for confirmation of a need you've already decided you can solve. Instead, focus on understanding the range of ways people carry out the activity and notice the range of problems without trying to find a solution to each one immediately.

If other technology products support the same or a similar need, use them and learn how they work. Watch people using those systems and see what works and what causes problems. Talk to people about which features they use so you get an initial sense of the features you need to include and features that might be cluttering those systems. Also, learn the conventional user interface behaviors for that type of application so you can follow them. People familiar with other applications should be able to transfer their knowledge to your system and not have to learn new techniques. You want to distinguish your product in terms of useful features and ease of use, not low-level user actions.

As valuable as it is to understand users' activities firsthand, it's also helpful to collect background information from other sources. Much of this information is collected by marketing organizations, but the rest of the team can benefit from it as well. There may be articles, reports, or even books about the activity you want to support. Look for market studies and newspaper or magazine articles characterizing the situation that would make your technology useful. If related products exist, you may be able to find current articles in trade magazines or technical journals about people's reactions to the existing technology.

Only after you've watched and spoken to at least 5–15 people should you start to look for patterns in the way people do things and the problems they encounter. At that point, start to come up with a list of *tasks* that your technology should support. The tendency is to jump immediately to features, but try to stay focused on people's activities and how they carry them out. Many teams use the task analysis to generate *use scenarios* that encapsulate the most important activities and users' expectations about how they should be done. For example, a scenario might be as follows: "Lillian arrives in her office after a meeting and sits down to work. She hears her colleague's Sound ID, which reminds her that she wanted to tell him some news from the meeting. He works in another time zone, so she looks to see where he is. She sees he's in his office, so she feels more comfortable contacting him with work talk. She sends him a sound message to get his attention, he quickly responds, and they get into a conversation."

These scenarios are used to generate the design and then to test the system to make sure the system supports them smoothly and easily. Some teams also generate *personas* or detailed descriptions of prototypical users, with the goal of keeping the team focused on the features that are most important to their customers rather than features that *some* people *might* want. Once you have a solid understanding of your users, their tasks, and how they go about them, think about how you could solve those problems with technology, and choose which type of hardware or software platform to build it on.

In the case of Hubbub, we had quite a bit of information before we began the project, which is not always the case. We had been studying informal communication for many years and had designed a few applications to support it using a range of technologies. We had also read many academic reports that characterized informal communication in the workplace and the role it plays. Through our experiences and these reports, we learned that groups located in the same hallway or work area maintain a background awareness of one another and have many unplanned interactions throughout the day. These interactions are critical for the smooth functioning of a group, even though people don't think of them as a "productive" means of communication. When we asked people how they communicate in the workplace, they talked about meetings and phone calls and e-mail, not the quick interactions that happen when they run into someone in the hallway or the lunchroom. Yet systematic studies show that more than half of all office interactions are impromptu, and people spend far more of their time in informal interactions than in planned ones. Furthermore, those who work at a distance don't work together as well as colocated groups even when they have just as many meetings, phone calls, and e-mails, largely because they miss out on the benefits of those quick, lightweight interactions.

Meanwhile, we read in the newspapers and in market reports that people are working at a distance from their colleagues because their company is distributing its workforce among multiple locations, or because they're working with people from other organizations, or because they or their team members are frequently on the road or working from home. We spoke with people who work from home who say they are more productive than they are at the office, but they miss the small daily updates from their colleagues, and they worry that others will think they're not working hard simply because they aren't visible. Most of the products on the market for distributed work teams focus on planned interactions (video conference rooms, e-mail, shared whiteboards, workflow, and so on). We wanted to find a way to help people who work at a distance to maintain an awareness of one another so that, first, they can feel more connected to one another, and second, they can have "opportunistic" conversations that are triggered because one person becomes aware of another at a time when they have something to discuss. Of course, people don't only interact with work colleagues. They also have informal interactions with friends and family who may be in different locations. As the lines between work and personal time blur, people are more likely to interact with friends and family while working as well as during personal time.

In the past, Ellen had worked on and studied the use of a desktop video conferencing system that made it quick and easy to establish a video connection with someone.[1] We had worked together on an online virtual world where people were represented by avatars who move around in a virtual neighborhood where they can "run into" people.[2] So we'd had some experience with different approaches to the problem of informal communication. Then instant messaging came along, and we became frequent users because it met a need of ours. Millions of other people also found it useful, and it quickly took off as a product. It occurred to us that, although existing IMs allow you to have quick, informal interactions, they don't do much to help you stay aware of other people or trigger opportunistic interactions. You can determine who is online, but not whether they're really at their computer. These IMs also don't help you notice when people are around; you have to look to see who's online. Some IMs play a sound when anyone comes online but you can't tell from the sound or by looking at the interface who just arrived (unless you can remember who wasn't there a few seconds earlier). And since many people stay online for days at a time, knowing when they come online isn't useful if you're trying to find a good time to talk. So we thought about how we could build awareness cues into an instant messenger.

[1] This application was called Montage. You can read about it and our experiences building it at www.uidesigns.com/bothsides/refs/montage/.

[2] This application was called Microcosm and you can read about it at www.uidesigns.com/bothsides/refs/cosm/.

Since we were considering building on an existing product, we started by learning about the other IMs on the market. At the time we came up with the idea, we had used ICQ, Yahoo! Messenger, and Excite PAL extensively in our work and personal lives, and we had experimented with a short-lived IM called Ding! We then tried AOL Instant Messenger (AIM) and Microsoft Messenger and used them for a while. We learned about many IM conventions as we used these systems with different people, but we also observed how other people used them and we talked with them about what they liked and didn't like about their experiences. We also read as many reports as we could about the use of IMs.

We saw cases where IM was used in the workplace to do such things as coordinate meetings or phone calls and to collaborate in real time (two people at their own desks working on their part of a task, using an IM to ask questions and update each other on their progress). We learned that spouses use IM to coordinate at the end of the day, arranging who should pick up the children or go to the market before dinner. Later we found out that teenagers use a form of phone-based IM for "micro-coordination," that is, coordinating as they go so they don't have to make plans in advance. For example, they might decide where to meet at a large venue only as both people converge on a location, or they may split up while shopping and then message each other to coordinate when they're ready to leave. We also observed some problems. For example, conversations often started with "Are you there?" indicating that people didn't have enough cues to figure out when the other person was available. People also complained that they couldn't tell whether the other person was typing or expecting them to type, and they didn't always know how to interpret long pauses. Also, people had trouble ending conversations for a variety of reasons.

So in our case, we had been aware of a need for some time, and we'd tried other approaches. When instant messaging came along, we gathered as much information as we could to help us understand how to adapt that technology to meet this need. Sometimes, you become aware of a need and have to go out to unfamiliar environments to understand it, perhaps setting up site visits or observing people in public places. Other times, you build a new technology and as people use it, they develop further needs. In all these cases, you should conduct firsthand observations, talk with people, and read reports about others' experiences and the broader market conditions. The critical thing for a user-centered approach is to mold your solution to match the need, rather than building something because you can and then hoping it solves a problem.

Once you've completed your task analysis, create an initial list of the tasks you would like your technology to support, called a *Task List*. Again, list tasks, not features. Doing so will help you stay focused on the user's purpose in using your technology rather than on features, which are of interest only to the extent that they help people achieve a goal. Your list should include many of the same tasks you observed people doing, and it will probably include other tasks that you believe will solve problems you observed or improve the way people achieve their goals. This list is the first step in the process of converting users' needs into a piece of technology.

Figure 5.1 shows the set of tasks we came up with for Hubbub based on our observations, our firsthand experience, and our readings. Our main focus was on helping distributed colleagues and friends feel connected to one another even when they were not interacting, and on supporting opportunistic interactions. After we fleshed out those tasks, we realized that we also had to consider the supporting tasks, such as getting set up, adding bubs to the list, and so on. We also wanted to be sensitive to social issues, such as protecting privacy, and since we knew Hubbub would be making use of sounds, we considered ways to help people easily control the sounds. As you can see, the list enumerates things you should be able to accomplish with Hubbub, not features.

5.1

The initial Task List for Hubbub, based on our analysis of user needs.

Hubbub Initial Task List

Using Hubbub, you should be able to:

Awareness

Look to see who "is around" and who's not, where people are (or just were), and how busy they may be

Check to see whether a certain person is around with the intention of contacting them

Hear someone log on or become active, and either know who it was, or if not, look to see

Decide to contact someone, evaluating whether they're likely to be there and how busy they are

Hear someone go idle or offline, and either know who it was, or look to see who it was

Adjust the order of your bub list, moving some people up and others down

See who is messaging with whom

Get a sense of how active each of your groups is right now

Sound Messaging

Receive a sound message, and either know what it means and who it's from, or glance to find out

Send a sound message

Turn off all sounds

Decide whose activity sounds you want to hear, and turn off those you don't

Exchange messages in a meeting where you've got sounds muted

Create a new sound

Import a new sound to Hubbub and send it to someone else

Receive a new sound message from someone and send it to someone else

Text Messaging

Receive a text message and know who it's from, and glance to see it

Send a text message

Quickly glance at a conversation screen and find the last message the other person sent

Have multiple IMs going at once, switching between them

Exchange messages with someone while doing other things, noticing when the other person is sending you a message, expecting you to respond, or off doing something else

Invite a third person to join your conversation

Carry on a multi-way conversation, then people leave until it's 2-way again

Arrive at a new location, start using your computer, and get a new message there without ever telling Hubbub where you are

Setup, Administration, Privacy

Register, choose a name, password, and Sound ID, and download the application

Log in, label the device

Find a Hubbub user and invite them to be your bub

Remove a bub

Create a group and put some bubs in it

Move a bub to another group

Use Hubbub from someone else's machine—log that person off, log on as yourself

Change your name, password, Sound ID, device label

Specify which bubs can see your activity/location or send you text/sound messages

Specify which bubs can see whom you're talking with in Hubbub

Help

Check online help

Use a tutorial to learn the sounds

This list is probably a little more complete than you would have at this phase. Sometimes you start with just the core tasks, and add other supporting tasks only later when you're figuring out the functional requirements. Since we had a lot of experience in this domain, we were able to anticipate the subsidiary tasks early on.

Specifying the Functional Requirements

Once your team agrees on the set of tasks you want to support with your technology, it's time to turn those tasks into specific product requirements, that is, functions the system needs to provide. To create an initial draft, you can go through each task on the list and come up with the requirements or functions that would support that task. Often it takes several functions to support a single task, and sometimes a single function can support multiple tasks. That is, there is not a one-to-one correspondence between each item on both lists, but you should track which functions support which tasks. (This will become important later when you design the UI.) You will also come up with some requirements that are not generated by a particular task but are part of the underlying support that enables tasks. Other requirements may arise as you investigate the technical capabilities of your platform and discover potential ways to support the tasks.

Requirements Guideline
The Functional Requirements Document lists the functions the system should perform. It should be generated primarily from the tasks you want users to be able to accomplish with the system. Some tasks will be supported by multiple functions, and some functions may support multiple tasks, so keep track of which functions support which tasks.

Usually, the product manager is responsible for generating this list and turning it into a document that is variously called the Functional Requirements Document, Functional Specification, Requirements List, or Market Requirements Document. Too often, project managers generate the Requirements List based primarily on competing products' features and sometimes in response to particularly vocal customers. Those sources provide important input, but they should not turn your focus away from supporting the tasks you determined were most important to users. One of the ways you want to distinguish your technology is by making it easier to use the features that most people need, not by jamming in a lot of features that few people use.

The Functional Requirements Document is the basis from which the underlying architecture and the user interface are designed. It's important, therefore, to make sure the items on this list do not specify architecture, engineering, or design details. They should be described in a way that allows for many different solutions on different platforms and with different UIs. We like to write them in terms of things the user can accomplish with the technology rather than how they accomplish those tasks.

Requirements Guideline
The Functional Requirements Document should list items in terms of requirements, independent of how they are designed or implemented. This allows the designer and the engineer the freedom to fulfill those requirements in the best way possible given other design and engineering constraints.

To return to our Hubbub example, take a look at Figure 5.2, which shows the initial Hubbub Functional Requirements Document. Notice how it provides a high-level description of each feature. It uses terms such as "ability to" and "indication of" without specifying how you might make that feature possible or how you might indicate that information. For example, one item under Text Messages is "Ability to visually differentiate each person's text" in a message. It doesn't say how the user interface should indicate each person's text. In fact, we used different methods on the PC (different colored text) and the Palm (bold versus non-bold). The requirement should specify only that there is a need to distinguish the information. Focusing on capabilities allows the designer to determine the best way to present the feature. If instead, you list requirements in terms of UI (for instance, "show different people's messages in different fonts and colors"), you predetermine the design before you understand how that feature fits in with the rest of the design. Also, the engineers will think in terms of that presentation, which may lead to wasted effort (they may spend time investigating font support when it may not be necessary, for example). Later, when the user interface and architecture are defined, you will generate a *Feature List* that does refer to design and implementation details. The Feature List translates the functional requirements into features that fulfill those requirements.

5.2

The initial Functional Requirements Document for Hubbub, after initial discussions within the team and feedback from colleagues.

Hubbub Functional Requirements

Proposed requirement

~~Requirement that was removed after initial investigations~~

Awareness—Visual

Bub list

Indication of whether each bub is active, idle, or offline

Indication of how long each bub has been active or idle

For active bubs, indication of level of activity:

>   Current level

>   Average over some period

Indication of which device each bub is on or was last on

Indication of each bub's location

Ability to manually order bubs within list

Indication of each group's average level of activity

Awareness—Sounds

Sound ID for each bub

Sounds to indicate when someone starts using computer (active sound) and goes idle (idle sound)

Sounds to indicate when someone starts or exits Hubbub (log in sound, log off sound)

Possibly, sound to indicate what device each bub became active on (device sound)

Visual indication of who went active/idle (to learn meaning of sounds)

Ability to tell if bub's device is muted

~~Sound to indicate when someone moves into or out of a "special zip code"~~

~~Sound to indicate when someone gets on/off a call~~

Sound Messages

Ability to send and receive sound messages

Visual indication of meaning of incoming sounds and who sent them

Ability to Mute All

Ability to mute each bub's activity sounds

Log of last N incoming sound messages

Ability to compose new Sound IDs

Ability to compose new Sound Instant Messages

Ability to test new sounds on Palm and PC

Ability to import new sound messages into Hubbub

Ability to send new sound messages to bubs

Text Messages
    Ability to send and receive text messages
    Visual indication of incoming text messages and who sent them
    Sound to announce arrival (and maybe sending) of each text contribution
    Ability to visually differentiate each person's text
    Indication of bub's window focus and typing activity during conversations
    Ability to have multiple IMs at once
    For other IMs not visible, ability to tell
        Window focus and typing status of bub
        Whether they've sent a contribution to which you haven't responded
    Time stamp of first message in conversation
    Ability to see who is messaging with whom
    Multi-way messaging

Mobility
    Ability to run Hubbub on a wireless device and a PC
    Ability to stay logged in from multiple clients at once
    Messages automatically "find you" as you move from device to device
    Ability to choose which device to send message to (if bub is on more than one)

Setup
    Ability to download and install the application
    Ability to register for an account
    Ability to choose a Hubbub name and password
    Ability to choose a sound to represent you (Sound ID)
    Ability to label the device
    Auto-login when you log on/turn on device
    Manual logon/off

Administration
    Ability to add bubs (requires permission)
    Ability to remove bubs
    Ability to grant/deny permission to add
    Reciprocal bub membership
    Ability to specify privacy settings when you add a bub
    Ability to create groups
    Ability to add/remove people to/from groups
    Ability to change your Hubbub name
    Ability to change your password
    Ability to change your Sound ID
    Ability to change device label

Privacy

Per person (and across clients), ability to specify whether you want to:

Provide active/idle info (per bub)

Provide location info (per bub)

Accept text messages (per bub)

Accept sound messages (per bub)

Provide info about whom you're messaging with

Other

Online help

Tutorial for learning sounds

Log of user actions (for usage study)

You can see how some tasks turned into multiple requirements. A good example is the initial task, "Look to see who 'is around' and who's not, where people are (or just were), and how busy they may be." By that task, we meant to convey that you should be able to glance at Hubbub and get a similar sense of the environment as you would at work if you popped your head up and looked around or took a quick walk through the hallway. To do this, you'll need a range of information, including who is working on their computers, where, how long they've been at it, and if someone is not there, where they last were and how long they've been away. The task expresses a single goal someone would have in looking at the application, and it maps to six requirements:

Task	Requirement
Look to see who "is around" and who's not, where people are (or just were), and how busy they may be	Bub list
	Indication of whether each bub is active, idle, or offline
	Indication of how long each bub has been active or idle
	For active bubs, indication of level of activity
	Indication of which device each bub is on or was last on
	Indication of each bub's location

On the other hand, the requirement, "Sound ID for each bub" helps support four tasks, all related to interpreting a message without looking. Our idea was that you would hear a Sound ID along with an event sound and be able to tell whom that event applied to.

Task	Requirement
Hear someone log on or become active, and either know who it was, or if not, look to see	Sound ID for each bub
Hear someone go idle or offline, and either know who it was, or look to see who it was	
Receive a sound message, and either know what it means and whom it's from, or glance to find out	
Receive a text message and know whom it's from, and glance to see it	

Requirements Guideline

The requirements will change during the development process as you learn more about implementation constraints and as you observe people using the system. You will discover that some requirements are not as important as you thought, others are more important, and some are too costly to provide given their value.

At this stage, some of the functional requirements may be tentative. For example, in Figure 5.2 under "Awareness—Sounds" is an item, "sound to indicate when someone moves into or out of a 'special zip code.'" This idea came from Alan's investigation of wireless PDA devices to determine which platform to build Hubbub on. He discovered that the Palm VII provides information that allows you to locate someone down to a specific zip code. This made us think of how people often use IMs to notify others when they are getting ready to leave or that they have just arrived. We thought it would be helpful for people to know when their spouse left work at the end of the day and when they arrived at home, or when their remote colleague arrived at their office, without that person having to update their location.

However, as he investigated further, Alan discovered that the pricing model for the Palm VII at the time allowed for only a few minutes of connection time per day without incurring further charges. Since Hubbub is intended as an awareness device, you have to be able to leave it on for long periods even when you're not actively using it to communicate. Meantime, Alan found that Omnisky, which offered a Minstrel wireless modem for the Palm V or Palm III, had an "all-you-can-eat" pricing model. Also, the Minstrel battery lasted for about eight hours—not ideal, but enough to leave it on for an all-day conference or a day away from the office. But it did not have the ability to pinpoint location. Given those tradeoffs, it was easy to decide to drop the zip code feature and choose the platform that better supported awareness. This was the first of many changes to our list of requirements. (In Figure 5.2 and other similar figures, we cross out items we dropped from the list rather than removing them so you can see the how the project evolved as we learned more.)

In other cases, we had a good idea of the basic design approach from the start, and that drove some decisions about the platform, which in turn affected the functional requirements. For example, we knew we wanted to use sounds to alert people about their bubs' comings and goings. Sounds are effective because people can notice them without having to focus their attention on them, which is important for an awareness device. So we knew we needed a platform that could support sounds, and specifically one that could play different sounds in response to different events. At that time, no cell phones had such support. Some cell phones allowed *users* to specify what rings to play for different callers, but a *program* couldn't trigger different sounds based on different events. So we had to postpone the phone client and focus instead on PDAs.

For yet other items, you may not yet have enough information to decide their potential effect on either the design or the implementation. Those items should be left in the Functional Requirements Document and resolved later when you build the feature list. You will create that list after you've worked out a design and an architecture, and better understand the tradeoffs involved in including each item and how best to do so.

One thing you might notice about the Hubbub requirements list is that it's relatively long. It has a lot of features for two engineers to implement. As long as it is, many of the other projects we've worked on have had much longer initial requirements lists relative to the size of the staff. At this early stage, everyone has a lot of good ideas about requirements that might be useful, and you'd really like to include them all. It isn't necessarily bad to include requirements that you won't implement in the first or even second release. When designing the architecture and user interface of the initial product, it can be helpful to know what's coming later so you can plan to handle the more peripheral requirements in the future. You don't build support for them initially, but you also don't make decisions that would make them difficult to add later, at least not without choosing to do so for a reason.

Prioritizing the Functional Requirements

The next stage is critical for setting yourself up to build something people will enjoy using. After generating the long list of requirements, you must prioritize them—and be ruthless about it. There are two reasons to create a prioritized functional requirements list. Most importantly, it helps the team communicate about its expectations as early as possible. It helps everyone understand what they are signing up for and what will be produced in the end. Secondly, prioritizing the list helps keep the team disciplined about working on the most important features. When prioritizing the functional requirements, it's critical to be conservative about the number of features you expect to build. The more features you set out to include, the less time you give yourself to do each feature well. And as we explained in Chapter 1, your users won't thank you for cramming lots of features into an unusable application. They'll thank you for making it pleasant to do the few things they need (or want) to do. The problem for many development teams is that they don't know which few key features to get right, so they build them all. By planning to do a usage study during development, you'll have the advantage of learning which are those key features.

Requirements Guideline
Divide your requirements into priority categories such as Core, Important, and Nice to Have, and get agreement on those priorities from the entire team. Be conservative as you assign categories. You should have strong evidence for each feature's necessity, so when in doubt, choose the lower priority. If the feature is really needed, you will find out during the usage study or usability testing.

Rather than fighting over the priority of every item, it helps to put the list into priority categories. In the case of Hubbub, we had three categories (shown in Figure 5.3): *Core*, *Important*, and *Nice to Have*. You may find a need for more priority levels, especially if you have a larger project. There is no magic formula for deciding which requirements go in which category. If you did a good job investigating users' needs and the tasks they perform to meet those needs, you'll have an easier time at this stage. When in doubt, choose the lower priority. You want strong evidence for each feature's necessity, so if you're not sure, be conservative.

Requirements Guideline

The Core requirements are the minimum features needed to use the system. This category should include the features with which users can start to try out the most basic aspects of the system, not the full set of useful features. The fewer items you put in the Core list, the more your development will be driven by real usage data rather than your perceptions of what users need or how they behave.

We think you should have at least one category called *Core Functionality*. This is the basic set of features you need to meaningfully use the application at all. By no means does it include all the features you need to ship. It includes only those features that make the application just barely functional so that you can try out its central functionality. In other words, the Core features are the ones you need to start testing the most basic aspects of the system with users. To use the system, you may need to fudge some aspects. Maybe you'll need to provide some fake data to work with. Or maybe you'll need to hard-code some attributes so you can get people set up. But once you have the Core features, you can start to test the system's ease of use by starting a usage study or running your first round of usability testing. Your goal is to have most of the development process guided by data from real usage rather than your notions of how users will behave, so try to put as few features as possible in the Core category. Then as you start testing with users, you'll get feedback about which features are truly important and which are nice to have.

5.3

Hubbub's initial Functional Requirements List, divided into priority categories (first pass).

Hubbub Prioritized Functional Requirements

Proposed requirement

~~Requirement that was removed after initial investigations~~

Core Functionality

Can't meaningfully start using application without:

Bub list

Indication of whether each bub is active, idle, or offline

Indication of how long each bub has been active or idle

Sound ID for each bub

Sounds to indicate when someone starts using computer (active sound) and goes idle (idle sound)

Visual indication of who went active/idle (to learn meaning of sounds)

Ability to send and receive sound messages

Visual indication of meaning of incoming sounds and who sent them

Ability to send and receive text messages

Visual indication of incoming text messages and who sent them

Ability to Mute All

Sound to announce arrival (and maybe sending) of each text contribution

Ability to run Hubbub on a wireless device and a PC

Ability to stay logged in from multiple clients at once

Messages automatically "find you" as you move from device to device

Important Functionality

Can't ship without:

For active bubs, indication of level of activity:

  Current level

  Average over some period

Indication of which device each bub is on or was last on

Indication of each bub's location

Sounds to indicate when someone starts or exits Hubbub (logon sound, logoff sound)

Ability to tell if bub's device is muted

Ability to mute each bub's activity sounds

Log of last *N* incoming sound messages

Ability to visually differentiate each person's text

Indication of bub's window focus and typing activity during conversation

Ability to have multiple IMs at once
Ability to choose which device to send message to (if bub is on more than one)
Ability to download and install the application
Ability to register for an account
Ability to choose a Hubbub name and password
Ability to choose a sound to represent you (Sound ID)
Ability to label the device
Auto-login when you log on/turn on device
Manual logon/off
Ability to add bubs (requires permission)
Ability to remove bubs
Ability to grant/deny permission to add
Reciprocal bub membership
Ability to specify privacy settings when you add a bub
Ability to change your Hubbub name
Ability to change your password
Ability to change your Sound ID
Ability to change device label
Per person (and across clients), ability to specify whether you want to:
    Provide active/idle info (per bub)
    Provide location info (per bub)
    Accept text messages (per bub)
    Accept sound messages (per bub)
    Provide info about whom you're messaging with
Online help
Log of user actions (for usage study)

Nice to Have Functionality

Great feature ideas that you can ship without. Evidence from real use can tell you whether to include them:

Possibly, sound to indicate what device each bub became active on (device sound)
Ability to manually order bubs within list
~~Sound to indicate when someone moves into or out of a "special zip code"~~
~~Sound to indicate when someone gets on/off a call~~
Ability to compose new Sound IDs
Ability to compose new Sound Instant Messages
Ability to test new sounds on Palm and PC
Ability to import new sound messages into Hubbub
Ability to send new sound messages to bubs

For other IMs not visible on Palm, ability to tell
    Window focus and typing status of bub
    Whether they've sent a contribution to which you haven't responded
Time stamp of first message in conversation
Ability to see who is messaging with whom
Multi-way messaging
Ability to create groups
Ability to add/remove people to/from groups
Indication of each group's average level of activity
Tutorial for learning sounds

Requirements Guideline

The Important require-ments category includes the minimal set of features needed to ship the application. Keep this list as small as possible so you have time to polish each feature, and so you can add items that usage feedback indicates are needed. The Important list will change during development, but it is helpful for the team to agree up front on which features are considered necessary to ship.

With Hubbub, the Core category certainly needed to include the buddy list (we call it a *bub list)* and the ability to send and receive text messages. Since awareness was the central distinguishing concept behind Hubbub, we included basic sound support and the ability to tell who is active or idle on their computer and for how long. Having these would allow us to understand early on what it was like to *hear* when someone becomes active or to send a sound instant message. We did not include things such as account setup or the ability to add and remove bubs. We figured we could hard-code the account information and the list of bubs, at least to start. We also did not include some of the features we considered innovative and were eager to try. For example, we wanted to experiment with ideas for showing each bub's level of activity at any given time or averaged over time. But we could get a meaningful experience using Hubbub without this capability, so it was not considered a Core feature.

The second category, Important, includes the minimum set needed to ship the application. If your project is large, you may decide to divide this category into a few subcategories to distinguish levels of importance. Defining this category is where the hard work is done. As we mentioned before, the more you load it down with features that really belong in the Nice to Have list, the less time you're giving yourself to build these features right. Also, keep in mind that this part of the list is the most likely to change once you get some experience using the application and watching others use it during development. In some cases, you'll include the first part of what you expect to be an extensive feature, only to find that people rarely use even the basic part, so you can trim most of the feature. (Yes, this really does happen.) Meanwhile, other features you hadn't thought of will seem obviously missing. If you keep this list as short as possible, you give yourself room to focus on the features that matter to people and to make sure you make them smooth and easy to use. The more you pack it with everyone's wish list, the more you set up everyone's expectation to rush through each feature to get to the next one. As we discuss our experience building Hubbub, you'll see how helpful it was to know that we would find out how users reacted during our usage study before we made final decisions.

Requirements Guideline

The Nice to Have requirements should include all the great ideas that could make the technology more interesting but are not required to ship. Most of them will not be included in the first release, but they may become important later as you get data from users.

Requirements Guideline

Users ask for features the way kids ask for candy. Don't be tempted to add too many requirements to your higher priority categories.

The Nice to Have list is the place to put all those great ideas that could turn out to be extremely useful but that you can live without at first. Once you run the usage study, you'll figure out which ones should be bumped up to the Important list, and some might even wind up distinguishing your product. But until you *know* that any of these features are truly necessary, keep track of them in the Nice to Have list. The Nice to Have list can be a good political mechanism as well, especially when people come up with new ideas after you've agreed on the prioritization of the requirements. Putting a requirement on the Nice to Have list acknowledges the idea and ensures that it won't be forgotten, but does not distract you from your highest priorities at that time. Keep in mind that it takes a lot less effort for someone to think up a feature than it does to design it, build it, test it, and polish it, even if you ignore the concern about how it affects other features. Just because someone can imagine that a feature "might be useful" doesn't mean it's worth your time to create it. We're reminded of a saying we once heard: "Users ask for features the way kids ask for candy."

In the end, you are likely to include few of your Nice to Have requirements, at least initially, and that's okay. You will end up providing other features instead. And because you'll be basing your feature decisions on real usage patterns, you'll know that you are spending your precious resources on the features that make a difference to people. If you want to look ahead to find out which requirements we ended up dropping, and which unanticipated ones we added, sneak a peak at Figure 10.17 in Chapter 10.

In the Hubbub list, the Core Functionality list is quite short, roughly half the size of the Important List, which is also longer than the Nice to Have list. The Nice to Have list should probably be longer than the Important list, especially if you were liberal about including potential requirements when creating the original list.

Designing the User Interface First

Design Guideline

To develop cooperative technology, you must design the user interface first and then design the architecture to support that user experience. If the engineers don't know how the system should behave up front, they unwittingly make design decisions that preclude satisfying basic user needs. If they have UI information up front, they can balance those constraints against all the other engineering constraints.

At this point, you're ready to begin the user interface design, *after* which you'll design the architecture. Unfortunately, it is common for people to either design the architecture next and then the UI, or to dispense with a UI Specification altogether. The UI is very much part of the functionality of the application, so you need to know what it is before designing the architecture to support that functionality. If you want to build cooperative technology, first create the Functional Requirements List, then the UI Spec, and then the System Architecture. Of course, creating these documents isn't purely a serial process and you have to iterate to get them right. But it's important to figure out how the user will interact with the technology before you decide how to support that interaction.

If you build your architecture first, you will inevitably run into situations where the design calls for a certain interaction approach that the architecture can't support cleanly, if at all. In most cases, if the architect had known the interaction need up front, it would have been easy to build in, but since they didn't anticipate the need, they made decisions that precluded it. For example, several years ago, one of the Web portals built its e-mail offering as a standalone site. Once it was released, the product managers quickly wanted to let people know whether they had new mail on the home page of the portal, rather than making people go to the e-mail site to check. The original design hadn't taken this into account, so it took a large group of people a few months to adjust the architecture to handle this simple (and in retrospect obvious) request. And even then, it worked only for those who registered for an account after that point, not for all the existing users.

If you design your user interface first, the engineer can treat the interaction requirements as a set of constraints on the system, much like memory and performance considerations, and design an architecture that handles them. This is not to say that the UI will always determine how the system is designed. Rather, you will be able to balance the UI considerations against others and make informed decisions instead of finding out after the fact that an early architecture decision precluded satisfying an important user need. One of the most important things you can do to improve the usability of your technology is to first specify how people will interact with the software and then construct an architecture that handles that interaction.

Using this approach does not mean that the engineering staff has to sit idle waiting for the designers to do their work. There is usually work that can be done independent of the UI, and many times the engineers need to investigate technical issues raised while listing the functional requirements or learn a new piece of technology for the project. Sometimes, the interaction designer can be working on the next phase of a project while the engineers are fixing bugs on the current release. In the case of Hubbub, during the three weeks that Ellen spent designing the first-pass UI, Alan looked into various wireless devices and, when we settled on Palm, started learning about Palm operating system development environments. For example, this was when Alan investigated the possible PDA and phone clients for Hubbub and narrowed our choice down to the Palm V, which removed a few tentative features from the list. As Ellen worked out the UI, we had a lot of quick conversations like this:

Ellen: Hey, can the Palm display italics?

Alan: I don't know, let me check.

Ellen: What about bold?

Alan: Yup, it's got a bold font built in.

In all of our experience, there has been productive work for the engineers to do while the initial design is being created. If you are both the designer and the engineer, we urge you to focus your efforts first on the interaction design and second on the architecture.

A View from Engineering

Before we roll up our sleeves to show you how Ellen designed the user interface (Chapters 6 and 7), let's take a quick look at Alan's take on the project so far. He's only got the Functional Requirements to work with, along with discussions we've been having about the underlying goals of the system. Without a detailed UI Spec, he can't design the architecture, but he is building a rough mental picture of the system's architecture. Alan's thinking is fluid enough at this point that he can adjust to handle different types of UI requirements once they are defined.

Alan: At this point in the project, I've got only a high-level notion of how the system will look. For instance, I know that Hubbub will need a server to handle coordination among clients. From the Functional Requirements, I know that there will be account management features (register for account, choose Sound ID, set permissions, add/remove bubs, and so on). This means that there will probably be some sort of database connected to the server.

I've got a picture in my head of messages being passed back and forth from client to server and from client to client. My guess is that the server will be the final authority on accounts and client authentication. Clients will need to tell the server that they're online, and the server can update them about their bubs. Text and Sound Instant Messages (SIMs) may be routed either through the server or passed from client to client directly; I'm not yet sure which is more appropriate. I will probably write the server in Java, since it's wonderful for whipping up back-end servers and I'm happy with its speed and stability in non-GUI situations. (As of this writing, I still wouldn't write a GUI with the standard Java toolkits. No sir. Not gonna happen.)

Since we'll be handling the same messages on at least three different platforms (PalmOS, Windows, and Java), I'll want to put some time into cleanly defining the messages and making them easy to handle. We also have security concerns, so I'll want to think about ways to prevent spoofing and eavesdropping.

A Word on Schedules

It's not uncommon for management to ask for a schedule at this stage. You've developed the Functional Requirements and agreed on which elements are critical for shipping, so (the theory goes) you should be able to give an idea of how long it will take to build. We believe any estimates at this point are mostly fiction. Until you know *how* you're going to provide the functionality, any estimates are based on wildly simplified ideas of what's involved in each component. Here, Alan explains what he would do if asked to come up with a time estimate for implementing Hubbub based on the functional requirements. Keep in mind that he has a lot of experience with similar applications, so he has confidence in his ability to learn quickly.

Alan: I'd read the Functional Requirements again, making sure that each item in it is at least possible (and not too unwieldy) to implement in my vague model. I don't know anything about PalmOS programming at this point so I can't judge the client side accurately, and I can't possibly anticipate all the implications of some of the items that will appear in the UI Spec, but that's OK. This is just a sanity check. I want to make sure that no requirements will obviously break my model. If that happens, my basic assumptions are wrong and I've got nothing to base a schedule on.

Once I've convinced myself that my notions are not obviously invalid, I start making wild guesses about time. Since I know I can't anticipate all the issues, I think in terms of weeks or months. I've done Java networking before, so I know it can move pretty fast. On the other hand, this server will need a database attached to it (because accounts need to be able to persist even when the server has stopped) and I haven't worked with JDBC (Java Database Connectivity) before. We're initially expecting to support thousands of users rather than millions, so I'm not going to worry too much about scaling for now. Say two weeks for the basic Java stuff, two weeks to get it working with a database, and then two more weeks of tweaking.

On the client side, we've settled on the Palm Vx and Omnisky Minstrel modem, but I have to think about building on those platforms. I'll have to learn both a new platform (PalmOS) and a new development environment. Since developing on the Palm is new to me (and I've read about various system constraints on memory, code segment size, and so on), I should take into account that progress may be slower than I'd like at first.

I know it'll take me at least a week, if not two, before I'm familiar with the new environment. So, say two weeks of learning, two weeks of getting basic functionality working, and then eight weeks of adding and tweaking various features. All I can do is guess at how long the various UI features (multiple IM windows, playing sounds, and so on) will take.

Scheduling Guideline
Don't try to estimate schedules based on the Functional Requirements. Until you know the details of the design and architecture, these estimates will be wildly optimistic. If you then commit to deadlines based on those estimates, you set yourself up to rush through the features and omit the work needed to make them easy to use. It will take only a little while longer to design the UI and architecture, so wait until you have that information.

Design Guideline
When designing a UI, focus mainly on providing the best possible user experience, forgetting all but the most basic platform constraints. Be willing to explore ideas that may be hard to implement; you may come up with great ideas that can be implemented another way. At this stage, your goal is to figure out how to cooperate with the user. Later you can adjust the design to accommodate engineering issues.

That's a total of six weeks for the server and 12 weeks for the client, for a total of about 4 1/2 months. This is without having a deep understanding of the issues that are bound to arise once implementation gets underway, so this estimate will be the low bound...

We've already mentioned that Hubbub took over a year to build, so you get an idea of how far off this estimate is. Alan promises that he was genuine in re-creating his thinking at this point, and having worked with him before, Ellen agrees that this is typical of his estimates. Maybe all this proves is that Alan is lousy at estimating schedules, but our experience has been that he is only slightly worse than average. Ellen spent nearly three years managing software projects and the common practice was to triple most engineers' estimates and consider that a best-case scenario. Our point is that if you want a more realistic schedule estimate, at least wait until after you have a UI Spec and an architecture, which should be ready in a matter of weeks.

Getting into the UI Designer Role

In the next two chapters, Ellen designs the user interface based on the Functional Requirements. If you are an engineer playing the role of a designer, the trick is to fully embrace that designer role for the time being. See the butler. *Be* the butler. Think about what would be most helpful and cooperative for the user, without, for the moment, rejecting anything on the basis of specific engineering constraints. If you allow yourself to try out an impossible-to-implement design, you might discover a more practical way to accomplish that goal with a different design. For the moment, your goal is to think solely about the users' needs and do your best to design for them.

If you are a designer working with an engineer, talk to the engineer to find out the basic constraints of your platform. Just as your UI design gives the engineer constraints from which to design the architecture, you need to know the underlying system constraints so you can come up with plausible designs. For example, if you're designing for a small device with limited memory and CPU, you'll want to minimize the amount of animation and graphics. If you're designing for a television set top box, there may be limited memory on the system, which will constrain how much you can remember about each user without going to the server to fetch the information, which takes time. Find out what's expensive in terms of performance, memory, disk space, bandwidth—whatever might be constrained. As you work through the UI, you'll have more questions, but start out with a basic understanding of the system.

In either case, you will likely feel a tension between brainstorming wonderful ideas that are unrealistic to implement and restricting your thinking to accommodate engineering constraints. Although there is no magic solution, during the design phase we tend to assume the limitations of the platform that can't be changed (memory, CPU, bandwidth, and so on), but then let our imagination wander about how the application might achieve different goals. Even if we come up with ideas that are too costly to implement, by working together we can often come up with variations that achieve a similar goal without taxing the system too much.

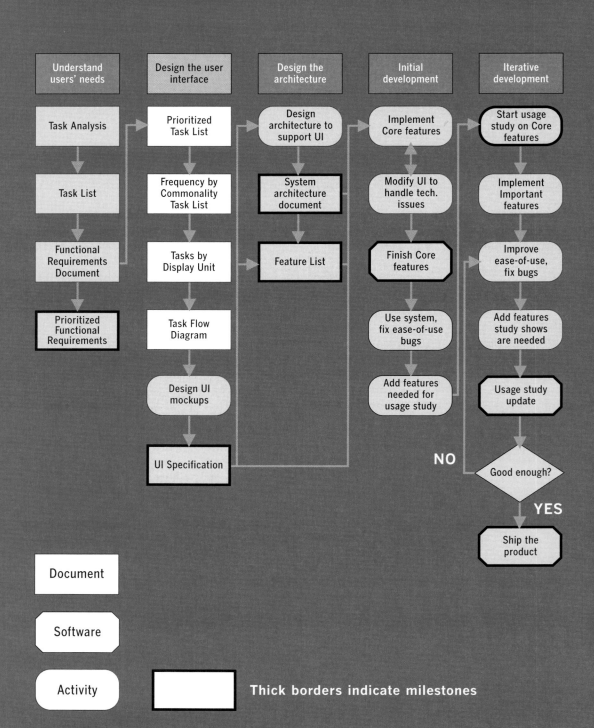

CHAPTER 6
Structuring the User Interface

Now the fun part begins. You've got your list of requirements and you need to turn it into a user interface design. In this chapter, Ellen explains how to do that.

The User Interface Spec

When you design a user interface, you need to capture it in a document called the *User Interface Specification*. UI Specs come in different forms, but typically they consist of many screen shots along with a description of how users manipulate the user interface components to accomplish their goals. You might think of a UI Spec as a storyboard or even a comic strip showing screen shots of critical steps in the process of doing each task, with text explaining what's happening. No matter how you handle the images, you need to write down all the aspects of the UI that are not easily conveyed in pictures. For example, if you want a PC application to remember the size, location, and configuration of each window (and you should), you need to specify that fact because your pictures won't convey it. Even if the screen shots do suggest an interaction, it's still worth articulating how it works, so it's clear that your picture isn't just one way to do it, but the approach you specifically chose. You can create a UI Spec in any number of formats, but make sure it is easily accessible to all the team members and easy for you to update.

On the Hubbub project, I wrote the UI Spec in HTML, included screen shots I'd created in Photoshop, and posted it to a protected Web site. I also checked it in to the source tree so we could keep track of versions, if need be. As we revised the features, I updated the screen shots and associated text to keep the document current. Several years ago while working on a large project with 30 engineers, I wrote the UI Spec as a text document with pictures and saved it in a directory accessible to everyone. Whenever I updated a section, I notified the associated engineer, who grabbed it from that directory. Another time when some colleagues and I designed a Web site, we created the design directly in

HTML and then wrote an accompanying document to spell out the interaction aspects that weren't clear from the static pages. The engineers started with the HTML we'd written and consulted the document to create the dynamic pages. In another situation, I was able to create the UI in a GUI builder, which generated its own code. This gave me full control over the layout, but I still had to write down the interaction design for the engineers to implement.

Design Guideline
It's very important to write a User Interface Spec that includes mockups of how the system should look as well as a written description of how it should behave. The UI Spec should be easy for the team to use. The more accessible it is, the more likely it is that the team will build the system as it was designed.

Writing a UI Spec may seem like a lot of work, but every time I've written down exactly how the user interface should work, the engineers have greatly appreciated having the document, and the resulting system has been much more consistent with my design. The Spec gave engineers something concrete to consult when making decisions, and it was available even when I wasn't. My experience has been that many engineers won't ask if they're not sure how to handle a UI issue because they're trained to figure things out for themselves. If there's a document answering the question, they'll use it; if not, they'll tend to come up with their own solution.

It's important to keep the UI Spec current so that the team members have confidence that they can always check the Spec to find out what they're supposed to build. During development, issues will come up that were not addressed in the Spec, so update the document to reflect the resolution so that others working on related parts have the new information. When you make a change, notify everyone who is affected by it. It can be a little hard to keep up with all the small changes, so I have found that over the course of a project, I wind up doing a few start-to-finish updates of the entire Spec to make sure it's current. When I do, I send e-mail to the entire team letting them know that a new version is available and pointing out the major areas of change.

Design Guideline
Keep the UI Spec updated as the design changes so that every-one on the team knows how each feature is supposed to behave. If used well, the UI Spec can help the team stay coordinated. It not only helps the engineers know what to build, but also helps the business team communicate the concept to interested parties, the testing team find features not implemented as designed, and the documentation team get started on manuals.

Keeping an updated UI Spec also helps members of the testing team, who can use it to make sure the application is behaving as designed, and the documentation writers, who can use it as a starting point for manuals. Even the business team benefits, because having detailed screen shots helps them present the technology to interested parties before it's working. Initially, they can communicate the concept using the design mockups, and gradually they can replace them with working demos as the components of the technology start to come to life.

I believe that the designer's job is not just to create the design, but also to communicate it to the team in a way that is easy to use. Communication can take a fair amount of time, especially with a large team, as you must check in with people, handle design issues, and make sure any changes are propagated to those who need to know. The time spent communicating about the design will not only help the team stay coordinated but it will also improve the chances that the system will be built as you designed it.

So how do you get from a prioritized Functional Requirements List to a UI Spec?

Start with Tasks

To decide how to design the system, you need to think in terms of the users' tasks. You aren't trying to figure out where to put the features, you're trying to figure out how to help people accomplish tasks. So start with a copy of the Task List, this time rearranged to reflect the priorities you agreed on when reordering the Functional Requirements Document. The prioritized Task List for Hubbub is shown in Figure 6.1.

6.1

The Hubbub prioritized Task List.

Hubbub Prioritized Task List

Core Tasks

Look to see who "is around" and who's not, where people are (or just were), and how busy they may be

Check to see whether a certain person is around with the intention of contacting them

Hear someone log on or become active, and either know who it was, or if not, look to see

Decide to contact someone, evaluating whether they're likely to be there and how busy they are

Hear someone go idle or offline, and either know who it was, or look to see who it was

Receive a sound message, and either know what it means and who it's from, or glance to find out

Send a sound message

Turn off all sounds

Exchange messages in a meeting where you've got sounds muted

Receive a text message and know who it's from, and glance to see it

Send a text message

Quickly glance at a conversation screen and find the last message the other person sent

Arrive at a new location, start using your computer, and get a new message there without ever telling Hubbub where you are

Important Tasks

Decide whose activity sounds you want to hear, and turn off those you don't

Have multiple IMs going at once, switching between them

Exchange messages with someone while doing other things, noticing when the other person is sending you a message, expecting you to respond, or off doing something else

Register, choose a name, password, and sound ID, and download the application

Log in, label the device

Find a Hubbub user and invite them to be your bub

Remove a bub

Use Hubbub from someone else's machine—log that person off, log on as youself

Change your name, password, Sound ID, device label

Specify which bubs can see your activity/location or send you text/sound messages

Check online help

Nice to Have Tasks

Adjust the order of your bub list, moving some people up and others down [may not be necessary if we have groups]

See who is messaging with whom

Get a sense of how active each of your groups is right now

Create a new sound

Import a new sound to Hubbub and send it to someone else

Receive a new sound message from someone and send it to someone else

Invite a third person to join your conversation

Carry on a multi-way conversation, then people leave until it's 2-way again

Create a group and put some bubs in it [may not be necessary if we allow ordering of bubs]

Move a bub to another group

Specify which bubs can see whom you're talking with in Hubbub

Use a tutorial to learn the sounds

The prioritized list reminds you to focus on making the higher priority tasks as simple and easy to accomplish as possible, if necessary at the expense of lower-priority items. However, the priority of the tasks was determined by many factors, only some of which are relevant to the user interface design. What you really want to know is how important each task is to the users as they accomplish their goals. To determine this, think about the tasks along two independent dimensions:

1. How often will people do the task?
2. How many of your users will do the task?

If you combine those two dimensions, you get four categories:

	By Many	By Few
Frequent	**Frequent by Many** Most people will do this task frequently (nearly every time they use the application)	**Frequent by Few** Only some people will do this task, but they will do it frequently
Occasional	**Occasional by Many** Most people will do this task, but only occasionally	**Occasional by Few** Only some people will do this task and only occasionally

Now assign each of your tasks to one of these categories. You'll have to use your judgment, again based on your analysis of user behavior during the initial phase of the project. The reason to categorize the tasks is that the tasks in each of these categories should be designed differently, as we'll illustrate shortly. First, let's explore these levels of priorities by looking at the Hubbub Task List reorganized into the four categories, shown in Figure 6.2. I didn't want to lose the overall priority, so I've indicated by the bullet type which ones are Core, Important, and Nice to Have. As you can see, they are related but not completely correlated. In particular, the Core tasks should fall mainly in the Frequent by Many category, the Important tasks should fall primarily in Frequent by Few and Occasional by Many, and the Nice to Have may be scattered among all the categories, but primarily in the latter three.

6.2

Hubbub Task List divided into the Frequency by Commonality categories.

Hubbub Task List, by Frequency and Commonality

- Core Functionality
- ■ Important Functionality
- ❖ Nice to Have Functionality

Frequent by Many

- Look to see who "is around" and who's not, where people are (or just were), and how busy they may be
- Check to see whether a certain person is around with the intention of contacting them
- Hear someone log on or become active, and either know who it was, or if not, look to see
- Decide to contact someone, evaluating whether they're likely to be there and how busy they are
- Hear someone go idle or offline, and either know who it was, or look to see who it was
- Send a sound message
- Receive a text message and know who it's from, and glance to see it
- Send a text message
- Receive a sound message, and either know what it means and who it's from, or glance to find out
- Quickly glance at a conversation screen and find the last message the other person sent
- ■ Exchange messages with someone while doing other things, noticing when the other person is sending you a message, expecting you to respond, or off doing something else
- ❖ See who is messaging with whom

Frequent by Few

- Arrive at a new location, start using your computer, and get a new message there without ever telling Hubbub where you are
- ■ Have multiple IMs going at once, switching between them

Occasional by Many

- Turn off all sounds
- Exchange messages in a meeting where you've got sounds muted
- ■ Decide whose activity sounds you want to hear, and turn off those you don't
- ■ Register, choose a name, password, and Sound ID, and download the application
- ■ Log in, label the device
- ■ Find a Hubbub user and invite them to be your bub
- ■ Remove a bub
- ❖ Adjust the order of your bub list, moving some people up and others down [may not be necessary if we have groups]
- ❖ Get a sense of how active each of your groups is right now

❖ Invite a third person to join your conversation
❖ Carry on a multi-way conversation, then people leave until it's 2-way again
❖ Create a group and put some bubs in it [may not be necessary if we allow ordering of bubs]
❖ Move a bub to another group

Occasional by Few

■ Use Hubbub from someone else's machine – log that person off, log on as youself
■ Change your name, password, Sound ID, device label
■ Specify which bubs can see your activity/location or send you text/sound messages
■ Check online help
❖ Create a new sound
❖ Import a new sound to Hubbub and send it to someone else
❖ Receive a new sound message from someone and send it to someone else
❖ Specify which bubs can see whom you're talking with in Hubbub
❖ Use a tutorial to learn the sounds

The Frequent by Many category is the most important. These are the tasks that nearly everyone will do nearly every time they use the application. For Hubbub, that includes checking to see who's around, hearing people coming and going in the background, and sending and receiving text and sound messages, all Core functionality. We don't think we have to show who is messaging with whom in the first release (it's a Nice to Have feature), but if we do, it's the type of activity many people will do often. You should spend most of your effort making sure that users can accomplish these all-the-time tasks smoothly and easily, without any breaks in flow. If people have trouble with these tasks, they won't like using your application.

Some tasks are performed all the time, but only by some people (Frequent by Few). In the case of Hubbub, our initial investigations indicated that some people will use Hubbub from multiple locations while others will use it from just one, so features related to multiple sites are Frequent by Few. Also, we found that some people carry on conversations with different people at the same time, whereas others don't like to multitask like that and will engage in only one conversation at a time, so features related to carrying on multiple conversations also fall into this category.

Other tasks are needed by everyone, but only occasionally (Occasional by Many). Good examples are installation and setup. Everyone has to do them, but they do them only once or twice. In Hubbub, everyone needs to add bubs, but they usually do so once at the beginning and then only occasionally as they encounter more people to add. Once they have enough bubs, they'll want to put them in groups or order them. (We're figuring we'll only have to do one of these features, not both.) And it should happen only occasionally that people have multiperson interactions, turning their instant messages into chat sessions.

Design Guideline
To determine the priorities of the tasks for the user interface, divide the tasks into those done (a) frequently by many, (b) frequently by few, (c) occasionally by many, and (d) occasionally by few. These categories will not only tell you which features you should concentrate on making smooth and easy to accomplish, but will also suggest where they should be placed in the interface and how they should be designed.

Finally, there are some tasks that few people use and even then, only rarely. This category (Occasional by Few) should consist only of tasks that you *can't not* provide. For example, if people can add a bub, they must be able to remove that bub, even if few ever will. Many privacy and security features fall into this category. Few people ever turn on privacy features, but they need to know that the features are available or they won't use the application. Help features also may be in Occasional by Few—you need them for those who seek them out, but most people don't. If you have any tasks in this list that are not strictly necessary, you should convince yourself that they're worth the time and effort to build if few people will ever use them.

In the case of Hubbub, most of the Occasional by Few features are of this "must have" nature, but we do have a few nonessential features that enable users to create new sound messages, import them, and send them to others. We justify these on the basis that they allow the few avid users to create a better experience for everyone else. If just a small group of people become excited about creating their own sounds, they'll send them to their bubs, who will send them on to others, and soon enough, many people's experience will be enhanced by the efforts of a few. However, those features are Nice to Have, so even though we keep them on the list, we're not likely to get to them in the first release unless we find from the usage study that there's a strong desire for them.

Map Priorities to Design

Now let's see how dividing the tasks into these four categories helps you design the interface. Each of the two dimensions maps to a different UI treatment:

- Tasks that people do frequently should require fewer clicks than those done less often.
- Tasks that most people do should be more visible than those done by few.

Design Guideline
Tasks done frequently should require fewer clicks than those done occasionally; tasks done by many people should be easier to find than those done by few. Therefore, Frequent by Many tasks should be visible and take few clicks; Frequent by Few tasks should take few clicks but may be a little harder to find; Occasional by Many tasks should be easy to find but may take more clicks; and Occasional by Few tasks should be hidden and may take more clicks.

These two rules tell us how to handle the four categories. Frequent by Many tasks should be visible and take a minimum of steps. Frequent by Few tasks should require a minimum of steps for those who use them all the time but can be suggested on the main screen or hidden so they don't clutter everyone's screen. Occasional by Many tasks can take more steps if necessary but they should be easy to find—they're not worth a lot of prime real estate, but you should be able to look at the main screen and have a good idea how to get started. Occasional by Few tasks should be hidden and might require more steps:

Of course, you'd like all your tasks to be visible and require few steps, but that's not possible for any but the simplest application. You're going to have to make tradeoffs, and this diagram is intended to help you determine the best way to make them. Keep in mind that the Frequency by Commonality guideline is just that. Sometimes you will be faced with other considerations when deciding how to handle a feature. But the guideline should serve as a helpful heuristic that applies in the majority of cases. (When I discuss the process of laying out Hubbub in Chapter 7, I'll explain how the Mute option was a case in which I made an exception to this guideline.)

Example: "Reverse Designing" Priorities

Let's get concrete. For the moment, we'll step away from Hubbub so we can compare two designs based on the same set of requirements:

the Palm Date Book and Microsoft Outlook Calendar. What are some of the Frequent by Many tasks that most people do most of the time when they use a calendar? Palm's Date Book's design (shown in Figure 6.3) treats the task of making a one-hour appointment for sometime this week as Frequent by Many. How can I tell? Let's look at what's involved in this task. When you turn on the Date Book, you see today's appointments, with one line for each hour. To add an appointment today, you tap the line by that hour and type the name—two clicks. (We count entering one text entry as one "click" since it's one mental event and users are in control of how much they enter.) If the appointment is on another day this week, you first tap that day, then the hour, and then type—three clicks. Even though the screen is relatively uncluttered, those two tasks are easily visible and they take few clicks. Making an appointment next week takes just one more tap to scroll the week. The scroll arrows are visible (suggesting the feature), but next week is hidden, so it is treated as an Occasional by Many task.

6.3

Palm Date Book. This design shows that entering a one-hour appointment for today or this week is considered a Frequent by Many task. Entering a one-hour appointment for another week is considered Occasional by Many.

On the other hand, Outlook Calendar (shown in Figure 6.4) is optimized to make half-hour appointments for some time during the next two months. If you're making a half-hour appointment today, you click on the time slot and type, the same two steps that the Palm requires (plus switching from the mouse to the keyboard). If you're making an appointment for any other day this or next month, it takes just one more click to first select that date, for a total of three clicks. Certainly three clicks is nice if you happen to be making a half-hour appointment for five weeks out. But we're guessing that few people do so on a regular basis, and the cost is the visual complexity of showing not one full month but two, which makes it harder to zero in on, say, tomorrow.

6.4

Microsoft Outlook Calendar. This design indicates that entering a half-hour appointment any time in the next two months is considered Frequent by Many, but making one-hour appointments is treated as Occasional by Many because it's visible but takes more steps.

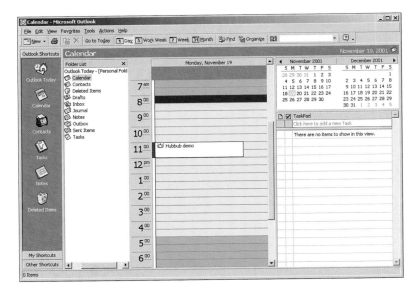

Let's look at how Outlook handles making a one-hour appointment for sometime this week. The quickest way is to click and drag to select one hour, and then type. Yes, it's just one more click than the Palm, but that extra drag and release costs most people extra effort every time they make a one-hour appointment. Perhaps Microsoft had data indicating that most people make half-hour appointments far more often than they make one-hour ones, but our experience indicates that the opposite is true. Yet making one-hour appointments not only requires extra physical effort and more manual dexterity, it also requires mental effort to figure out the drag shortcut. This shortcut is typical of the kind offered for Frequent by Few tasks: Once you figure it out, it's quick, but you need to be more motivated to figure it out. We suspect many people don't figure out this drag-select option, and instead use the standard method of double-clicking on the first half-hour to launch a huge popup cluttered with menus, buttons, tabs, and other widgets, shown in Figure 6.5. From there you enter the appointment name and change the end time using a pull-down menu. Using this method, it takes five steps and two mode switches to create a one-hour appointment, indicating that it is considered an Occasional by Many task.

6.5

Microsoft Outlook Appointment Editor. Making a one-hour appointment with this editor takes five clicks and two mode switches. The window is cluttered, making it harder for people to focus on the important elements.

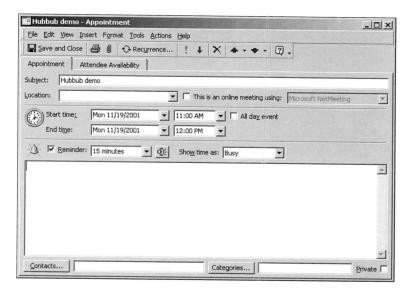

Why did the Outlook designers choose this approach? My guess is because this design is more flexible. It's just as easy to make an appointment for one hour as it is to make one for an hour and a half, two hours, or even two days, all of which are just a little more work than a half-hour appointment. But everyone pays the price for that flexibility every time they make a one-hour appointment because they have to drag and select.[1] Palm's Date Book sacrifices the half-hour task in favor of the one-hour one. To make appointments for more or less than an hour, it takes a lot more work. First you tap the start time to view a time editor (see Figure 6.6), then you tap the end time, then you tap once or twice more to adjust the end time, tap the OK button, and finally type your appointment. That method takes five or six steps to create a non-one-hour appointment, about the same as the standard Outlook method for creating non-half-hour appointments, and with far less clutter.

---

[1] One way to be more cooperative would be to default appointments started on the hour to one hour, but appointments started on the half-hour to 30 minutes, especially if there is another appointment already scheduled starting at the next hour. You would need to observe real calendar use to decide whether this would be more helpful than bothersome, but it might be a good idea for a widgetless feature. (Thanks to Leysia Palen for this idea.)

6.6

Palm Date Book Time Editor. Making an appointment that is anything other than an hour long requires five to six taps and requires using this screen. Palm optimized the design for one-hour appointments, but when users make appointments for other durations, it takes no more clicks than Outlook's standard method.

Design Guideline
You can "reverse design" an application to figure out which tasks were placed in which Frequency by Commonality category. Make sure your design reflects the priorities you set out to achieve.

These examples show how your priorities will be reflected directly in your design. You can even "reverse design" an application to figure out the priorities of the designers. Whether you plan it or not, fast, obvious tasks imply that you expect most people to do them all the time; fast, less obvious tasks indicate that you expect only some people to do them frequently; slower, more obvious tasks indicate that you expect most people to do them occasionally; and slower, hidden tasks imply that you expect few people to do them and only rarely. If you understand how to prioritize your tasks and reflect them in the design, it will be easier to design your application to behave like a butler.

Once you put your tasks into your Frequency by Commonality categories, show the list to the rest of the team and make clear the design implications for each category. This is an important list to get right and to agree on as a team. Discussing what goes where helps everyone think about the application from the user's standpoint and sets everyone's expectations about the UI. It also gives everyone a common basis for evaluating how well the user interface is doing its job. Later, when someone (possibly even you) wants to add a new feature because *someone might* want to use it *sometimes*, the list will show you that it belongs in the Occasional by Few category, which tells you that it may not be worth doing. (If you do decide to do it anyway, you know it should be hidden and can take more steps to complete.) Or maybe once you see people using your system you'll discover that some people are using it differently than you expected, so maybe it's time to add a requirement to support that activity and design it as a Frequent by Few task.

As you design more interfaces, you should find yourself thinking in terms of frequency and commonality all the time. Even then, it's worth creating the Frequency by Commonality Task List as a useful communication tool for your team.

Organize the Tasks into Display Units

Now it's time to figure out where to present your tasks. Most applications have a main screen that is the starting point and may be visible most of the time when the application is running. Subsidiary screens allow people to carry out tasks suggested on the main screen. Even on the main screen, some things are immediately accessible and others require opening menus. You need to decide which tasks go on the main screen, and of those, which ones users can access without having to reveal hidden information. Then you need to decide how to organize the subsidiary tasks that are not on the main screen.

Design Guideline

The main screen is the place to put Frequent by Many tasks, and to offer at least the first step in Occasional by Many tasks. Frequent by Few tasks can be placed on another screen, but they should be easy to access, perhaps with shortcuts. Occasional by Few tasks should not be on the main screen.

Tasks that most people use (Frequent by Many and Occasional by Many) are your candidates for the main screen. You'd like people to be able to accomplish Frequent by Many tasks without going to subsequent screens, whereas Occasional by Many tasks can require additional screens as long as it's clear how to get to them from the main screen. Frequent by Few tasks need to be easy to accomplish without cluttering the screen. If there's a way to offer these tasks cleanly on the main screen, that's good, but if not, put them on another screen and offer shortcuts that enable quick access to them. Also, make sure the shortcuts are easy to discover when doing the task the longer way, so the frequent users can quickly learn the fast method. Occasional by Few tasks shouldn't have visible elements on the main screen, they should be revealed only when users open a menu or follow the path of a related task. No matter what category a task is in, though, you want it to be as smooth as possible, so you need to group related tasks and arrange them so that accomplishing the task is as straightforward as possible.

Design Guideline

In your first design pass, try to include all features, including Nice to Have ones, so that you can make sure your design will accommodate a range of features. Then pull out the Nice to Have features to make sure the design still works without them.

At this stage, include all the tasks on your list, from Core down to Nice to Have, even though you won't implement them all right away. You want to make sure they all fit into your design model. You don't want to wind up shoving a feature into an awkward place because you hadn't planned for it. And if you try to fit in all the features from the start, you'll learn whether you have too many and whether some should be dropped or lowered in priority purely for design reasons. Some features may not fit into your approach, some may be too complicated to communicate, and some may clutter the screen more than they add value. (We'll see some examples of this from the Hubbub project in the next chapter.) The earlier you figure this out, the better, so you can adjust your list and save engineering effort. Once you've added all the features, make sure that your design still holds together without the Nice to Have features, since few of them will be available initially.

Let's walk through the process of grouping tasks into screens or sets of screens (or windows, pages, or whatever display unit is appropriate for you). At this point, you need to go back to the Functional Requirements rather than the Task List because you need to decide what user interface elements to provide to support each requirement, which in turn supports the tasks. This is where you need to know which requirements were intended to support which tasks, so you can group the related UI elements.

I'll use the Hubbub Palm client to illustrate. From Figure 6.2, it's clear that the two primary activities in Hubbub are about maintaining an awareness of bubs and exchanging messages with them. I'll need a screen for each of these activities, since you can't conduct a conversation on the same screen where you see your list of bubs. (These two windows are standard on IMs.) There are other support screens (for example, to set privacy controls and add/remove bubs), and those will be used much less frequently than the first two. Figure 6.7 shows how I organized the set of requirements from the Functional Requirements Document into screens or related functions. You can see that the Core functionality is located on the two primary screens. The Important and Nice to Have features are distributed among many screens, although items in each category tend to be grouped together. At this stage, you may not be certain that you've put all the items in the right places, and that's okay. Things should fall into place later as you work through the details.

6.7

Functional Requirements List reorganized by related functions or screens. Core functionality is located in the Main screen and the Message screen, while Important and Nice to Have features are distributed among many screens.

Hubbub Functional Requirements Grouped into Screens

- • Core Functionality
- ■ Important Functionality
- ❖ Nice to Have Functionality

Main (Awareness) Screen
- • Bub list
- • Indication of whether each bub is active, idle, or offline
- • Indication of how long each bub has been active or idle
- ■ For active bubs, indication of level of activity:
    - ■ Current level
    - ■ Average over some period
- ■ Indication of which device each bub is on or was last on
- ■ Indication of each bub's location
- • Sound ID for each bub
- • Sounds to indicate when someone starts using computer (active sound) and goes idle (idle sound)
- ■ Sounds to indicate when someone starts or exits Hubbub (logon sound, logoff sound)
- ❖ Possibly, sound to indicate what device each bub became active on (device sound)
- • Visual indication of who went active/idle (to learn meaning of sounds)
- • Ability to Mute All
- ■ Ability to mute each bub's activity sounds
- ■ Auto-login when you log on/turn on device
- ■ Manual logon/off
- ❖ Ability to manually order bubs within list
- ❖ Ability to see who is messaging with whom
- ❖ Indication of each group's average level of activity

Message Screen
- • Ability to send and receive sound messages
- • Visual indication of meaning of incoming sound messages and who sent them
- • Ability to send and receive text messages
- • Sound to announce arrival (and maybe sending) of each text contribution
- • Visual indication of incoming text messages and who sent them
- ■ Ability to visually differentiate each person's text

- Ability to choose which device to send message to (if bub is on more than one)
- Indication of bub's window focus and typing activity during conversation
- Ability to have multiple IMs at once
- Ability to tell if bub's device is muted
- ❖ Ability to send new sound messages to bubs
- ❖ For other IMs not visible on Palm, ability to tell
  - ❖ Window focus and typing status of bub
  - ❖ Whether they've sent a contribution to which you haven't responded
- ❖ Time stamp of first message in conversation
- ❖ Multi-way messaging

Message Log Screen
- Log of last N incoming sound messages

Setup Screen
- Ability to download and install the application
- Ability to register for an account
- Ability to choose a Hubbub name and password
- Ability to choose a sound to represent you (Sound ID)
- Ability to label the device

Account Administration Screen
- Ability to change your Hubbub name
- Ability to change your password
- Ability to change your Sound ID
- Ability to change device label

Add/Remove Bubs Screens
- Ability to add bubs (requires permission)
- Ability to remove bubs
- Ability to grant/deny permission to add
- Reciprocal bub membership
- Ability to specify privacy settings when you add a bub

Bub Management Screen
- Per person (and across clients), ability to specify whether you want to:
  - Provide active/idle info (per bub)
  - Provide location info (per bub)
  - Accept text messages (per bub)
  - Accept sound messages (per bub)
  - Provide info about whom you're messaging with

Group Management Screens

- ❖ Ability to create groups
- ❖ Ability to add/remove people to/from groups

Help

- ■ Online help
- ❖ Tutorial for learning sounds

Sound Creation Screen

- ❖ Ability to compose new Sound IDs
- ❖ Ability to compose new Sound Instant Messages
- ❖ Ability to test new sounds on Palm and PC
- ❖ Ability to import new sound messages into Hubbub

My initial focus is on the Main screen and the Message screen. On the Main screen, I need to allow users to glance at the screen and get a sense of everyone's status, which means I need to include a bub list that shows which bubs are active, idle, or offline, for how long, from where, on what device, and how active the active bubs are right now. (All of those items came from the requirements generated by the "see who's around" task.) It also has to be trivial to send a sound or text message, since you'll initiate those actions from this screen. The sound features are a little unusual, since sounds announcing other people's activity can play regardless of what screen you're on, but I'm grouping them with the Main screen because that's where it makes sense to put visual cues about what an incoming sound means. Since sounds can be annoying if they play at the wrong time, I need to make it especially easy to turn them off at any time. Finally, if a user ever wants to explicitly log off (which shouldn't happen often on a single-user device like the Palm), they should be able to do so from the Main screen.

The Message screen includes everything related to a particular conversation: sending and receiving text and sound messages, distinguishing your text from the other person's, seeing whether the other person is focused or typing in your conversation window, information about when the conversation began, and so on. We'll have one screen per conversation, so I'll need a way to switch to any other conversation from the current one.

The rest of the screens are fairly straightforward. There's a screen to set up an account, a screen to manage your own information, a screen to add and remove bubs, a screen to edit each bub's permissions, a screen to create and manage groups, a help screen, and a screen to create new sounds (which may become its own application). At this point, I'm not worrying about how to lay out each of these screens, or even whether they might consist of several subscreens. I'm just focusing on grouping them into functionally related units.

Create a Task Flow Diagram

Once you have a sense of what goes on in each screen, create a diagram that shows how the screens relate to one another. This is called a *Task Flow Diagram*, or sometimes a *Flow of Control Diagram*. It is used to help you figure out (and illustrate to others) how users walk through the screens to accomplish any given task. Again, don't worry about what UI widget they use to move from one screen to another. Just go through the tasks and determine the screen or screens where the tasks take place. If more than one screen is involved, show the users' path through them to accomplish that task. As you drill down to design each of these screens, you might find that you need additional screens to support certain tasks, so you'll go back and add them to the Task Flow Diagram.

Design Guideline
Create a Task Flow Diagram that shows the set of screens and the user's path through the screens for each task. As with engineering architectures, try to make the design architecture as clean and simple as possible.

Task Flow Diagrams are similar to engineering architecture diagrams in that they give a quick overview of the structure of the system and the relationships between the components. By working with a Task Flow Diagram, you can see at a glance how many screens the application has, and the complexity of the relationships among them. As with engineering architectures, the simpler you can make the diagram and the shorter the path for most tasks, the better—given that you are maximizing efficiency of the high priority tasks. As you walk through different tasks, move features around until you think you've optimized the flow. If you wait until code has been written to work out the flow, it gets expensive and sometimes even impossible to make changes.

6.8

Initial Hubbub Task Flow Diagram for the Palm client.

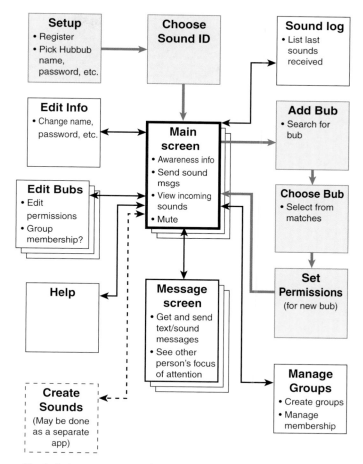

Setup	Choose	Sound log
• Register	Sound ID	• List last
• Pick Hubbub		sounds
name,		received
password, etc.		

Edit Info
• Change name, password, etc.

Main screen
• Awareness info
• Send sound msgs
• View incoming sounds
• Mute

Add Bub
• Search for bub

Edit Bubs
• Edit permissions
• Group membership?

Choose Bub
• Select from matches

Help

Set Permissions
(for new bub)

Message screen
• Get and send text/sound messages
• See other person's focus of attention

Create Sounds
(May be done as a separate app)

Manage Groups
• Create groups
• Manage membership

Blue indicates screens appear in sequence

Figure 6.8 shows the initial Task Flow Diagram for Hubbub's Palm client. The two principal screens are the Main screen and the Message screen. The Main screen is shown as a "stack" of screens to indicate that you can have multiple groups, and you can flip from one group to another. The Message screen is also a stack because you can have many two-person conversations at once and flip among them. So far, most of the rest of the screens are one tap away, which is good because it means fewer steps to do the associated tasks. The only tasks that go through a linear sequence of screens are those that logically require multiple steps (shown in blue). For example, when adding a new bub, you can add only those who have existing accounts. So you first need to search for a bub, then the system has to display possible matches, then you have to indicate which one you want to add. We want you to explicitly set permissions for each person (offering defaults, of course), so we make that the last step. When you're done, you return to the Main screen.

As you can see in Figure 6.8, I haven't yet tried to figure out how users will get from one screen to the next. Maybe they'll press a button or maybe they'll choose an item from a menu. Right now, I'm just trying to get an overall sense of where things go. But I've made sure to look at every task on the Task List and figure out where it would take place. Most of the tasks in Hubbub will be done on one screen, which is ideal. Others require moving among screens, and I've done my best at this point to keep those hops to a minimum.

I've done a lot of work already and I haven't even begun to figure out what the user interface will look like. This is because I want to make sure I've got a solid structure for the UI before worrying about the UI controls. Although you do iterate the design quite a bit, it is much more difficult to change the underlying UI structure than it is to adjust the widgets and the layout within that structure. In practice, we've rarely seen major changes to the UI structure once the architecture has been designed to support it and implementation has begun. Often people feel the pressure of the schedule, and the evidence that the design is not working is not strong enough to slip the schedule. It's worth the effort to work it out as thoroughly as possible. In the next chapter, I'll pick up the process from here and lay out the UI controls to finish the initial user interface design.

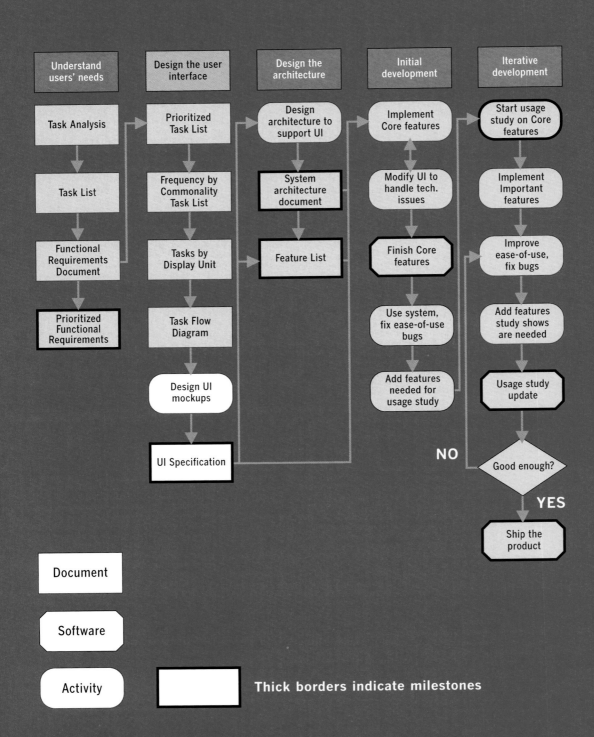

Understand users' needs

- Task Analysis
- Task List
- Functional Requirements Document
- Prioritized Functional Requirements

Design the user interface

- Prioritized Task List
- Frequency by Commonality Task List
- Tasks by Display Unit
- Task Flow Diagram
- Design UI mockups
- UI Specification

Design the architecture

- Design architecture to support UI
- System architecture document
- Feature List

Initial development

- Implement Core features
- Modify UI to handle tech. issues
- Finish Core features
- Use system, fix ease-of-use bugs
- Add features needed for usage study

Iterative development

- Start usage study on Core features
- Implement Important features
- Improve ease-of-use, fix bugs
- Add features study shows are needed
- Usage study update
- Good enough?
  - NO
  - YES
- Ship the product

Document

Software

Activity

Thick borders indicate milestones

CHAPTER 7

Laying Out the User Interface

Now that the features are organized into screens, it's time to drill down to each screen and figure out which controls to use and how to lay them out. The idea is to design each screen so it communicates to users how to carry out their tasks. You want them to be able to look at a user interface with a goal in mind and have a good idea of how to get started. As they go through each step, it should become clear what to do next until the task is done.

Communicating Visually

This part of UI design is perhaps the most like an art. But it is an art more similar to writing nonfiction books than to, say, painting in that its main goal is to communicate. It should also be aesthetically pleasing, but the aesthetics need to support the communication. A writer's tools are words plus conventions about how to put those words together. Change the wording of a sentence slightly, and the meaning changes. Similarly, a designer's tools are UI widgets (such as menus, check boxes, and buttons), the labels of those widgets, and rules about how to put them together. Your goal is to use those tools to communicate to users how they can accomplish their tasks.

At this stage in the process you should work with a graphic designer. Graphic designers are skilled not just at making things "look good," but in communicating visually—presenting visual information so that people understand its meaning. In my experience, I've usually drafted the user interface architecture (that is, the set of screens, the flow from one screen to another and within each one, the approach to representing and manipulating information, and so on), and then worked with a graphic designer to lay out the screens. The layout needs to communicate the flow you have in mind and make it easy for people to interpret the information on each screen. Depending on the type of system you're building, you may also want the design to express a certain attitude or personality. All of this is the domain of graphic designers. Of course, they can also design icons and logos, but that's only a part of their contribution.[1]

Most computer users can't articulate the meaning of UI controls, but they have developed expectations about how those controls behave. For example, a button conveys that pressing it will cause an action. A check box or radio button lets you choose an attribute or option associated with an object. Radio buttons offer exclusive choices (you can pick only one), whereas check boxes offer nonexclusive choices (you can choose as many as you like). People also understand rules about how widgets are put together. If three items are grouped together and separated from two other elements, they infer that the items in each group are related to each other and are different somehow from those in the other group (see Figure 7.1). In most cultures, items laid out vertically tell people to look at the top items first and work their way to the lower items. The items at the top are probably more important, or maybe changing them affects items lower down. The more you understand about the language of user interfaces, the better you will be able to visually communicate what you want people to do to accomplish a task.

7.1

Grouping elements tells people what is related and what is not. In group A, you assume that the first three items are related and the second two are related. In group B, all five elements appear to be related.

I won't cover the list of all UI controls and how to use them. Most platforms have a Style Guide that explains the meaning of each of its user interface widgets and provides guidelines on how to use them.

---

[1] The basic distinction between a user interface designer and a graphic designer is that UI designers are trained in understanding user *behavior* and in designing the technology's *interaction* with users to make it easy for them achieve their goals. Graphic designers are trained in *visual communication* and are skilled at using visual characteristics such as shape, size, color, position, orientation, and so on to communicate meaning. Of course, some people are trained in both, but most designers tend more toward one set of skills than the other.

Read the Style Guide and become familiar with other applications on your platform so you can see how the rules are applied. I also recommend an excellent book on visual design by Kevin Mullet and Darrell Sano called *Designing Visual Interfaces,* which gives many before-and-after examples of screen layouts to help you understand how to communicate visually.

The best way I know to teach someone to lay out a user interface is to show examples and explain the reasoning that went into them. Here, I work through a few examples from Hubbub. Through these examples, I hope you can pick up the patterns and the type of thinking that drives design decisions. I also note in the margins instances where I'm applying design principles from the first part of the book. Even though I've designed many user interfaces, you'll see that I often didn't get the design right the first time. Most of these screens took a few iterations until the pieces of the puzzle started to fit together. And even then, as you'll see in Chapter 10, many aspects of the interaction design needed to be changed once we started using Hubbub and especially once we observed others using it during the usage study. This is to be expected, since it is an iterative process that takes feedback from many sources.

When creating a layout, I often start by sketching the screen on a piece of paper, which allows me to quickly visualize my ideas. (Alan will attest to my lack of drawing ability, so it's clear that anyone can do this.) Once I've done a few iterations on paper, I move to the computer to create detailed screenshots. I try to make them as realistic as possible, partially to make sure I'm working with the proportions of the real screen and partially so that the engineer can see the details of what I have in mind. I prefer to work closely with a graphic designer at this stage, but we did not have one on the Hubbub team, so I did all of the design myself. (I'll point out some mistakes I made that a graphic designer would not have made.) I used Photoshop for the screenshots in this chapter, but there are many image editing tools available, so use whichever works best for you.

In designing Hubbub, I needed to create two versions of the same interface on two platforms. I decided to start with the Palm because it is more limited in space and encourages a sparser interface, but I kept the PC constraints in mind as I made decisions. The first two examples focus on the Palm, and then I move on to show how I mapped that design to the PC and then adjusted both designs for the sake of consistency.

Example 1: Focusing on Frequent by Many Features

I always start by focusing on the Frequent by Many tasks. Let's look at the first two, which are to give people a sense of who's around and to help them decide whether now is a good time to contact someone. I know we're going to have a list of bubs (as all IMs do), and I want to design it so you can accomplish these goals without taking any physical action beyond glancing at the screen. **[Treat Clicks as Sacred]** Here's the information we want to make visible at a glance:

- List of bubs
- Which bubs are active, idle, or offline
- How long each bub has been active or idle
- How active each bub is right now (if they are active)
- What device each bub is on
- Each bub's location

Design Guideline
Try to use visual cues that are easy to interpret without conscious thought. For example, bold and larger type convey more importance, motion conveys activity, fading an item out conveys that it went away or was deleted.

The first item is the most important one: showing whether each bub is active, idle, or offline. If someone is offline, you can't contact them, and if they're idle, they may not be available for an interaction (although they may in fact be at their computer without using it). So I want to make their activity status a prominent cue, something you don't even have to think about consciously to interpret. **[Respect Mental Effort]** I chose to put the active bubs in bold and the idle bubs in regular font so that you can quickly glance at the list to see who's active. Since bold is more prominent and captures your attention, it gives a good mapping to the meaning I'm trying to convey.

What about those bubs who are offline? I could choose a different font to convey that they are not available. I thought about italics, but when I checked with Alan, he said there's no built-in support for italics on the Palm. Also, it's visually complicated to have three font styles on one screen. And since we're working with a small display that can show only a limited number of people, I don't want to use up precious space listing people you can't contact. So I decided to display people who are logged in (either active or idle) at the top of the list, with offline people below. When someone comes online, their entry moves to the top section of the list. This way, your display automatically shows people who are "around." Figure 7.2 shows my design of the bub list at this point.

7.2

In-progress design of Hubbub's Main screen. So far, it handles showing who's active, idle, and offline at a glance. Active and idle bubs are alphabetized at the top, with active bubs in bold. Offline bubs are alphabetized at the bottom of the list.

In this design, if you're looking for a particular person (also a Frequent by Many task) who happens to be offline, you'll have to scroll down to find their name, which requires more physical effort than I'd like for such a common task. **[Make Common Tasks Visible]** But if we alphabetize the list, you'll know that someone is offline if you don't see their name in the appropriate place in the top list. If their name begins with a letter near the end of the alphabet, you may need to scroll a little, but only if more than a screen's worth of people are currently online. In many cases, though, you'll be able to look and see that someone is not available without tapping.

Design Guideline
Try to use different types of visual cues (font, color, position, borders, text, icons, and so on) so that you don't overload one type with too much information.

I'd have a better idea whether this approach would work if I knew roughly how many bubs people are likely to have and how many are likely to be online at any time. Statistics from a few studies indicate that people using other instant messengers have an average of 14 buddies. I don't have information about how many are usually online at any given time, but 2/3 is probably a generous estimate. That tells me that if we can show 9 or 10 bubs on the screen, most people will be able to look at the screen most of the time and get a good idea of which bubs are online. So it seems like a good approach to put online people at the top and alphabetize the online people separately from the offline people. It uses only one font characteristic (bold versus nonbold) and relies on position to convey important information. This design seemed to work and it's one we stuck with throughout the whole project.

Design Guideline
Use icons alone if people can understand their meaning without a label or if the information represented is not critical and doesn't have to be interpreted immediately. If people need to interpret an icon quickly, combine it with a label. If you plan to internationalize the interface, keep in mind that labels will probably get longer in other languages, and you may have to modify icons if there are culture-specific references.

On the other hand, it took several iterations to work out how to display the four other pieces of information about each bub: time active/idle, level of activity, device, and location. This is a lot of information and I'm concerned that visual clutter will distract people from seeing the basic information: who's around. **[Use Visual Elements Sparingly | Make Common Tasks Visible; Hide Infrequent Tasks]** I started by putting most of this information right next to each bub's name, in parentheses to help separate it from the bub name. Figure 7.3 shows my attempt at the Main screen with additional information. Next to each name is the amount of time that bub has been active or idle in hr:min:sec (or just min:sec if it's been less than an hour), followed by an icon indicating their device, followed by the label of the device. I hoped using an icon for the device type (Palm, PC, phone) would help break up all that text information. Also, to cut down on clutter and because the Palm screen is so small, I decided to use just two letter labels for the location, which should be enough to convey Home (Hm), Work (Wk), School (Sc), or perhaps the abbreviation of a state (CA) or country (UK).

7.3

In-progress design of Hubbub's bub list on the Palm with all the activity information.

The remaining awareness item is *how* active each bub is. We wanted to provide this information for two reasons. First, we wanted to provide a better idea of whether someone is really there when you initiate an interaction. Our initial investigations indicated that many IM conversations start with something like, "Are you there?" because people can't tell from the cues they have. Second, we thought it would add to the feeling of awareness if you could glance at your list and get a sense of how actively people were typing, clicking, or tapping away. (This feature would reduce users' privacy, but we figured we would handle that by allowing people more control than other IMs offer in deciding who can watch them and how much information they can see. Our goal was to see how well we could support groups of friends and colleagues who want to stay closely connected from distributed locations.) Since the screen was already getting cluttered, I decided to create a very small "activity meter" that would reflect the level of activity—empty would mean no activity and full would mean a lot. I made it very small, just three pixels wide and eight high, and put it just to the left of each active bub's name (see Figure 7.3). My thinking was as follows. As you look at the screen, the activity meter updates every few seconds (say 10 or 20) to show your bubs' current level of activity. Even if you don't know exactly what the meter means at first, (a) you'll get a general sense of activity among those bubs who are active, and (b) it's relatively easy to ignore the meters because they are neatly lined up to the left of each bub's name. Figure 7.3 shows how the bub list looked at this point, with all the activity information included.

We had originally thought about showing two types of information with this meter: current activity (within the last 10 to 20 seconds) and average activity over, say, 5 minutes. We thought it might be helpful to know that, for example, although someone wasn't typing right then, they'd been very active over the last few minutes. When I showed the design to Alan, though, it was apparent that the screen was getting pretty complex and there wasn't much room left to work with. We agreed that the value of knowing activity over time as well as at the moment didn't seem worth the visual complexity, so we dropped the "average activity" feature to reduce the mental effort of interpreting the screen. **[Use Visual Elements Sparingly]** This was one example of eliminating a feature for complexity-of-design reasons.

Design Guideline
Information is easier to comprehend if it's laid out in rows and columns. A grid structure helps organize the information, and it helps people to focus on certain pieces of information while ignoring others.

As the design stood, it had all the information but it was very busy looking. I showed it to some colleagues, and they said they had a hard time interpreting all the information next to each person's name. One person suggested that it might be easier to read if I created a column for each piece of information. (Here was a case where a graphic designer would have gotten it right the first time. A basic tenet of graphic design is to lay out items on a grid.) I tried that and indeed the activity information became easier to interpret (or to ignore if you weren't interested at the moment). The problem was that space was getting tight, since I had to leave the maximum room for each column. Earlier, when I'd showed the design to Alan, he had said he was concerned about the performance and battery life implications of showing the active or idle time in seconds because it meant redrawing much of the screen every second. If we simplified the time to show just hours and minutes, we could improve performance, make the column narrower, and generally reduce visual complexity. This was one of those happy decisions that improves both the design and the implementation. We would lose precision, but I figured that a minute was sufficient granularity for learning how long someone has been active or idle. So now that I had created columns and reduced the active/idle time (and made a few other small changes), the display looked like Figure 7.4.

7.4

In-progress draft of Hubbub's bub list on the Palm. In addition to showing all the activity information, this one also includes a way to turn each bub's activity sounds on or off, a groups menu (Pals) with a group activity meter, a way to add a new bub (New button), a way to view the sound messages you might have missed (Last Msgs button), and an indicator of whether you have an active IM conversation with someone (in this case, Ellen).

As it turned out, the bub list essentially kept this structure over time, although we needed to make a few small changes to it. For example, when we started using it, we found that we had trouble reading the activity meter, so we widened it to 4 pixels, which helped its readability and reduced mental effort. In Chapter 10, we'll discuss how we adjusted the location indicator once we saw how other people used this feature.

Example 2: Following Platform Conventions

Although I had used the Palm for several years, this was the first time I had designed an application for it. It took some work to adjust my design approach from the desktop style to the Palm style. This example illustrates how I had to make a major change to the design after I realized I had not followed the Palm style conventions.

One of the challenges of designing Hubbub was deciding how to initiate a sound or text message. I wanted it to be trivial to send a sound message, so I started by putting the sound icons on the Main screen underneath the names, as shown in Figure 7.5A. This reduces the number of bubs you can see at a glance, but it makes it easy to send someone a message. You tap a name and then tap a sound message button to send that sound to that bub. I made the sound icons as small as I could while still providing a hittable target (assuming the button clicks when you tap it) and a readable label (creating 13×13 pixel buttons). I could fit only seven icons, but we knew we wanted to provide more, so I thought maybe we could hide the lesser-used ones behind a menu. **[Make Common Tasks Visible; Hide Infrequent Tasks]** I put a menu arrow to the right of the sound icons, which would bring up a menu of another seven icons, shown in Figure 7.5B. So sending the most commonly used sound messages would take two taps (tap on name and then on sound icon) and less common sounds would take three (an extra one to open the menu). I figured we'd learn which sounds were most commonly used during the Hubbub usage study.

7.5

First draft of Hubbub's Main screen with the sound message buttons. To send a sound message, you tap a bub name and then a sound button (A). More sound messages are revealed when you tap the left-facing arrow to the right of the LOL button (B).

A

B

Now I needed an easy way to send a text message too. Realizing I was going to need space to scroll the bub list, I created a scroll bar and then placed an IM button next to it to initiate a text message. To start a text message, you'd tap a name and then tap the IM button (next to the New button). I wasn't happy with all the wasted space above the sound message buttons in this design, but I wasn't finished with all the features, so I figured I'd see how I might be able to use that space.

After a while, I revisited the Palm Style Guide[2] and other Palm applications, and I realized that my design violated Palm's conventions. **[Follow Conventions]** I'd used the desktop select-and-operate approach. On the Palm, tapping on a noneditable item takes you to another

---

[2] The *Palm OS Programmer's Companion* contains a section titled "User Interface Guidelines." It is available from www.palmos.com.

screen with further information and commands associated with that entry. (See the Address Book for a good example.) Only if the Main screen items are editable can you select one and then choose a command, but even then, tapping an item places the cursor there rather than highlighting it. (The Date Book is a good example of this style.) Also, the Style Guide says never to display buttons that aren't available. So if no bub name were selected, the sound message buttons shouldn't appear, since you first have to specify whom you're sending a message to. I didn't want those buttons to appear and disappear depending on whether you had a name selected. Not only is that too much visual activity, but it would mean covering up names at the bottom of the list, which would cause more problems.

7.6

Second draft of Hubbub Main screen (A). If you tap a bub's name, you see a newly created Bub screen (B). If you then enter a text message and tap Send, you move to the Message screen, shown in Figure 7.7.

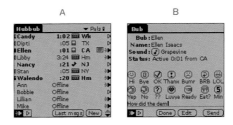

I revised the Main screen (see Figure 7.6A) so that tapping a name would display a newly created *Bub screen*, which includes all 14 sound messages and a text entry field for starting a text message (see Figure 7.6B). You tap someone's name and their Bub screen appears. I thought this was a big improvement for several reasons. First, it allowed me to show more bubs on the Main screen. Second, you could now get to all 14 sound messages in two taps. **[Treat Clicks as Sacred]** Third, it gave me room to include a text entry field on this screen, which reduced the number of clicks needed to send a text message. Instead of tapping a name, then tapping an IM button, then entering text, you could just tap a name and enter text, assuming we automatically put text focus in the text field when you arrived on the Bub screen. As soon as you sent the message, you would move to the Message screen, shown in Figure 7.7A. Fourth, it gave me a place to put more information about each bub that isn't important enough to go on the Main screen. For example, I used the Bub screen to display a Sound ID button that lets you play some-one's Sound ID at any time and an Edit button that takes you to a screen to edit their permissions. **[Make Common Tasks Visible; Hide Infrequent Tasks]** The Edit button on your own Bub screen takes you to a screen to edit information about yourself. The main drawback with this new approach is that it creates a new screen, which means you're changing contexts when you tap a name. But since this follows the Palm convention and solves so many problems, it is definitely a net win.

7.7

Draft of Hubbub Message screen (A). In this example, Walendo (Alan's Hubbub name) is interacting with Ellen; her text is in bold, his in regular type. To send a sound message, you tap the sound menu button, launched by tapping the up arrow in the lower left of the screen (B). The Done button takes you back to the Main screen and removes the conversation. Hold takes you back to the Main screen but preserves the conversation so you can return to this conversation screen.

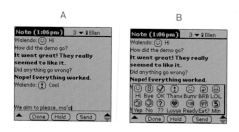

A   B

Design Guideline
Try to keep menus and menu items to a minimum. As common as they are, people often don't hunt around in them for features.

Since I had added a new screen, I went back and modified my Task Flow diagram, shown in Figure 7.8. I was pleased to discover that this new design was going to allow access to all the Hubbub functionality without creating any menus and with most functionality within two screens of the Main screen. I prefer to avoid menus because I have found that people often don't find things in them, or even look in them. People are especially unlikely to look in menus on the Palm, but they often don't open them in PC applications either. (As surprising as that may sound, when application providers request feedback from users, people commonly ask for functionality that is already available in a menu—not even a submenu—and yet they have never found it. This is because people are focused on their task, and hunting around in menus is a distraction that often does not feel worth the effort.)

7.8

Revised Task Flow Diagram that shows the new Bub screen. (Blue indicates a sequence of screens.)

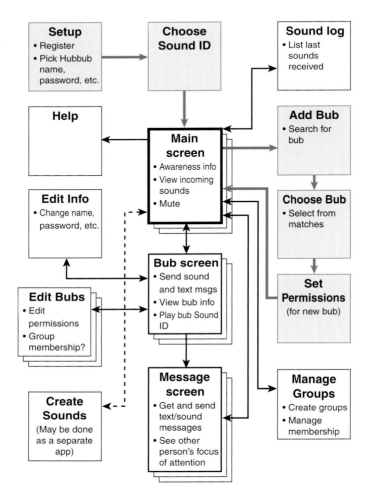

Again, this structure worked well for us throughout the project, although we later made a number of small changes during the usage study. And as you'll see in the next few examples, I had more tweaking to do to finish the design of the Main screen.

Example 3: Designing for Multiple Platforms

So far I've been discussing only the Palm client. I also needed to design a PC client that would be as similar as possible to the Palm client while still observing PC conventions. Although I had more flexibility on the PC—more room, more colors—I still wanted to keep the design as small and simple as possible. We expected people to run Hubbub all the time to stay aware of their bubs, so we didn't want to hog too much of their desktop (or CPU or memory for that matter).

Figure 7.9 shows my initial version of Hubbub on the PC. The Main screen information is organized just as it is on the Palm. Now that I'd moved the activity information into columns, it was even easier to map this to the PC, which already has a convention of creating columns of information associated with an entry. (The file explorer has a very similar design.) I labeled the columns since that is part of the convention and I hoped the labels would help people interpret the information more easily. (As it turned out, it took several tries to get the right labels. For example, when I showed this design to some colleagues, they didn't understand the label Activity, and they were unsure if the time was Minutes: Seconds or Hours: Minutes. So I changed the label of the column to Hrs: Mins, which helped but didn't completely explain the meaning of the column.)

7.9

First draft of the Hubbub Main screen on the PC.

Since I was designing for the PC, I went back to the select-and-operate approach, making all the sound messages available from a toolbar at the top. **[Follow Conventions]** To send a sound message, you select a bub and click on a sound message. To send a text message, you double-click on a bub name to open a text window, which is the convention across all instant messengers and is consistent with the PC convention of double-clicking to act on an item. So sending either a sound or text message still requires only two clicks, which is good. Since I was concerned about space, I decided to label the sound buttons with ToolTips, which you see when you roll your cursor over the buttons. (The ToolTip for the Bye button is shown in Figure 7.9.) This allowed me to get all 14 sound buttons on one toolbar. (You might notice that this violates the guideline mentioned earlier about adding labels to icons when their meaning is not clear and they need to be recognized quickly. We discovered that this was a mistake when we did the usage study, as we'll explain in Chapter 10.) Because the window is resizable, I didn't have to worry about how many bubs would appear on the Main window. People can adjust the window size based on how many bubs they have or how many are online. I made a note to specify that the window size and location should be remembered across sessions. **[Remember Where They Put Things]** Still, many people never adjust the default window size, so I wanted it to fit about 10 bubs. **[Keep Preferences to a Minimum; Give Smart Defaults]**

Design Guideline

When using color, try to make color redundant with some other cue (such as size, position, or font). Some people have trouble distinguishing certain colors, so make sure they can still use all the important features of your application.

Since on the PC I have color at my disposal, I used it to reinforce information rather than to introduce new information. Whenever working with color, I remind myself that color-blind people can't distinguish certain colors, so I try to use it as a redundant cue. For example, active bubs are bold *and* green, idle users are black, and offline bubs are at the bottom of the list *and* gray. The activity meter has three colors associated with the three levels (low, medium, and high) so it's easier to tell how high the meter is. I colored the sound message icons so you can more easily find the one you want, and made the text on the Mute button red so you can find the button easily when you want to turn off sound.

I was reasonably pleased with this initial PC design, but I was still unhappy that the window was so wide. So I showed it to people and got some good ideas. Dipti, the engineer who was implementing the PC client, pointed out that the "on" and "off" labels next to the speaker icons weren't very helpful. She also didn't find my column labels very clear. We played around with the design for a while, and realized that if we took the on/off labels away, we could move the sound icons to the left of the activity meter and remove an entire column. **[Use Visual Elements Sparingly]** To make the window narrower, we'd have to split the sound message buttons into two toolbars with seven each and stack them vertically. Now that the sound icons were on the left, I flipped them to face right so they wouldn't be pointing away from the bub name. Figure 7.10A shows the new version. Since I'd changed the PC version, I went back and revised the Palm version to remain as consistent as possible (see Figure 7.10B).

A

B

7.10

Later draft of the Hubbub Main screen on the PC (A) and Palm (B).

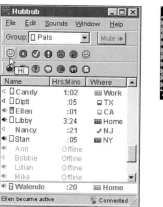

As you can see, the PC and Palm versions of the Main screen are fairly similar. It should be easy enough to move from one to the other and still interpret the information and know how to send a message. **[Be Predictable]**

Example 4: Handling Differences in Platform Conventions

There were a number of cases where I had to handle the same functionality differently on the PC and the Palm. The following examples show how the conventions of the platform can affect design problems.

Providing the Ability to Mute

The first example is the Mute feature. It's important for Mute to be easily accessible and instantly recognizable so that you can mute as soon as you need quiet. So it needs to be on the Main screen and one click away. (Earlier I mentioned that the Frequency by Commonality guidelines have exceptions, and this is one. Most people mute only sometimes, so it should be an Occasional by Many feature, and yet it is so important to be able to stop unwanted sounds quickly that I believe it should be designed as a Frequent by Many feature.) On the Palm, the convention for toggling between two states (mute and unmute) is to use the radio button. **[Follow Conventions]** I used the standard speaker icon with or without sound waves coming out, shown in Figure 7.11A. On the PC, the radio button takes up more room and is more visually complex than I wanted, since you have to label both states (see Figure 7.11B). Instead, the appropriate control on the PC is a single toggle button that stays depressed when you click it (see Figure 7.11C). But when I showed that to people, they had trouble telling whether the button was pressed in, simply because of the visual design of the button, which is determined by the Windows UI Specification. At Dipti's suggestion, I changed the control to a check box (see Figure 7.11D), which makes it clear whether the application is muted or not, but feels like a violation of the convention. Check boxes should modify an attribute, not issue a command. Still, when we tried it out, it was much clearer to users, so we went with it. (I wasn't happy about violating a convention, but my first priority is to make sure people can mute quickly. Also, these toggle buttons are not commonly used, which was some consolation.) I looked at other audio applications, and many of them use the toggle button but replace the button design with an image of a speaker either on or off. At this point, we did not want to create our own custom button, although it probably would have been the best solution.

A   B   C   D

7.11

Options for the Mute feature on Palm and PC. The Mute/Unmute radio button on the Palm (A) works well. PC radio buttons (B) take up too much room and make it harder to find Mute quickly. Because of the visual design of Windows push buttons (C), people found it hard to interpret the button's on and off positions. A Mute check box (D) is easier to interpret, but it is not a conventional use of a check box.

Muting any individual bub was again easier on the Palm than on the PC. On the Palm, I made the sound icon next to each bub toggle between on and off. To turn off someone's sound, you tap their sound icon; to turn it back on you tap it again (see Figure 7.10B). But on the PC, you can't click directly on the icon to change its state. Instead, you have to use the conventional approach of selecting the name in the bub list and then choosing a menu item to mute a bub's activity sounds. [Follow Conventions] This meant I needed an Edit menu with an item to Turn Off Bub's Activity Sounds. I also created a pop-up menu that appears if you point to a bub and right-click, making Turn Off Bub's Activity Sounds the first item. (Not all computer users use pop-up menus, but for those who do, this is a nice shortcut.) So it took three clicks to turn off a bub's sounds through the Edit menu and two clicks through the bub pop-up menu. In this case, a very simple action ended up requiring more effort on the PC than on the Palm.

Providing Status Information

Design Guideline
On desktop computers, use footers to provide dynamic status information. Footers are useful because people don't notice them when all is well, but they often find them when something is wrong and/or they're looking for an explanation of what's happening or has just happened.

On the other hand, it was much harder to give status on the Palm than on the PC. One of our Frequent by Many tasks was to allow people to see what a sound meant whenever one played (for instance, Russ became active, Libby said "hi"). Again, I want people to be able to quickly glance to see what the sound meant—if they have to go digging around in menus, they won't bother. The PC has a convention of putting dynamic information such as this in the footer. My experience in observing users is that they don't notice footers unless they're wondering what is happening or just happened. This is the effect I wanted, so it was an easy decision to use a footer here (see Figure 7.10A). On the Palm, though, there is no such status area, so I had to create another solution.

In the very first iteration of the Palm Main screen, I considered indicating the meaning of the most recent sound in the whitespace just above the sound message buttons, but I didn't like that solution because it seemed to be floating in space (see Figure 7.12A). Once I changed the design to meet other needs, there was no space left (see Figure 7.12B). The only place where any "status-like" information is presented is the header, which labels the screen. I wondered if we could temporarily flash the meaning of the sound in that area, say for three seconds. I asked Alan if that was possible and he determined that he could do it by creating another small form (screen) that would overlay just the header area of the current screen (see Figure 7.12C). So I went with that, still concerned that it might not work.

7.12

An early version of the Palm Main screen design (A), which has an area for status information such as "Ellen became active." However, it seems to be floating in space and isn't easy to locate. When Hubbub evolved (B), there was no place left for status information. We wound up flashing a message over the header area of the screen (C).

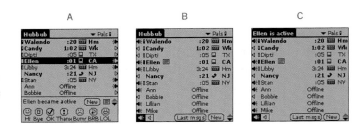

A   B   C

We found out later that this did not work well. After we had started using Hubbub ourselves, we found that the status message grabbed the input focus, so if you were entering text when a sound arrived, your characters stopped appearing in the text entry area. This was confusing and frustrating. **[Show Signs of Progress]** You had to wait until the message stopped flashing. Since there's no good way to find out whether someone is entering text (or is about to), we experimented with ways to let users get rid of the message quickly. First we tried tapping the message itself to remove it, but as we used it more, we found that our instinct was to tap the text entry area again (to put focus back in it), so we made that work. Still, having to interrupt text entry to stop a status message from flashing was a big break in flow. We finally decided not to present the message when you're in a text entry screen (the Bub screen or the Message screen). This approach avoids the interruption, which is critical, but it means you miss some status messages. In the end, we never found an ideal solution. Because the PC has a conventional status area and the Palm does not, it's much easier in Hubbub to find out what a sound means when you hear it on the PC than it is on the Palm.

Distinguishing Participants' Messages

In yet another situation, I used a slightly different design to better suit the constraints of each platform without violating either platform's conventions. The Functional Requirements indicated that while in a conversation, it should be easy to distinguish each participant's messages. People need to be able to look back at the last few messages and quickly identify who said what. On the PC, most instant messengers put the sender's name in front of each message and some reinforce that cue by using a different color for each person. I went with that approach on the PC, using color and labeling each message with the bub name in bold so it would be easier to spot (see Figure

7.13A). On the small Palm screen, though, we didn't have color[3] and I didn't want to use up precious space repeating the bub name in front of every message. Instead, I used font weight as a cue. The other person's messages appear in bold, so they're easier to spot, and your messages appear in regular font, as shown in Figure 7.13B. I wasn't concerned that people wouldn't be able to remember whose messages were whose, since their messages would be fresh in their minds.

7.13

Design of the Message screen on the PC (A) and the Palm (B). On the PC, each person's message is identified using a label and a color. On the Palm, where space is more limited, the labels are removed except for sound messages. Instead, the other person's messages appear in bold and yours appear in regular font, allowing more of the messages to appear.

A   B

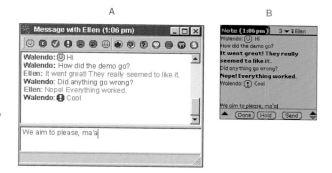

I was concerned that it might be difficult to tell who sent a sound message, since you can't make an icon bold and some of the labels can be very short ("Hi," for instance). So I did include the sender's name in front of sound messages. Since they always appear on a separate line, they still take up only one line.[4] The use of font weight to distinguish both parties' messages on the Palm worked very well. It allowed us to show more message text per screen, and we later discovered that no one had trouble interpreting the screen or figuring out who sent which messages. (We stuck with color and a label on the PC since it was the convention.)

---

[3] Some Palms do have color, but they were not available when we were designing Hubbub. Even now, the battery life on color models is fairly short, so we would probably still go with black and white until the color models could last for eight hours straight.

[4] I had wanted to incorporate the sound messages directly into text messages, but the engineers said that doing so would be more complex to implement. We agreed to try sending sound messages separately to see whether this would be an acceptable solution before spending the implementation time. It turned out that this approach worked well enough, although it did surprise some users.

Example 5: Removing a Feature

There were some cases where we decided to remove an entire feature primarily for design reasons. I've already mentioned one example—removing the indication of average activity over time. Another example was removing the ability to tell who is messaging with whom. This feature is hard to design because you may not have both people in your list. For example, you might have Stan in your list, but not Bobbie. When Stan talks to Bobbie, how can you see whom he's talking with? I could show that Stan is interacting with someone, but not whom. But we had other worries about this feature because it's not clear how to control permissions. Suppose Stan and Bobbie both have Cyrus in their bub lists. Stan has given Cyrus permission to know whom he interacts with, but Bobbie has not. If Stan interacts with Bobbie, what does Cyrus see? That Stan is interacting with someone whose identity isn't shown? Maybe he doesn't see that Stan is interacting with anyone. The first option can be confusing and the second is misleading.

Another problem is that it's complicated to communicate visually who is interacting with whom. We could draw a line between interacting bubs, but we don't have much room and if a few people are interacting at once, it could get very visually complex, especially if some bubs are scrolled off the screen. **[Use Visual Elements Sparingly]** Color is a possibility, but again, we didn't have color on the Palm. Since this was a Nice to Have feature, I proposed that we drop it for design reasons. We agreed that it wasn't worth the complexity, even though it would increase awareness to know who was interacting with whom. Of course, if the usage studies indicated that people wanted this information, we would re-evaluate. (As it turned out, no one ever asked for it, or described a problem that would have been solved if they'd had that information.) This was one of the harder features for me to strike from the list because it was a personal favorite, but it's a good example of letting go of pet features for the sake of simplicity.

These are just a few examples of laying out a UI, mostly focusing on the primary screens. Designing the rest of the application consisted of going through the rest of the tasks and figuring out which UI widgets to use, how to lay them out, and how to transition across screens, if necessary. Each time, I worked through as many issues as I could, keeping in mind which tasks were in which Frequency by Commonality category, and their relative priority. Once I'd settled on a design or component of a design, I showed it to colleagues and incorporated their feedback, going through several iterations even before implementation began. As you saw, sometimes the feedback led to relatively major changes, which affected the design of other features, so I had to keep checking the Task List to make sure everything was still covered. It was especially important to check with Alan regularly, so he could point out problems early (for example, the performance problem with updating the active/idle time every second). This way, I was able to design around some engineering problems before any code was written. My main goal was to make sure that the UI architecture was solid, since that's expensive to fix once implementation begins. If I'd gotten some of the details wrong, it was a comfort to know that there would be time to make smaller adjustments once we ran the Hubbub usage study.

Walk Through the Tasks

There is one final step you can take during the design phase to make sure you've accounted for all the tasks and optimized the design for the most common and frequent ones: Walk through the tasks. That is, try to carry out each task using the design to see how well it supports the intended tasks and whether it appropriately reflects the priority of the features. It's much easier to revise a UI Spec than it is to rewrite code, so it's worth spending a little more time up front to refine the design. It doesn't have to take long—you can do it as formally or informally as you like, spending anywhere from a few hours to a few days. But trying out the design can help you find problems early. It's a bit like cross-checking your figures by adding them up in a different order.

There are several techniques you can use to do this. One technique, called a *cognitive walkthrough*, requires walking through each task ensuring that the flow makes sense, that it's clear how to move from one step to the next, that there's sufficient feedback along the way, and so on. Another technique, called a *heuristic evaluation*, can be used at this phase as well, although it is intended for those trained in interaction design. Again, the tester goes through the interface looking for specific types of problems that might slow down or confuse users.[5]

---

[5] To learn more about these methods, see *Usability Inspection Methods* by Jakob Nielsen and Robert L. Mack.

I believe that much of the value of these techniques is in forcing you to explicitly walk through each step in the process of accomplishing the tasks supported by the technology. Go back to your Task List organized by frequency and commonality and, with your design mock-ups in front of you, pretend to select items, press buttons, pop up windows, and so on as if you were really doing each task. When you do this, you can't help noticing problems that weren't as obvious when you were deciding what widgets to put where. I've found it helpful when walking through the tasks to keep in mind these questions:

1. How many steps is it taking to accomplish this task?
2. How visible is the first step in the process of doing this task?
3. Once you start the task, how clear is each next step in the process?
4. Is the effort and visibility matching the Frequency by Commonality priority of this task?

In other words, you're asking yourself whether you met your goal of making Frequent by Many and Occasional by Many tasks as efficient as possible, and making Frequent by Many and Frequent by Few tasks as obvious as possible.

Design Guideline
After laying out the UI, walk through each of the tasks using the mock-ups. Look for tasks with too many clicks, no visible cues, awkward flow, and so on. Walk through the clean version of each task, and then think of common nonstandard scenarios and things that might go wrong. As you find problems, adjust the design and walk through the tasks again. This technique can help you find problems very early, when it's fast and cheap to fix them.

It is helpful to think about at least two scenarios for each task. Start with the clean case where everything is set up just right and everything goes well. Then think about other common contexts and ways that things might go wrong. Don't conjure up bizarre scenarios that could conceivably crop up; think of ordinary variations that will probably occur. For example, suppose you've designed a mechanism to enter phone numbers into a cell phone. The clean case is when someone enters one number and returns to the Main screen. But what about entering a lot of numbers in one sitting: How smooth is that process? This won't happen all the time but it will happen to everyone when they first get the phone, and occasionally when they add one person's multiple numbers (home, work, cell, and so on). Also, think about some things that can go wrong. What if they enter a name that already exists: How easy is it to recover? Do you show the number already entered for that name, so they can decide whether to replace it? It helps to walk through various "nonstandard" scenarios like this and notice how many extra steps they take and how easily you can figure out what to do. You'll probably realize you can make small design adjustments to smooth out those nonstandard cases. By anticipating these cases early, you can start to make sure your technology will behave like a butler. As you make changes, you may need to go back and walk through tasks that are affected by those changes. Keep going through the Task List until you're able to walk through all the tasks without changing anything.

Here's an example of a problem I found in Hubbub's design by walking through the task, "Find a Hubbub user and invite them to be your bub." First, I started from the Main screen and went through the steps of getting to the Add Bub screen, entering a name, getting some matches back, and choosing one. It was pretty clear how to get started on the task, and it took 6 taps in the cleanest possible case, which seemed acceptable for an Occasional by Many task. Figure 7.14 shows the steps in this process and how I counted them.

7.14

Steps in the task of finding a user and inviting them to be your bub.

A

1. Tap New

B

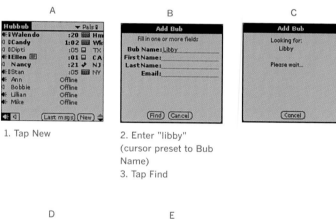

2. Enter "libby"
(cursor preset to Bub Name)
3. Tap Find

C

D

Add Bub

Please select the bub you want to add:

Libby   Libby Tarian
Libbylaw   Mike Sourdough
LibbyLou   Monica Sullivan

(Add) (Cancel)

4. Select name
5. Tap Add

E

Add Bub

Adding Libby (Libby Tarian)

Group: ▼ Pals
Accept: ☑ Text messages
              ☑ Sound messages
Provide: ☑ My idle/active info
              ☑ My location
Presence: ☑ Play sounds when
              they go idle/active

(Add) (Cancel)

6. Tap Add
(Group set to current group; permissions same as last Bub)

But then I wondered what would happen if the system didn't find the person you had in mind. Right away, I realized I needed a New button on screen D to start a new search, which would take you back to screen B. When I pretended to tap that, I realized that information entered in the previous search should be repeated in the text fields so you won't have to start from scratch, especially since entering text on the Palm is slow and error-prone. **[Remember What They Told You]** In many cases, if the system finds no match it's because you made a typo or got some part of the name wrong. If the information is still available, you can see what's wrong, fix it, and search again. So I added a New button to the design, and indicated in the UI Spec that the information from the previous search should be filled in to the new form. Since this change was local to the process of adding bubs, no other task was affected by it.

Going through the exercise of walking through each task as if you were the user is like doing a very early round of testing. Some people even do usability testing with real users at this stage, using just the mock-ups. You can't simulate the real experience, but you can find some problems you hadn't anticipated. This is an especially good way to find out whether the UI has any underlying structural problems. As I mentioned earlier, development teams usually resist making large changes once implementation begins, so now is a great time to find those types of major problems. It will cost you only a few days or a week instead of weeks or months. Even if you find that the UI structure appears to be sound, walking through the UI helps you refine the interaction before you've written any code. You'll be that much closer to making your technology behave like a butler.

Once you finish creating all the screenshots and walking through the tasks, it's time to write up the User Interface Spec. Don't give in to the temptation to stop at this point, posting the mock-ups and expecting the engineers to work from there. The mock-ups show only the look of the design. You cannot determine most of the behavior by looking at them. Since so much of your users' experience is in their *interaction* with the system, you need to make sure the intended behavior is well specified so the engineering team can design the architecture and build the system to support that interaction. As we mentioned, you can create UI Specs in any of a variety of formats. The most important thing is to make it easy to read so that people are willing to read it, and easily accessible so that anyone on the team can quickly pull it up to check on a specific point. Choose the format that works best for your organization.

The Hubbub UI Spec is too long to reproduce in this book. However, if you're interested in seeing what a UI Spec looks like, we've made it available on our Web site, www.uidesigns.com. I wrote it as a set of Web pages, so you'll be able to skim through it to see how it was organized and what type of information was included.

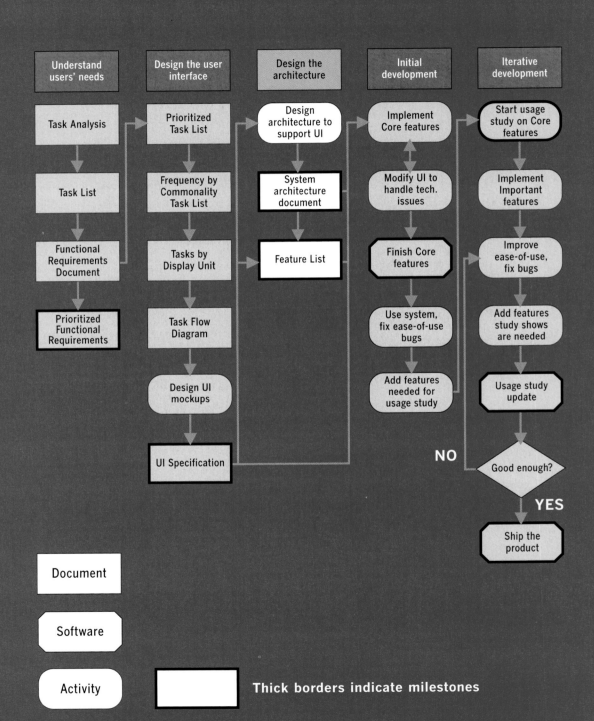

CHAPTER 8
Architecting with the UI in Mind

Now that we have a UI design, it's time to work out how to build the system. When engineers architect a system, they first make sure that they understand its underlying constraints (operating system, CPU, memory, bandwidth, available storage, and so on). Designing the system is a matter of balancing all those constraints against other issues, such as simplicity and ease of maintenance. If you have a UI design available at this point, the UI becomes another one of the constraints to factor into the equation. This doesn't mean you'll always do what's best for the UI, but you're in a position to weigh the implications of the UI for other parts of the system and vice versa. Certainly, all else being equal, you should do what works for the UI. And in cases where you feel you need to weight another factor more heavily, you'll be aware of the UI cost and the options to work around it, rather than finding out the hard way. Just as knowing the range of CPUs that you're building for makes it easier to design a system that will run quickly, having a UI Spec makes it much more likely that you'll build something usable.

In this chapter, Alan explains how the UI affected the design of the Hubbub architecture. As you'll see, often the system was designed primarily to meet the needs of the UI design, but sometimes system constraints affected the UI. If you're an engineer, we hope you'll learn more about incorporating UI concerns into your system architecture. If you're a designer, we hope you'll understand more about the many concerns engineers have to balance when considering UI issues.

Alan: In the following sections, I don't try to explain Hubbub's complete architecture, I just point out some examples of how the UI affected our decisions. This requires getting into some Hubbub details. While you don't have to follow everything, it might help to get the gist of the technical issues so you can understand how we balanced them against UI concerns.

Our first task was to figure out Hubbub's network architecture, which led to the design of the server and its communication with the clients. (In the next several sections, "we" refers to Dipti and me.) We then figured out how Hubbub was going to run on multiple devices, supporting multiple clients per user. Finally, as Dipti worked on the PC client, I focused on the Palm client and worked out my design for supporting its UI. The following sections describe each of these tasks.

Network Architecture

At the highest level, Hubbub consists of many clients sending and receiving updates about each other. That tells us that they will be networked, but not much else. Should they talk directly to each other or pass messages through a server? What types of data need to be sent around and when? Before doing any implementation, we had to make some basic networking decisions and start defining the Hubbub protocol. The UI Spec drove much of the network architecture. For instance, it indicated the types of data we needed to send over the network and the paths the data would take.

UI Drives Architecture

Like most instant messenger clients, Hubbub clients need to receive updated lists containing each bub's *Hubbub name* and status, and they need to send and receive text instant messages. Unlike most instant messengers, however, Hubbub needs to allow users to see how active their bubs have been in the last 10 to 20 seconds. And because the UI Spec indicates that the activity level of each bub is displayed continuously on the Main screen (as opposed to only being displayed when the user requests it), clients need to be updated several times a minute. Since these constant updates result in a lot of network traffic, we spent a lot of time finding the most efficient approach.

The simplest method is to have each client send its *activity level* to each of its bubs every few seconds (see Figure 8.1). It's straightforward, but puts a large load on the network. Let's say activity updates are sent every 15 seconds. If 10 users, each a bub of the others, have one client online, each client would send 9 update messages (one to each of its bubs, but not to itself). That translates to 90 activity messages every 15 seconds, or 6 messages per second generated by just 10 users!

8.1

One possible architecture for passing around Hubbub activity messages is to use a client-to-client model. It is straightforward but puts a heavy load on the network.

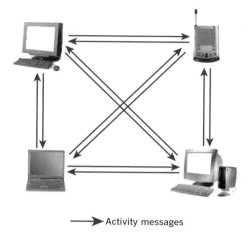

Activity messages

It made more sense to have each client update a server, which responds with the last reported activity of each of the user's bubs. The server combines multiple activity messages into one response (see Figure 8.2), which means that the delivery of activity information is delayed slightly, but the result is a huge reduction in network traffic. Now, instead of 90 activity messages every 15 seconds, we have 20 (one from each of the 10 clients to the server and one from the server back to each of the clients). Even better, this approach scales linearly instead of exponentially as more bubs and clients are added to the system. We also decided to have the server send updates only in response to receiving an update itself, which makes it less likely that the server will send messages to clients that have gone offline or out of coverage. So in this case, we started with the UI requirement of updating activity every several seconds and came up with a network design that supported it while alleviating our concerns about bandwidth and device connectivity.

8.2

We decided to go with this client-server architecture for passing around Hubbub activity messages because it keeps network traffic down.

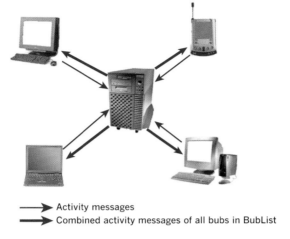

———▶ Activity messages
━━━▶ Combined activity messages of all bubs in BubList

Although Dipti and I decided to use a client-server model for sending bub lists and bub activity updates to reduce our network traffic, at first we assumed that client-to-client messages, such as text and sound, would be sent directly from one client to another (see Figure 8.3). These messages must be delivered to a single client immediately, and unlike activity messages, multiple client-to-client messages cannot be combined at the server. In fact, sending them through the server would increase its load and could delay their arrival.

8.3

We initially expected to send text and sound messages directly between clients, as shown here.

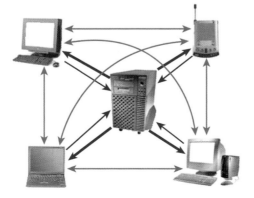

———▶ Text and sound messages
———▶ Activity messages
━━━▶ Combined activity messages of all bubs in BubList

However, allowing the clients to contact each other directly means there are more potential privacy problems. For instance, the UI Spec says that when you remove a bub, they are removed from all of your clients and you are removed from all of theirs. The problem is that once a (possibly malicious) client is given your client's IP address, you can't rely on it to stop sending you messages when you ask it to. You can certainly ignore those messages, but the burden is now on you and your client. If all messages are routed through a trustworthy server and you tell the server to stop allowing messages from an ex-Bub, the burden now lies with the server. Since I'm paranoid about exposing someone's IP address to the world, and since we can upgrade and patch the Hubbub server more easily than the clients, we decided to have all messages pass through the server (see Figure 8.4). With the server handling permissions and authenticating messages, there would be less chance of a malicious client sending spoofed or unwanted messages. Everything we wanted to do could be done in a peer-to-peer scheme, but it would add a lot of complexity and a greater risk that we would miss something.

8.4

We decided to go with a pure client-server approach to sending text and sound messages because it allowed us to more easily handle other features, such as privacy and security.

⟶ Text and sound messages
⟶ Activity messages
⟶ Text, sound, and activity messages

Engineering Guideline
When designing an
architecture, start with
the behavior specified
in the UI Spec and
build the system to
support it.

Having all messages pass through the server would also give us the ability to generate comprehensive logs that show how people use (and do not use) Hubbub features. This information is important for our method of development because it helps us fine-tune the UI based on which features are being used and how. Plus, we envision Hubbub as a workplace tool, and using a central server makes it easier to run behind corporate firewalls. So based on UI issues, the value of being able to track usage information, and our limited development resources, it made sense to go with a pure client-server model. We'd just have to use other techniques to make sure we could handle the load and still scale to a reasonable size.

Architecture Drives UI

In other cases, we had to make decisions based on technical considerations that would have had negative implications for the UI. When this happened, the three of us (Dipti, Alan, and Ellen) worked together to figure out how to resolve those issues. Sometimes we came up with a technical solution and sometimes we adjusted the UI enough to handle the technical issue without hurting the user experience. One technical decision that affected the UI was our decision to use UDP (User Datagram Protocol) instead of TCP (Transmission Control Protocol) as our data transport mechanism.

The major difference between the two is that TCP requires a "connection" between two devices whereas UDP does not. TCP is a streaming connection, similar to a phone call between two people. Once established, the connection is reliable in that if you push a message in one side, you can expect it to come out the other. The downside is that keeping a TCP connection open requires the device to remain continuously accessible to the network. Portable devices such as wireless Palms often go in and out of coverage as people put them in their pockets or walk into elevators. Using TCP would mean the added complexity and expense of handling and re-establishing broken connections frequently. And, on the server side, it would also mean having to handle many TCP connections, which is a project in itself.

UDP, on the other hand, is more like the postal service. Messages are small, individual packets that you address and send. No direct connection is necessary; once you've mailed them, they are in the system and make their way to their destination. UDP is also like postal mail in that there is no guarantee when packets will arrive, if ever! The good news is that, since there's no connection to maintain, there is much less networking code to write. The implementation downside of UDP is that, since packets are not guaranteed to arrive, or to arrive in the order in which they were sent, the application has to handle those cases gracefully. And, since messages are passed around in small packets, either an application's messages must be small enough to fit into one packet or the application must reassemble multiple UDP packets—which can be complex, given their unreliable nature. (There are other technical downsides to UDP as compared to TCP, such as the lack of built-in congestion control, but we felt that these were acceptable for the scope of this project.)

Since Hubbub was designed for use on portable wireless devices as well as on desktop PCs, we knew we were going to have to handle the problems of flaky connectivity and dropped messages no matter what. Our plan was to make the protocol as simple and as stateless as possible. Each message must contain all the information needed for the recipient to fully process it upon arrival. One message cannot depend on the arrival of another message, or depend on the system being in a certain state when it arrives. If a message is lost (the device loses coverage, the PC crashes, your cat chews through your network cable), Hubbub clients should never need to stop and wait, or become otherwise confused. The worst that should happen is a small delay while the message is re-sent, or the display of slightly out-of-date data for a few seconds.

As we spent more time defining the messages required by the UI Spec, it became clear that the messages could be kept both small and self-contained, which meant UDP was a viable option. Since we were already planning to handle lost messages—UDP's primary drawback—and because implementing on top of UDP was much simpler, we decided it was a better choice than TCP. This decision to go with UDP had some significant implications for the UI that came up throughout the project. One major issue was this: Since there's no "connection" to other clients, how do we tell whether a message was delivered? And what does this mean to the user?

In talking to Ellen, we realized that only some messages need to get through reliably. Text and sound messages always need to be delivered because it's very disruptive to a conversation if any are dropped. It's also very important that both sides of a conversation get feedback indicating whether a text or sound message has been delivered, for the same reason. It's difficult to have a conversation when each person has a different notion of who has seen which messages. Other messages aren't as important, such as the client activity messages that indicate how actively someone is using their computer. Those are meant as background information to help people stay aware of one another, but no one message is critical, especially since a new one will arrive every few seconds. So we needed a mechanism to ensure reliability, but it could be selective.

We decided to go with a standard method for handling reliability with UDP. Figure 8.5 shows the flow of events for text and sound messages. The sending client assigns a unique sequence number to each message it generates. In the case of text and sound messages, which must get through, the sending client also sets a flag that requests an acknowl-edgment (ACK) from the recipient. If the sender does not receive an ACK in a certain amount of time, it re-sends the original message. The responsibility for re-sending important messages lies completely with the originating client. The server knows nothing about re-sending, and simply passes messages through as they arrive. We decided to have Hubbub clients attempt to send the message every three seconds until one minute has passed or until it receives an ACK for that message. Because the returning ACK messages include the sequence number of the message being acknowledged in their data (and because the Hubbub protocol is stateless), the sender does not need to stop everything and wait for a particular ACK. The client is free to send other messages. With this mechanism in place, there is still no guarantee that a message will get through, but the odds are increased (because of the re-sending), and at least both clients know whether a given message has been received.

Since re-sending may cause multiple copies of a message to be received, clients also need to be smart enough not to display messages they've already seen. We started by having Hubbub clients keep track of the last hundred or so message sequence numbers they've seen from each bub. If a duplicate is received, it is acknowledged and ignored.

8.5

This flow diagram shows how Hubbub increases the reliability of text and sound messages and lets the user know when messages reach their destination. Activity messages don't need to be reliable so they do not go through this process.

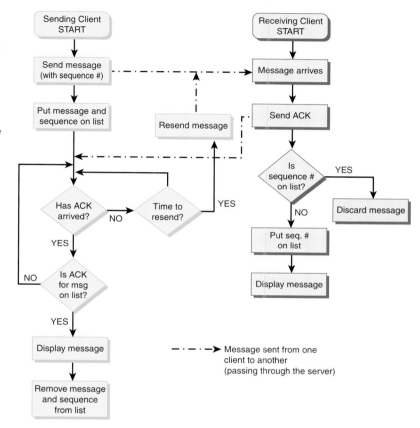

A major UI implication is that some messages might not get through. But, as Ellen explained, the most important thing is for the sender of a text or sound message to *know* whether the other person got it. You'd prefer that all messages get through immediately, but if they don't, people at least need to know so they can adjust. The worst thing is for someone to send a message, get no response, and then jump to a conclusion about the other person's intentions. (Now *that* would reduce tolerance capital.) So in the UI, Ellen decided we could delay displaying the message in the conversation until the recipient has seen it (that is, until the sender's client has gotten an ACK). This way, when a message occasionally gets dropped and is re-sent, people will think the system is a little slow but they won't misinterpret each other's behavior. (Later we came up with a UI refinement that helped people better interpret this lag, but for now, we had the critical UI issue covered. We'll describe the refinement in Chapter 10.)

Engineering Guideline
If there are technical reasons not to support the UI as specified, find out which behavior is critical to the user experience and then adjust the architecture and UI to support it. You may need to adjust the way that the UI deals with noncritical behaviors to handle the technical constraints.

If we hadn't been able to come up with a good way to let both people know if and when messages arrive, we wouldn't have used UDP. After all, the whole point of building Hubbub was to support the features in a way that people can use. Nonetheless, as was the case in this example, if we had a technical reason to do something a certain way, Ellen was usually able to adjust the UI constraints to accommodate while still addressing user concerns.

Multiplatform Architecture

From the beginning, the team wanted users to be able to have multiple Hubbub clients running on multiple devices and even multiple PCs. Having used ICQ, AIM, and Yahoo! Messenger in the past, we wanted to avoid the problem they all have when you switch machines. Since they allow you to be connected from only one location at a time, you have to log in every time you come in to work or arrive home after work. And the "You have logged on at another location, so you have been logged off here" dialog box is annoying. Worse yet, if you leave the office for the day and someone sends you a message, even if you log on from home, you won't see it until you get back to work the next morning.

Okay, so we want people to be able to stay logged on from multiple places at once and not have to do anything when they switch from one device to another. But how should that work? How do we make sure people get their messages wherever they are? What happens when they're idle on all clients? What do their bubs see about their location and active/idle time as they move around? We spent a lot of time discussing scenarios involving multiple clients and figuring out the experience we wanted users to have, and then Ellen updated the UI Spec to reflect the behavior we settled on. Having a detailed description of the interaction design allowed us to design the architecture to support that behavior.

Here's what we came up with. We created the concept of a *Last Active Client*, which is the client on which a user last moved the mouse or hit a key (PC) or tapped the screen (Palm). Internally, the Hubbub server keeps track of all the places where a user is logged on, but the Last Active Client is the one whose information is passed to the user's bubs.

When a text or sound message is sent to someone who has multiple clients logged on, the server must decide which client should receive the message. The algorithm is simple: if the Last Active Client is currently active (meaning that there has been mouse, keyboard, or pen activity within the last few minutes), the message is sent there. If the Last Active Client is idle (there has been no input activity within the last few minutes), the message is sent to all the user's clients. Our reasoning is that since all the clients are idle, we don't know which one the user will see next. And it's better to receive a message in multiple locations than to miss one entirely.

To illustrate, suppose I have Hubbub running on both my home and office PCs, with their locations set to "Hm" and "Wk," respectively. Let's say I go to a meeting about trademarks, turn on my Palm and set my location to "TM." Now my Palm becomes my Last Active Client and my bubs will see "TM" as my location (see Figure 8.6). As the meeting drags on (and on…) they will see how long I've been active or idle on my Palm.

8.6

When a user is active on one of several clients, that one becomes the Last Active Client. Others see the location and the length of time that the client has been active or idle.

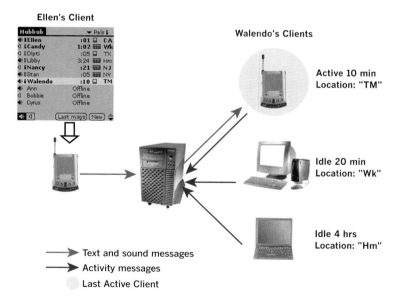

Ellen's Client

Walendo's Clients

Active 10 min
Location: "TM"

Idle 20 min
Location: "Wk"

Idle 4 hrs
Location: "Hm"

Text and sound messages
Activity messages
Last Active Client

Now imagine that I become idle on my Palm during the endless meeting. Everyone still sees my location as "TM" because it's still my Last Active Client, but now if Ellen sends me a message, it will go to *all* my clients because I'm idle on all of them (see Figure 8.7).

8.7

If a user is idle on all their clients, their bubs still see the location and activity of their Last Active Client. Text and sound messages are sent to all idle clients to ensure that the recipient will see them no matter where they become active next.

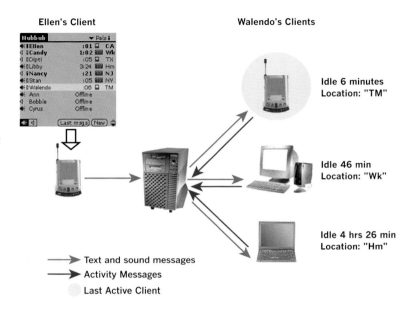

Ellen's Client   Walendo's Clients

Idle 6 minutes
Location: "TM"

Idle 46 min
Location: "Wk"

Idle 4 hrs 26 min
Location: "Hm"

⟶ Text and sound messages
⟶ Activity Messages
⬤ Last Active Client

Finally, when they let me out and I go back to my office PC, others see me become active at "Wk" and any new messages will arrive there (see Figure 8.8).

8.8

When a user becomes active on a new client, the server updates the Last Active Client. That user's bubs see the location and activity information from that newly active client, and text and sound messages are sent there.

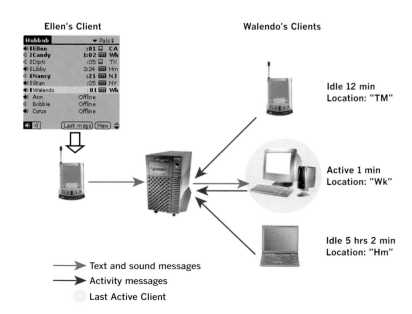

Ellen's Client   Walendo's Clients

Idle 12 min
Location: "TM"

Active 1 min
Location: "Wk"

Idle 5 hrs 2 min
Location: "Hm"

⟶ Text and sound messages
⟶ Activity messages
⬤ Last Active Client

In this last case, Ellen specified the experience users should have when running multiple Hubbub clients (with our input), and we designed the architecture to support that. Sometimes, though, the UI was limited because of technical constraints. For instance, sounds play a large part of the Hubbub experience, so we naturally wanted them to be as pleasing as possible. Since Hubbub runs on the Palm and the PC, we had to pick a sound solution that worked on both so that the same sound messages could be used on either platform. Modern PCs generally have excellent sound support and can play complex compositions in many formats. PalmOS, on the other hand, only supports simple single-instrument MIDI compositions with no chords. We could have come up with a scheme for sending different MIDI files to different devices depending on their capabilities, but to reduce technical (and administrative) complexity, we decided to limit ourselves to the Palm client's capabilities. We also hoped to allow people to create and add their own sounds to the system (a Nice to Have feature), and we all agreed that it would be too much to ask people to create two versions of every sound, one for each device. The downside of using simple sounds is that the Hubbub PC client sounds fairly primitive. So here, the user experience suffered somewhat because of technical constraints, but we all agreed that the UI cost was much lower than the implementation cost of working around it. If it turned out later that users hated the sounds, we could reconsider.

Palm Client Architecture

Once Dipti and I had worked out Hubbub's overall architecture, she started working on the Windows client and I focused on designing the Palm client. When coding an application like Hubbub, I try to start with the core data structures and work outward. Since we had been working on the UI Spec for a while, I already had a rough idea of what would be needed. The "finally-I-get-to-code-something" half of my brain wanted to jump right into *vi*[1] and start typing. But the "oh-yeah-users-matter" half of my brain knew I should start by looking at the UI Spec to make sure my assumptions about the data structures were right.

---

[1] You got a problem with *vi*?

Palm applications differ from desktop applications in that they tend to be *form* based (that is, a form defines how to present and interact with data). A typical Palm application has multiple forms that the user can switch between. For instance, the Address Book consists of an Address List form that lists a single line for each address entry in your list, an Address View form that displays all the information about a specific entry, and an Address Edit form that lets you update a specific entry or add a new one.

From the UI Spec, I saw that the three primary forms used in Hubbub would be what we call the Main form, which displays a list of bubs and their current status; the Bub form, which displays more detailed information about a particular bub and allows the user to initiate text and sound messages; and the Message form, which displays the conversation and allows users to send more text and sound messages. Since most Hubbub features involve displaying or interacting with bubs, it was clear that one of the Palm client's core data structures would be the *BubList*. In it, I would keep all the information the server sends about each bub: handle, first name, last name, e-mail address, location, activity level, duration of active or idle time, and so on. Once I knew that, I could define the interfaces to allow the forms to access the BubList as necessary.

Since PalmOS devices typically have very little dynamic memory available to applications, another issue we faced was deciding where in memory to keep the BubList. For Hubbub, we were using the Palm Vx with PalmOS 3.3. According to the *Palm OS Programmer's Companion* (available from www.palmos.com), Hubbub would have only about 36Kb of dynamic heap memory to work with. The alternative is the storage heap, where applications can store data in PalmOS "databases," which are the PalmOS analog to files. The storage heap is much larger, and data persists between sessions. This means that you can leave data there and it will be available the next time you run your application. The drawback to the storage heap is that you have to access your data through the PalmOS Data Manager, which may take longer than accessing the dynamic heap.

Engineering Guideline
Consider UI require-ments along with system constraints when making technical decisions.

I knew that the BubList could grow fairly large since it would contain all the information for each bub. That was a good reason to put it in the storage heap. On the other hand, it would also be continuously displayed and updated, so I didn't want it to be expensive to access. That was a good reason to put it in the dynamic heap. And since the server sends an updated BubList each time a client logs on, the transient nature of the dynamic heap wouldn't be a problem. I could have gone either way at that point, so I went back and looked at the UI Spec. It specified that we would be saving some per-bub state information locally (such as whether or not you had a bub muted) each time the user exited Hubbub. By putting the BubList in the storage heap, where it would persist between sessions, I could avoid doing the extra work of saving that state somewhere else. I then remembered that we'd only be updating the BubList every 15 seconds or so, which is not frequently enough to worry about the performance hit of using the Data Manager. Decision made: we went with the Data Manager.

Although I'm implying that I diligently refer to the UI Spec for all my decisions, this is not really the case. The truth is that my instinct is still to go off and make it work the way I assume it should. I've been known to forget to check the Spec, and once the UI designer calms down ☺, I have to go back and build it again. I've built up a lot of general-purpose programming knowledge over the years and, like all programmers, I use that knowledge instinctively as I write code. I make assumptions without realizing it and I make decisions based on those assumptions. Because the UI Spec is an external source of information, I need to remind myself to look at it before diving in.

Engineering Guideline
Remember to check the UI Spec often so that you don't base your technical decisions on implicit engineering assumptions about how a feature should behave. Understand the specified behavior first and then design the system to support it.

I could easily have caused myself extra work when I was deciding how to implement the Main form. This form displays the list of bub handles, locations, and active/idle times. PalmOS supports two constructs for displaying information in rows, the List and the Table. It's fairly easy to display lines of text in either, but since Tables don't have built-in support for scrolling, I planned to use a List. The UI Spec showed that I'd need to display bitmaps (the activity meters, the device icons, and the per-bub mute status indicators) on each line (see Figure 8.9). Okay, that could still be done with a List. I'd just need to implement a custom drawing function (which I'd have to do even if I used a Table). But wait, the mute status bitmap is really supposed to act like a button. When the user taps it, it toggles. If I used a List, the whole line would be selected, which isn't the effect we wanted. In the end, the better decision was to use a Table even though it meant I'd have to add scrolling support myself. If the UI Spec hadn't been as detailed as it was, and if I hadn't looked at it closely, I would have used a List for the first implementation and then would have had to go back and do it again with a Table.

8.9

Each bub entry in the BubList has several icons, including the speaker icon that acts as a toggle button to turn on and off that bub's activity sounds.

Designing an application's architecture is a series of big decisions, and coding an application is a series of small decisions. Programmers are continuously weighing one approach against another when writing code, and often the wrong approach seems just as valid as the correct one until later when some obscure detail becomes apparent. Having a detailed UI Spec available can help reduce the number of wrong decisions—especially if you can get the programmers to read it.

The Feature List

Once Alan and Dipti finished designing and writing up the system architecture, we were finally ready to produce a Feature List. The Feature List itemizes all of the features to be implemented, this time making specific reference to their UI and implementation now that those are defined. The Feature List is used mainly as a project management tool to help the team keep track of what needs to be done and what has been completed. It is often very long, since it accounts for all of the features, from the underpinnings up through the UI details. It is also a useful communication tool that informs everyone about what will (and won't) be built and how much effort is involved. Usually, you create the Feature List by going through all of the items in the Functional Requirements and then using the UI Spec and the architecture document to translate them into specific features to be implemented. In our experience, each engineer has written up the features on the items assigned to them and then the designer has gone through the list to add UI-specific items that the engineers may have overlooked. The project manager usually coordinates this process.

There are, of course, many ways to organize a software project, and this book is not about project management. But there are a few things to note about how your project management approach can affect the UI. We've been saying that to build cooperative technology, you should aim to provide fewer features but design them well. Providing fewer features means that you need to make sure you're building the right ones, and designing them well means that you need to plan to spend time iterating them as you get usability feedback. Your scheduling mechanism should be designed to support these goals. The next few sections discuss several things you can do to make effective use of your time and effort.

Work in Priority Order

Project Management Guideline

Implement features in priority order, building Core features first, so you can try out the system with users as soon as possible. Prioritizing will help you avoid working on features that turn out not to be needed, giving you more time to work on those that are.

Earlier we talked about the importance of prioritizing the requirements into Core features (ones you absolutely need to meaningfully run the application yourselves), Important features (ones you minimally need to ship), and Nice to Have features (ones that enhance the application but are not strictly required). The Feature List should retain these prioritization categories. Most of the features should reflect the category of the functional requirement that generated the feature, but you should look over the entire list at once to see if you need to make adjustments. Again, it's important for the team to reach agreement on which features are in which category, and then to stick with those priorities. Your goal is to get the Core features done as soon as you can so that you can start to use the application and get some early information about what's working and what's not. You'll want to fix problems right away. Once you're using the application, you'll get a feel for which Important features you need to add, if any, before you can start a usage study or usability test. Again, your goal is to get that feedback as early as possible so that you can find out what you need to change. If you build features out of order, you'll be spending more time on features that may not be needed, and you'll have less time to polish the ones that are.

Of course, things can change, and your priorities might change along with them. That's fine, as long as you keep the prioritized Feature List up to date so you can make sure that people are working on the highest priority tasks.

Estimate a Schedule Based on Detailed Feature Descriptions

We saw in Chapter 5 what happens if you ask someone to estimate how long it will take to build a feature based on a general description. They vastly underestimate, because people are notoriously bad at thinking about all the details that go into a task, and they don't anticipate the problems that inevitably get in the way. You want as accurate a schedule as you can get so that you don't overestimate what you can accomplish in the time you have. When you overcommit yourself, you end up trying to throw in all the features you promised without spending time to polish them, and you have to throw away your goal of making your technology cooperative.

Once you have a Feature List, you can use it to get a more accurate schedule estimate. It will still give you a low estimate, but at least it will be closer to the truth. The trick is to include as many details about the feature as possible in its description. The engineers should break down the features into multiple implementation steps, and the designer should spell out the UI attributes of each feature that are likely to be overlooked. Then, have the assigned engineer estimate each of the component tasks rather than the overall feature. By including feature attributes, you accomplish two things. First, you get a better time estimate, and second, you can keep track of the tasks more accurately. You'll know why it's taking so long to do a particular feature—perhaps because it includes many hidden tasks that help smooth out the user's interaction. Project management tools often allow you to "open up" a task to see the subtasks associated with it. It can be helpful to use this mechanism to list the ease-of-use components of a task.

Figure 8.10 shows a small portion of the Hubbub Feature List. This one is for the Palm client only and it shows the tasks for just a few features: the Bub List Infrastructure, the Bub List UI, and the Mute feature, divided into Core and Important categories. These features are broken down into specific elements, and some of them have subitems associated with them. For example, under the feature "Bub List," all the components of the bub list are listed separately (the indication of who is active, the active or idle duration, current device, current location, and so on). The "Bubs are listed" item is broken down further into five tasks, three referring to the technical work required to display the bubs, and two specifying the ordering method. The bub list is not done when the bubs are listed; they must be listed in the proper order. If Alan had just been estimating the time needed to display the bub list, he might not have remembered to include the ordering in his estimate and he would have been off by half a day. Add up enough of those omissions by multiple engineers, and you'll be off by weeks or months.

8.10

A small section of the Hubbub Feature List showing the Bub List and Mute features. We generally rounded up to the nearest half day for each higher-level task. This list shows actual estimates, before we doubled them to account for "slop time" in the engineer's estimates and then added more time for ease-of-use refinements. (A plus sign indicates that there are subtasks hidden "inside" a feature; a minus sign indicates that a feature is "opened up" to show all its subtasks.)

Hubbub Feature List: Palm Client

Core Features

	Engineer	Time
- Bub List Infrastructure	Alan	10 days
- Create connection	Alan	1 day
- Send and receive messages	Alan	7 days
+ Support code for sending & receiving msgs	Alan	1 day
+ Package messages	Alan	3 days
+ Parse messages	Alan	3 days
+ Create bub list class to manage bubs in a db	Alan	2 days
- Bub List	Alan	3.5 days
- Bubs are listed	Alan	2 days
Create Bub List form	Alan	1 day
Create table that is Bub List	Alan	2 hours
Populate the Bub List from the bubs db	Alan	2 hours
Alphabetize list with self at top	Alan	2 hours
Online bubs listed above offline bubs	Alan	2 hours
Active bubs listed in bold, idle & offline in regular font	Alan	2 hours
Active/idle duration is displayed	Alan	4 hours
Each bub's current device is displayed	Alan	2 hours
Each bub's current location is displayed	Alan	10 mins
Activity meter is displayed when someone is online	Alan	2 hours
- Mute	Alan	2 hours
Mute All/Unmute All radio button	Alan	2 hours

Important Features		
- Bub List	Alan	2 days
Header flashes when someone goes active/idle	Alan	1 day
- Return to existing Message screens	Alan	1 day
Display text icon next to bubs with open conversations	Alan	2 hours
Tapping icon goes to Message screen with that bub	Alan	2 hours
Icon to take you to the last open Message screen	Alan	2 hours
- Mute	Alan	1 day
Mute each bub	Alan	1 day

Of course, these estimates didn't turn out to be accurate. That half a day error turned out to be more like a day. And of course, unanticipated tasks always crop up. For example, object code on the Palm needs to be organized so that the CPU never jumps more than 32K at a time, and code resources are also limited in size. We were aware of these limits early on, but we didn't know whether we'd hit them, so they didn't make it onto the task list. Of course we did hit them, and it took a few unplanned-for days to reorganize the code.

Project Management Guideline
Estimate the schedule based on detailed descriptions of each feature. Have each person estimate the time it will take to complete their components, and then double their estimates to account for inevitable inaccuracies.

Also, when engineers estimate a feature, they're imagining the time it would take if they were working without interruption. Suppose they think it would take about a day to do a feature. They're imagining getting into the office bright and early at 10 a.m. and sitting at their desks programming for eight hours straight. They're not thinking about the time they'll spend responding to e-mail, talking with colleagues who stop by with questions, going to dreaded status meetings, running into someone at the soda machine and getting into an interesting conversation, or dealing with any other interruptions during the day. They're also probably forgetting about the time needed to plan the feature or discuss it with other team members (which affects the schedules of those other team members who also didn't plan to talk about it). So really, if they think it will take a day of coding time, it will probably take two to three days of elapsed time. Even if someone is aware of all this, no one wants to put down on paper that it will take two days to do something that seems doable in one. For all these reasons, it will serve you well to double each engineer's estimate to allow for "slop time" (you can adjust up or down as you learn each engineer's track record for estimating their tasks). Then you need to add time to address ease-of-use problems, which we'll discuss next.

Plan Time to Polish Each Feature

The most important thing the project manager can do to ensure that you'll build a cooperative piece of technology is to build in a mechanism to add "ease-of-use features"—features that polish the functionality and remove breaks in flow. When you first list a feature, you won't know what tasks you'll need to do to smooth it out. Sometimes you get lucky and it works beautifully the first time. But most often, as soon as you start using or testing a feature, you'll find problems that need to be fixed or related features that need to be added or adjusted.

In his highly regarded book *Debugging the Development Process,* Steve Maguire discusses the importance of fixing bugs as you go rather than waiting until the end. He gives four reasons:

- It's harder to fix bugs in code you wrote a long time ago than it is to modify code you just wrote.

- If you're forced to fix your mistakes early, you'll learn from them and won't make them again.

- Those who write sloppy code will spend more of their time fixing bugs than working on cool new features, so fixing bugs as you go becomes a positive reinforcement mechanism.

- You'll be better able to predict when you'll finish because each feature is done before you move on to the next; you don't have to guess how long it will take to fix the bugs in all the unfinished features. You can also more easily ship on time by dropping unfinished features.

Project Management Guideline
The final schedule estimate should be triple the cumulative estimate for all the tasks. Double the estimate to account for estimate inaccuracies, and then add the same amount again for making ease-of-use adjustments.

This is excellent advice, and we believe it holds true for "ease-of-use bugs" as well as "functionality bugs." If a feature is technically working but people consistently have trouble using it, it has ease-of-use bugs and it is not done. If you don't move on to new features until you've fixed all the bugs in the current ones, and you consider ease-of-use bugs just as important as functionality bugs, you can be sure that you will build a usable, cooperative product. Again, your application won't have as many features as some others, but the features it has will be a pleasure to use. In all, we recommend tripling the total cumulative estimate if you want to create cooperative technology: Double the engineer's initial estimate and then add the same amount of time again to polish it.

You want to find the ease-of-use bugs as quickly as you can after building the feature. Most software teams test the functionality as it's being developed, and we advocate testing ease of use as the features are developed as well. You can do this with usability testing (in which you ask people to complete certain prespecified tasks using your technology) or with a usage study (in which you give people your technology to use in their own setting as part of their ongoing activities). Or you can do both. Just don't do neither. And don't do one so late in the development cycle that you can incorporate only the most trivial of changes. To incorporate testing into the project, you'll need someone to coordinate it on an ongoing basis, and you'll need to keep feeding the findings back into the Feature List to make sure they are addressed before you take on big new features. Since we are partial to usage studies, and since there is more information already available about usability testing methods[2], in Chapter 10 we focus on how to run a usage study.

On some projects, you might want to consider the tasks associated with implementing ease-of-use features as new subtasks associated with a feature. On other projects, you might want to consider them ease-of-use bugs that are entered into the bug database and prioritized along with all the others. Other projects may take a different approach. The important thing is to expect that your testing will reveal many ease-of-use problems. You should plan to spend time fixing them before considering a feature done.

To give you a sense of how your Feature List might change as you get feedback from a usage study, Figure 8.11 presents the same section of the Hubbub Feature List shown in Figure 8.10 as it appeared late in the project. The items in italics are the refinements we made to features after we discovered problems in use. For example, under Important features, we included items that addressed the problem of the status header stealing focus when you were typing. We added one task, and when that didn't resolve it, we added another, and finally a third until we could get the feature to work as intended. We also discovered that we needed to add a feature that would let people mute all activity sounds at once (rather than turning off each person's sounds individually). That became an entirely new feature within the Mute category.

---

[2] See recommended usability testing resources in Appendix B, "Recommended Readings." Also, Chapter 9 discusses how we did some quick-and-dirty usability testing during the Hubbub project.

8.11

The same section of the Hubbub Feature List after ease-of-use refinements have been added. The Time column indicates Alan's revised estimates for the features, although in reality they took longer to implement. (A plus sign indicates that there are subtasks hidden "inside" a feature; a minus sign indicates that a feature is "opened up" to show all its subtasks.)

Hubbub Feature List: Palm Client

Original feature
Additional feature added based on usage study feedback

Core Features

	Engineer	Time
- Bub List Infrastructure	Alan	10 days
- Create connection	Alan	1 day
- Send and receive messages	Alan	7 days
+ Support code for sending & receiving msgs	Alan	1 day
+ Package messages	Alan	3 days
+ Parse messages	Alan	3 days
+ Create bub list class to manage bubs in a db	Alan	2 days
- Bub List	Alan	4 days
- Bubs are listed	Alan	2.5 days
Create Bub List form	Alan	1 day
Create table that is bub list	Alan	2 hours
Populate the bub list from the bubs db	Alan	2 hours
List sorted with self at top, online bubs, then offline	Alan	2 hours
Truncate bub name if necessary	Alan	*2 hours*
Scroll bub list	Alan	*2 hours*
Active bubs listed in bold, idle & offline in regular font	Alan	2 hours
- Active/idle duration is displayed	Alan	4 hours
Idle time has minus sign in front of it	Alan	*10 mins*
- Each bub's current device is displayed	Alan	2 hours
Change PC icon to be as narrow as Palm icon	Alan	*10 mins*
- Each bub's current location is displayed	Alan	3 hours
Long location on Main & Bub screens	Alan	*2 hours*
- Activity meter is displayed when someone is online	Alan	2 hours
Widen activity meter to make it more visible	Alan	*10 mins*
- Mute	Alan	2 hours
Mute All/Unmute All radio button	Alan	2 hours

Important Features

	Engineer	Time
- Bub List	Alan	2 days
- Header flashes when someone goes active/idle	Alan	1.5 days
Initial attempt	Alan	1 day
Tapping header stops flashing	*Alan*	*2 hours*
Tapping text field stops flashing	*Alan*	*2 hours*
No flashing when on text entry screens	*Alan*	*10 mins*
- Display text icon next to bubs with open conversations	Alan	2 hours
Tapping icon takes you to conversation w/ that bub	Alan	2 hours
- Mute	Alan	7.5 days
- Mute each bub	Alan	7 days
Fake speaker button	Alan	1 day
Saved per client	Alan	1 day
- Saved across clients	Alan	5 days
Add new protocol message	Alan	2 days
Add Server resending	Alan	2 days
Add to login state bundle	Alan	1 day
Mute all activity sounds at once	*Alan*	*4 hours*

As we discovered the need for each new feature, we added it to the list and Alan estimated how long it would take to implement. Even though he had more information about the code at this stage, he still under-estimated. For example, he thought it would take two hours to modify the Main and Bub screens to display the longer locations, but it turned out that it took about a day because he had to truncate locations that wouldn't fit on the Main screen. We decided to put "…" on the end of truncated locations to indicate that there was more to them (shown on the Bub screen), and since we were using a variable-width font, Alan had to calculate where to start truncating. It wasn't a huge effort, but it took time. This is typical of the additional work you don't anticipate when considering what's involved in implementing or modifying a feature. Even the tasks he estimated at 10 minutes took longer because he was thinking only about the simple modification (replacing the activity meter icon with a wider one, replacing the PC device icon with a narrower one, putting a minus sign in front of the idle times) and forgot that he'd have to adjust the layout of the other elements on the screen to space out the columns properly. All this extra time adds up.

Project Management Guideline

Treat ease-of-use improvements as features in the Feature List or as ease-of-use bugs in the bug database. Either way, you should plan time to fix them before moving on to new features, just as you should fix functionality bugs before moving on. Doing so ensures that whatever you ship will behave cooperatively, even if it has fewer features than its competitors.

In practice, sometimes we added an ease-of-use refinement to the Feature List and sometimes we added it to the bug database. It depended on whether we perceived it as a new feature or feature component, or as a problem with an existing feature. For example, the first time someone chose a Hubbub name that started with a lowercase letter, we found that all lowercase names were listed after all capitalized names. We entered a bug specifying that alphabetization should not be case sensitive, although we could just as easily have made it a subitem of the Bub List feature.

However you track these ease-of-use refinements, plan your schedule to include them right from the start so that there are no surprises. It will seem painful at first to estimate so much time for what seems like so few features. But it's much better to insist on realistic times and then finish on schedule with a high quality product than it is to please management with a low initial estimate but then slip repeatedly while you cram lots of features into a shoddy product. Once you start getting usage feedback, list the changes to be made explicitly, just as you would other types of bugs, and fix them before moving on to other features. And finally, make sure that you reward people for fixing ease-of-use problems rather than criticizing them for not adding more features.

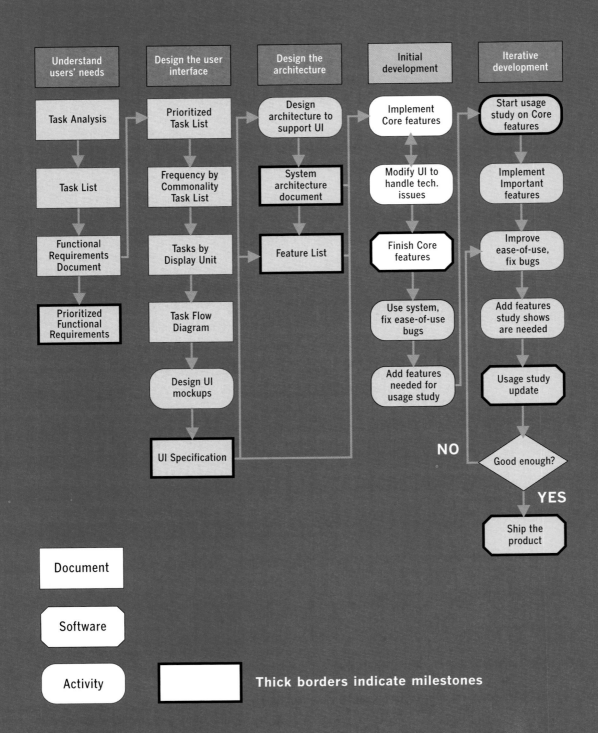

Understand users' needs
- Task Analysis
- Task List
- Functional Requirements Document
- Prioritized Functional Requirements

Design the user interface
- Prioritized Task List
- Frequency by Commonality Task List
- Tasks by Display Unit
- Task Flow Diagram
- Design UI mockups
- UI Specification

Design the architecture
- Design architecture to support UI
- System architecture document
- Feature List

Initial development
- Implement Core features
- Modify UI to handle tech. issues
- Finish Core features
- Use system, fix ease-of-use bugs
- Add features needed for usage study

Iterative development
- Start usage study on Core features
- Implement Important features
- Improve ease-of-use, fix bugs
- Add features study shows are needed
- Usage study update

NO

Good enough?

YES

Ship the product

Document

Software

Activity

Thick borders indicate milestones

CHAPTER 9
Initial Development

Finally, implementation begins! You've designed a UI Spec based on the Functional Requirements, you've designed the underlying architecture based on both of those, and you've worked out some of the engineering details needed to support the UI requirements. You've got a Feature List divided into priority categories, and you're ready to start the Initial Development phase.

We make a distinction between the *Initial Development* phase and the *Iterative Development* phase. In the Initial Development phase, you build the features as they were designed. You start with the Core features (the ones you absolutely need to start using the technology in a meaningful way) but without the supporting features that make the application more interesting to use. Once you have the Core set, you start to use the system yourself and build whatever Important features you need, if any, to let other people start testing it. Once you start to get usage feedback, you begin the Iterative Development phase on those initial features, while you also do Initial Development on other Important features. So every feature has an Initial phase, when it is first built, and most go through an Iteration phase, during which they are revised and polished to make them smooth and cooperative. The first half of implementation consists mainly of Initial Development, and gradually you shift more toward Iterative Development of existing features until all the features are implemented and polished. This chapter focuses on Initial Development, and as you'll see, some of the examples took place after we had collected information from the usage study on related features we had already implemented.

This phase is an exciting time when your technology starts to come to life, but it also involves a lot of heads-down development to get the basic system working as designed. It seems pretty straightforward, except that as features start working, you find that certain aspects of your design won't work the way you'd hoped, so you have to adjust. This phase is when collaboration between the designer and engineer becomes especially close, as you work together to resolve problems so that both parties' concerns are addressed as well as possible. It usually takes some work to understand the crux of each other's concerns, but once you do, you can usually find an alternative approach that is acceptable to both. If an engineer designed your technology's user interface, that engineer needs to play the role of the designer when issues arise. Of course, that can be difficult if the issues involve that engineer's features, which is why it helps to have someone dedicated to the designer role. If you can't manage that, perhaps another engineer on the project can play the role of user advocate on technical issues that arise in the engineer-designer's features.

In the following sections, we discuss examples from Hubbub, focusing on unanticipated issues that affected the user interface and how we handled them. We describe some cases where we resolved the issues on engineering grounds, working around them in the UI, and some cases where we did the reverse. Sometimes UI issues arose that Ellen hadn't anticipated in the UI Spec. Other times Alan didn't foresee the implications of his decisions for the UI, but later we discovered unanticipated effects (not always negative, as it turned out). We discuss these types of examples and others, focusing on how we tried to resolve the issues by balancing the cost of engineering with the value of the usability improvement. These examples illustrate some lessons we've learned about managing this delicate balance, and about the process of collaborating to make these decisions.

Issues Resolved on Engineering Grounds

Initially, Alan and Dipti were able to get the Core features working as planned. After all, we'd spent a lot of time planning the UI design and architecture to make sure that these features could be implemented. But then a few issues started to arise—issues that affected either subtle aspects of Core features or more obvious components of Important features (which got less attention during our planning phase). In the majority of cases, we were able to modify the UI to accommodate the engineering issue while still behaving like a butler.

Example: Edge Cases Versus Common Cases

A simple example arose because of the Palm's memory limitations. The UI Spec indicates that users can scroll back through any conversation to its beginning. They can also hold multiple conversations at once, putting as many as they want "on hold" while they view other screens. This concerned Alan. Here's how our discussion went:

Alan: I'm a little worried that if we keep around all the messages from all the conversations, we might run out of memory. Do we have to let people scroll back all the way to the beginning of their conversations?

Ellen: Well, on the small Palm screen we can't fit as many messages, so I think people will be scrolling back more than they would on the PC. Plus, they might miss some messages that arrived in another conversation. They need to be able to scroll back to see what they missed.

Alan: I'm not objecting to people scrolling back, I'm objecting to people being able to scroll back indefinitely.

Ellen: Well, how far back can you let people scroll without worrying about running out of memory?

Alan: How about something like 100 messages per conversation, about 15 or 20 screens?

Ellen: Oh, 100 messages would be okay. I was expecting you to say something like 10 or 15. I think it would be pretty rare for anyone to need to go back that far on a Palm.

Alan: Okay, good. As long as we're limiting their maximum size, I'm happy.

Ellen: If they try to go back further, the messages just aren't there, right? There's no annoying error message popping up, complaining that we've run out of room. [Solve Problems; Don't Complain or Pass the Buck]

Alan: Right.

Ellen: Great. What would happen if they had 100 messages in a conversation and they scrolled all the way to the beginning and stayed there as new messages came in?

Alan: The text would scroll up, pushing the oldest message off the top.

Ellen: Okay, that's good.

Collaboration Guideline
When rare but possible cases arise, remember that you don't have to design for those scenarios, you just need to handle them gracefully.

This conversation was representative of many we've had. Alan is concerned about the edge cases—someone having dozens of conversation screens open, each with thousands of messages in them, and never closing any of them. He's worried about having no limit at all. Ellen is thinking about the common case—figuring that Palm users may have as many as five or six simultaneous conversations at the outside, with few of them going longer than, say, 50 messages. Neither

Collaboration Guideline
When conflicts emerge between design and engineering goals, get concrete and specific about your concerns. Try to clarify the crux of the engineering concern and the key elements of the user experience. Don't assume you're imagining the same constraints on the feature. And don't assume the feature has to be implemented literally as first designed. Instead, work together to find an alternative design that is acceptable from both perspectives.

Collaboration Guideline
Designers should take time to learn the basics of the technical issues affecting their system so that they can understand the engineering constraints and communicate user needs more effectively. Engineers should assume that the designer knows more about user behavior than they do, even though they are users too.

of us says so explicitly. Instead, Alan just asks about scrolling back to the beginning of conversations, which Ellen thinks is important in her scenario. By getting specific about numbers, we realize that we're worrying about different orders of magnitude. Setting a high limit by Ellen's standards makes both of us happy because Alan gets his limit and Ellen handles the vast majority of cases. Remember, you might be able to construct a scenario of the rare case happening, but you don't have to design for that case, you just need to handle it. In other words, those cases shouldn't cause the system to break, but don't sacrifice the user experience in the common case to handle those rare cases.

We've seen many cases when a designer shows or describes a design to an engineer, who assumes it has to be implemented literally as described, and then declares that it can't be done. While it may be impossible to implement as described, you can usually find a design that would provide the important attributes of the feature. If the engineer can explain which aspects of the design they object to, and if the designer can explain which parts are critical for the experience they're trying to create, they can usually find a variation that works reasonably well for both. This is why it helps for designers to develop a general understanding of the relevant technical issues. If they don't, they will have trouble communicating their needs in terms the engineers can work with. On the other hand, engineers should respect the designer's judgment on issues relating to user behavior. Since everyone is technically a "user," many people are tempted to assume that they know how users behave, but it is the designer's job to know, so their judgment should prevail unless solid evidence indicates otherwise.

Example: Implementation Effort Versus Usability Value

It is very common to have to decide whether the effort required to implement a feature is justified by its value to the user experience. A problem like this emerged early on when Dipti was learning how to implement applications using the Microsoft Foundation Classes. The design of the PC Main screen called for a separate "Self pane" at the bottom where the user's own entry would appear, as shown in Figure 9.1.

9.1

The initial design of the Windows Hubbub client included a separate Self pane for the user's own entry so that it would stand out and would not scroll off the screen. However, this proved to be a bear to implement and we agreed that the value of the feature wasn't worth the effort, especially since the Palm didn't have a Self entry area.

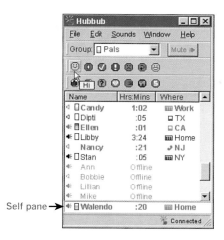

Self pane →

The goal of the design was to let users see how they appeared to others at all times. The reason for this is that people are less likely to feel that their privacy is violated if they can see and therefore control the information others can act upon. The important thing was to make sure users could see their own entry, and the split pane had the nice attribute of making sure it never scrolled out of view. After a little while, Dipti showed Ellen an interim version of the client with the Self pane partially implemented.

Ellen: I noticed that the Self pane has a few problems. Do you know why it's gray instead of white? Also, I noticed that you can resize the pane, but it should stay a fixed size.

Dipti: Well, I tried to make it so that you can't edit the name, but that made the pane gray. It could be just my ignorance, but I'm also having trouble figuring out how to make one half of a split pane a fixed size, and prevent it from growing when you resize the window.

Ellen: How long have you been struggling with this?

Dipti: Um, a few days? [Meekly] Okay, a week.

Ellen: Oh, geez. This isn't worth that much time! You know, we've already decided to put the Self entry at the top of the list on the Palm (since it doesn't support the concept of panes at all), so we could just do that on the PC. Would that make all the problems go away?

Dipti: Yes! Yes!

Ellen: Okay, let's do that. It'll mean that your own name can scroll off the top, but the most important thing is that the information is available, and usually people keep the list scrolled to the top anyway. Keeping the name in view sure isn't worth all the effort this turned out to be.

Dipti: That's great. Now I can go battle Windows over some other feature!

Here was a case where the effort was not worth the value of the design. Probably this design could have been implemented more quickly if Dipti had been further along her learning curve, but the engineer's level of experience is just another variable. We didn't know up front that this design would prove to be problematic, but once we found that it was, we modified the UI to avoid the engineering issue.

Collaboration Guideline
If the effort required to implement a feature outweighs the value it provides the user, redesign it so that it's easier to implement or don't offer it.

Effort versus value is a common tradeoff. It's often difficult to anticipate the problems you'll encounter, so it helps for the designer and engineer to stay in close touch so you can jointly decide to adjust the UI if the initial approach turns out to involve more effort than it's worth. Some engineers will take it as a challenge to make the software bend to their will, but it's more important to spend your energy on the work that is most likely to help users.

Example: Implementation Time Versus Usability Value

Related to implementation effort is implementation time. Often, implementation time comes into play when the engineer starts to plan the details of a feature's implementation, especially when you're deciding among alternative approaches. You want the value of a feature to be worth the time it takes to implement, because time spent on one feature is time not spent on another.

This example came up after we'd finished the Core features and were starting on the Important features. The UI Spec indicated that a user could turn off the sounds of individual bubs, and that those settings would be remembered across all of that user's clients.

Alan: How important is it that setting the mute state on one client sets the mute state on all of that user's clients?

Ellen: It's somewhat important. Someone might install Hubbub on their work machine and spend time deciding which bubs to turn on and off. Then when they install a client at home, they'd be pretty frustrated if they had to do it all over again. **[Remember What They Told You]** Why do you ask?

Alan: Well, it's pretty easy to save mute states per client, but it'll take a lot more time to save them across all clients.

Ellen: Any sense of how long it'll take for each?

Alan: To do it locally will take just a couple of hours, and we just have to modify both the PC and Palm clients. If we have to do it across all clients, it'll take at least a few days if not a week. It involves adding a new message to the protocol, adding message re-sending to the server so it can be sure the state change is reliably delivered to all clients, and updating both clients to deal with the changes.

Ellen: Hmm. That's a lot of extra time. I'm not even sure how many people will run Hubbub in multiple places.

Alan: Are you sure we need to do this? I could even imagine that someone might want different settings for different clients, say on their Palm versus their PC.

Ellen: That's possible. I suppose we could do the per-client version now, and then we'll see if we need to save it across clients once we give it to people.

Alan: Good plan. *(Excellent! I'll have to remember that "change to the protocol" excuse...)*

Ellen: [in project manager role] What's the cost of doing the per-client version now and then changing it later versus just doing the cross-client version now?

Alan: Not much. We're going to want the clients to save the state locally for startup anyway, so we wouldn't be doing throwaway work.

Ellen: Okay, good. But don't think I'm going to forget to check whether we need to save across clients...

As it turned out, during the usage study we found that it wasn't necessary to save per-bub mute status across clients. Although some people were surprised at first that their settings weren't preserved on

Collaboration Guideline
Time spent on one feature is time not spent on another. Spend your time on the features that you're confident will add the most value for users.

Collaboration Guideline
If you're not sure of the value of a feature, build a simple version of it and find out from usage testing whether a more complex version is needed.

Collaboration Guideline
People like to work on things they believe will be used. Once you have real usage data indicating that a feature is needed, it's much easier to reach agreement that the effort is justified.

another client, as Alan guessed, they soon found it handy to set them differently on different machines. For example, one usage study participant on the East Coast worked with colleagues on the West Coast, three hours behind her. On her work machine, she turned on the sounds of most of her colleagues. At home, she turned off the sounds of many of her East Coast colleagues, figuring she didn't need to stay in touch with them after work. But she did listen to the sounds of her West Coast colleagues because it helped her stay in touch with them while they were still at work. This is just the type of scenario that's hard to predict in advance.

In this case, we saved time by implementing the simple version of a feature, figuring we would build the more complex version if it became clear that it was worth the effort. We were fortunate that the code to do the simple version would still be needed for the complex version. It would have been a harder decision if the complex version would entirely replace the simple one, but it still might have been worth it.

This is also a wonderful example of the value of studying the system in use before releasing a product. Knowing we'd be getting real user data during the usage study made it easier for the team to reach agreement, and in the end, it saved us the implementation effort of doing the complex version of this feature. There were other cases when it turned out that we did have to handle the more complex case, but at least we knew that the time and effort were well spent. Still, it's surprising how often the simple version of a feature is sufficient.

Example: Expediency Versus Ideal User Experience

In all the cases where we made changes to the UI based on engineering concerns, the changes were relatively minor. There was only one case where we agreed to make a major change to the UI for technical reasons. This involved moving the account administration and permissions components to the Web rather than implementing them on each client.

Alan: Why don't we just do the administration stuff on the Web? Otherwise, we'll have to do it separately on both clients. Everybody uses the Web for this stuff now. **[Follow Conventions]**

Ellen: Well, if we do it on the Web, Palm users can't do things like add or remove bubs or set permissions while they're away from their PCs. Also, I think it's rude for an application to change the page of your browser when you choose a menu item. What if you were looking at something important? **[Don't Impose]**

Alan: You can hit the Back button.

Ellen: If you realize that's what just happened. And besides, you might be on a page that was generated, and sometimes you can't go back and restore your context. Remember that time you were filling out a form, you had gotten all that data together, and then when you had to refresh the page it didn't restore the data? How would you have liked it if that page had been changed under you by another application? *(Got him there!)*

Alan: How about if we pop up a new browser?

Ellen: No, that doesn't work either. Many people display their browsers in full-screen mode, so a new browser just looks like another page, and even worse, the Back button is disabled since this is the first page in that window. So then they're even more confused. **[Be Predictable | Don't Mislead]**

Alan: How the heck are they using Hubbub if they're using their browser in full-screen mode? *(Ha!)*

Ellen: You've heard of multitasking, right? [in project manager role] Never mind, we won't be getting to this feature for some time. We don't have to resolve it right now. Let's keep going and see where we are when it's time to implement the administration features.

Alan: I can live with that.

Collaboration Guideline
Sometimes it's worth providing an acceptable if not ideal user experience to keep the project moving and to meet deadlines.

Time passed. We began the usage study, and a few months into it we needed to let the participants manage their accounts (add and remove bubs, change their passwords, and so on) rather than handling their requests manually. Still, we had more work to do to refine existing features, and an experienced Web engineer contacted us looking for contract work. We decided to implement the administration features on the Web for reasons of expediency. This meant Ellen had to design the Web site to handle those features, and then work with the contractor as he implemented them. Ellen is still not delighted that we used a browser to handle adding and removing bubs, setting permissions, changing account information, and so on, but it did allow us to release Hubbub sooner. It also allowed us to iterate and add new administration features without having to make people upgrade to a new client.

Issues Resolved on UI Grounds

In the previous examples, the engineers ran into a problem that made it difficult to implement the UI as specified, and we adjusted the UI to accommodate the concern. In other cases, an engineering issue arose but we decided to stick with the UI design and work around the engineering problem. Usually, the objection was not so much with the difficulty of implementation but with the amount of effort, usually tedious effort. Again, the engineers wanted justification that the effort was worth the usability gain.

Example: Tedious Work Versus Polish

Very early in development, Alan got text messages working on the Palm. You could send someone a message and it would appear in a Message screen. It was exciting to see it working, but there was a problem with the scrolling behavior (see Figure 9.2).

9.2

The Palm Message screen with messages starting out at the bottom rather than the top.

Ellen: Did you notice that the messages are starting out at the bottom of the screen and moving up?

Alan: That's what messages do, right? They start at the bottom and scroll off the top.

Ellen: No, not really. The first messages appear at the top, and the new ones appear below them.

Alan: Oh, right. And once the screen fills up, *then* they appear at the bottom and roll up.

Ellen: Huh, that's interesting. I never realized that there are two stages to this.

Alan: Can I do it later? I'd rather get on to something new than fuss with this appearance issue. I mean, it works, doesn't it?

Ellen: [in project manager role] Well, I'd really rather that we get this working properly before moving on to something new. We can keep pushing it off, but it's not as if you're ever going to want to do it.

Alan: Grrr. Okay, but you're directly responsible for decreasing my employee satisfaction quotient.

Ellen: I can live with that.

Example: More Tedious Work Versus Completeness

Much later in the process, the tedium of implementing scrolling reared its head again. Toward the end of development, we implemented a feature on the Palm that allows you to send an e-mail to a bub who is offline, since you can't send them an instant message if they're not online. The UI design is shown in Figure 9.3.

9.3

The Bub screen for a bub who is offline. Users can send their bubs an e-mail rather than an instant message.

Ellen: I was playing with the offline e-mail feature and I realized that once you've written a sixth line, you don't get a scrollbar, so there's no way to scroll back up to the first line. Doesn't the toolkit automatically display a scrollbar when a text area extends beyond the space provided?

Alan: Nope.

Ellen: Really? They sure don't make life easy for you guys. Well, we're going to need scrolling.

Alan: Who in their right mind would write a long e-mail on the Palm? It's not that easy to enter text.

Ellen: The thing is, we can't just not give them a way to scroll back. That's just broken. **[Be Predictable]**

Alan: Why not just limit them to five lines?

Ellen: We could…. How much effort is it to add a scrollbar?

Alan: It's not that bad…. Okay, okay, I'll go do it.

Collaboration Guideline
Sometimes you just have to do boring work to make features operate smoothly. Get it over with before moving on to the next feature rather than putting it off until the end.

In both of these cases, Alan resisted because it meant doing tedious implementation work rather than more interesting features. Often, development toolkits handle things such as scrolling, but when they don't, the application engineer gets stuck with the duties. In these cases, we agreed that making the features behave cooperatively was worth the effort. (We wouldn't expect a butler to tell us that we can't edit the early part of our messages.) We also agreed to stick to our guns and not put off the work off until later.

In preparing to write this chapter, we made a long list of the issues that arose because of engineering concerns, and we were surprised to find that nearly every time, we resolved the issue by modifying the UI. It was hard to find cases where we stuck with the UI as it was, and those usually came about because the platform didn't include support for UI behavior that was just plain boring to implement. Nonetheless, Ellen is hardly known for being a pushover and she certainly felt as though Hubbub was being built as she had designed it. We realized this happened because the UI had been specified up front and the architecture had been built to support it, so the critical aspects of the user experience were built into the system. When issues arose, they involved features that were less critical to the system's usability and so there was room to compromise.

Unanticipated UI Issues and Adjustments

Collaboration Guideline
When a UI issue arises that isn't covered in the UI Spec, work together to come up with a solution. Engineers shouldn't just do whatever's easiest, and designers should be receptive to engineers' suggestions.

During development, engineers inevitably discover situations that are not handled in the UI Spec. Engineers tend to think about all possible cases, and designers often don't anticipate them all. Each time such an issue arose, Alan or Dipti brought it to Ellen's attention and the three of us worked together to figure out how to handle it.

Example: Designing a Case Not Covered in the UI Spec

A good example of an unanticipated UI problem was the case of sending long text messages on the Palm. Figure 9.4A shows the UI for entering a text message. You can see that it has room for only a few words of text, so we needed a way to allow people to write longer messages. Figure 9.4B shows the solution we came up with.

Alan: Hey, El? What happens when a user is typing a message and hits the end of the entry line?

Ellen: Hmm, good question. I guess I should have thought about that. Could we have the line scroll horizontally?

Alan: What do you mean? How would that look?

Ellen: As you type past the end of the line, your text scrolls to the left, and a little arrow appears at the left end of the text. If you tap the arrow the text moves left, and an arrow appears on the right side as well. As long as there's hidden text on either end, the appropriate arrow appears.

Alan: Hmm, that'd be kind of painful to implement.

Ellen: I don't even like that solution that much since you could only see a portion of your message at a time. What else could we do?

Alan: How about if we pop up a multiline text entry form when they hit the end of the line? **[Look for "Widgetless Features"]**

Ellen: Oh, that's cool! But you'd need to make sure the text they've already entered is there in the form, and they can just keep writing. **[Remember What They Told You]**

Alan: Right, I think I can do that.

Ellen: Hey! You just invented a widgetless feature!

A   B

9.4

The initial design (A) did not handle text messages that exceeded the space provided. We came up with a design (B) that pops up a multiline text pane when you get to the end of the text entry area.

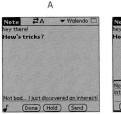

Example: Handling Small Issues as They Arise

When engineers encounter small issues not addressed in the UI Spec, the temptation is to handle them as they think best rather than stopping their work to ask the designer how the system should behave. Most often they'll wind up having to go back and change the code later, so it's best to either ask for help right then, or keep track of these small questions and ask them all at once at a more convenient time.

Here's one amusing case when this happened with Hubbub. Dipti was handling the case of someone writing a text message that is bigger than can be transmitted in one packet (message unit). She knew to program Hubbub not to pop up a message complaining, but instead to put a message in the Message window footer, and to beep and stop echoing characters if they tried to add more. **[Treat Clicks as Sacred | Prevent Errors]** She tried to think of a message that would make sense to users, and came up with, "Maximum number of characters reached." After Dipti checked in the code, Ellen saw the message and wondered, "What's this!?" She checked with Dipti.

Ellen: Where did this "Maximum number of characters reached" message come from?

Dipti: I wrote it! I worked really hard to avoid using geeky language. What do you think?

Ellen: Well, it's not bad, but it's kind of written from the program's perspective. This happens when the user's message is too long, right?

Dipti: Right.

Ellen: Maybe we could just say, "Message is too long." **[Explain in Plain Language]**

Dipti: Doh! And I thought I had done so well.

Ellen: Well, you were close. What was your first attempt?

Dipti: "Maximum buffer size exceeded."

Ellen: [laughing] Well, you're right, the version you came up with is much better!

Dipti: [sighing] Okay, I'll change it.

Example: Assessing the Impact of a New Design

In some cases, the designer may want to change a design before its implementation has begun. They may realize a problem with their design or they may realize that they haven't covered something. When this happens, it's important to check in with the engineer who will implement it to make sure that the change can be accommodated and to determine its effect on the system and the schedule. If the change is big, other team members should be brought in to make a priority call based on the value of the change versus its costs. In the following example, Ellen wanted to make sure her design could accommodate one of the Nice to Have features. The design she had in mind was directly affected by the architectural decision to update activity information every 15 seconds to minimize bandwidth, so we worked together to find a way to support the feature within those constraints.

Ellen: I realized that we don't have a way to tell whether someone has Hubbub muted before you send them a message. How hard would it be to display that on the Bub screen, after you tap on their name to send them a message? **[Offer Sufficient Information Early and in Context]**

Alan: Well, let's see, we could do it in one of two ways. We could either have each client regularly update the server with its mute status, or we could ask that bub's client when we need to display the information.

Ellen: What are the tradeoffs?

Alan: If we sent periodic updates, we could display the bub's mute state immediately, but the data would be 15 seconds old, so if someone just muted you, you wouldn't know it for 15 seconds.

Ellen: (I'm not going to worry about that case, since it would be very rare for someone to mute you just *before you selected their name.)*

Alan: And we'd be using a lot of bandwidth for information that wouldn't be displayed very often. Or we could ask the client when we need the information, but then we couldn't display it immediately because it would take some time to get the answer back.

Ellen: Okay, so we can either have accurate information slowly with little bandwidth impact, or quick information that costs more bandwidth. How long would it take to ask for the mute state?

Alan: It depends. It could be a few hundred milliseconds, it could be five seconds.

Ellen: (Can't he ever think about what will really happen?) Okay, what would be the *typical* response time?

Alan: Probably under a second.

Ellen: Oh, good, that's within tolerance. It's fine if you're entering text, since that takes time anyway, but sometimes it'll be a little slow if you're sending someone a sound message. Still, that's not too bad.

Alan: *(Swell. Now she's going to come whining to me every time it takes five seconds!)*

Ellen: [in project manager role] Which takes more effort to implement?

Alan: The periodic update is probably twice as much work.

Ellen: Okay, then when we get to this, I think we should go with the ask-when-needed approach.

Alan: Sounds good. Where does that fall on the priority list?

Ellen: Not high. It's Nice to Have, so we'll see whether it becomes a problem during testing.

Alan: Okay, sounds good.

While we think this would be a nice feature, it's still sitting on our Nice to Have list. Other features have always been more important.

Example: Revising a Design After Implementation

Collaboration Guideline
If you want to change a design after implementation has begun, you should be reasonably sure that the usability improvement is worth the additional estimated effort. If not, wait until you have evidence from usage data that the change is necessary. (If you decide it's worth it, it helps to bribe engineers with food and drinks.)

Sometimes, designers realize a problem with their design after the engineers have begun implementing it. If the problem could have been anticipated and the change is significant, they should proceed with caution when asking for a change. It can drive engineers crazy to keep changing the design in midstream, and it costs the team time. Before making a change that takes more than a minor amount of work, the team needs to be reasonably sure that the improvement from the design change will be worth the additional effort. If not, you should probably wait until you have stronger evidence from real usage data that the change is needed. Here's an example where Ellen asked for a change to the number of characters people could use to indicate their location. The initial design specified that Palm users would see two characters and PC users would see six, and Ellen realized that this would cause problems when prompting the user for their location. She suggested a change that turned out to be relatively easy to incorporate.

Ellen: You want a soda?

Alan: [suspiciously] What do you want?

Ellen: Since you asked…I

Alan: No!

Ellen: Just hear me out for a second. You might not mind this.

Alan: Okaaaaay…

Ellen: You know how we have six characters for the location field on the PC and two on the Palm? I realized that this means people are going to have to enter two locations each time, which is too much effort to ask. **[Respect Physical Effort]** It especially won't make sense to people who've never even seen Hubbub on the Palm. **[Respect Mental Effort]**

Alan: True.

Ellen: So I went back to the Palm and realized we probably could fit four characters in the location field if we shorten the name field a little. So I was thinking we could have just one four-character location for both clients.

Alan: Okay, that's not really a problem. That'll even save bandwidth since we won't have to pass around two locations.

Ellen: How bad is this? How many beers do I owe you?

Alan: Unfortunately, this one's easy. It is a change to the protocol, but a minor one.

Ellen: Cool. Thanks.

Alan: Sure. *(Maybe I should just leave it and wait for her to change her mind again...)*

Hidden UI Implications

Many times, engineers make decisions that don't appear to have implications for the user experience, but then later turn out to affect the user. Given all the tiny decisions engineers make every day, this is bound to happen. But to guard against it, keep in mind that the user experience encompasses more than just the widgets on the screen and how they behave. It also includes things such as performance, error handling, and machine resource usage. If the system runs slowly, the user's flow is easily broken. If users encounter many error messages, even nicely worded ones, their experience is degraded. If the application hogs system resources and isn't polite about releasing them, the user will have a hard time using other applications. So try to think broadly about how engineering decisions affect users. Of course, this also means that designers should be as concerned as engineers about designs that slow down the system or require complex code to support, since more complexity leads to more error conditions.

The following sections give two examples of situations when Alan made decisions that affected the UI without realizing it. One caused an ease-of-use bug, the other helped improve the user experience.

Example: Thinking Through Multiple Scenarios When Fixing a Bug

While testing the multiple client feature, Alan noticed a bug. Say you were running Hubbub on a Palm and a PC. You were last active on your PC, but became idle on both machines. If you picked up the Palm and immediately sent a text message to someone, the Palm would never display the message you just sent on your screen. This is because the server does not keep track of which client is waiting for an ACK. It simply decides where messages should be sent as they come in. The server assumed that a message requiring an ACK would be generated by an active client, so it sent all ACKs back to the Last Active Client. In this case, though, since clients update their activity only every 15 seconds, the server might still consider your Palm idle when you sent the text message and the returning ACK would be sent to your PC because it was your Last Active Client (see Figure 9.5). The PC would ignore it, and the Palm would not display the message you sent because it would be waiting for the ACK. Alan decided he could easily fix the problem by sending the ACK to all clients if they're all idle. Problem solved—or so he thought.

9.5

This figure shows what happens when Alan picks up his Palm and immediately sends a message to Ellen (step 1)—before the Palm client informs the server that it is active at its next 15-second update (step 3). Ellen's ACK (step 2) will go back to Alan's desktop client because it is still the Last Active Client, and his Palm client will never display the message. It also appears to Ellen that she is getting a message from Alan while he is idle on his desktop client, which seems strange to her.

Ellen's Client

Walendo's Clients

Idle 12 min
Location: "TM"
(Walendo picks it up and sends Ellen a mesage before activity update is sent)

Idle 4 min
Location: "Wk"

Idle 5 hrs 2 min
Location: "Hm"

Text and sound messages
Message acknowledgement (ACK)
Activity messages
Last Active Client

Collaboration Guideline
Designers and engineers should check in with each other frequently. Doing so will allow you to work around implementation issues as they arise while avoiding ease-of-use problems.

Later, when we were using Hubbub ourselves, Ellen noticed that you could receive a message from someone who appeared to be idle. This happened when they sent you a message immediately after starting to use their computer. They would become active shortly after you got the message, but the message would arrive before that happened. This is not a functionality bug because the message does get through, but it is an ease-of-use bug because it's strange to receive a message from someone who appears to be idle. **[Be Predictable | Don't Mislead]** She talked to Alan about it, and he realized that this was related to the earlier bug. A better solution would have been for the server to consider an idle client active if it sends a message, rather than waiting for the 15-second update. This way, the person would go active as soon as they sent the message, not a few seconds later, and the ACK would go back to the now-active client. Had Alan discussed the first bug with Ellen, it's likely that she would have brought up the problem of getting a message from someone who appears to be idle, and we would have figured out the better fix the first time.

This is not to say that engineers need to discuss every single bug with the designer, but if you are working together closely you'll likely have many quick conversations about situations like this, and you're more likely to uncover UI consequences that the engineer alone might not think about.

Example: Anticipating and Gracefully Handling Any Eventuality

Here's a case where Alan's approach to handling a technical concern greatly improved the user experience. Alan was concerned about the edge case of a wireless client going out of coverage long enough that the server would consider it offline, and then coming back into coverage. Once the client came back online, it would start sending messages to the server, which wouldn't recognize them because it would have removed that client from its tables. To handle this case, Alan added a mechanism enabling the server to request that an unrecognized client log in again. When a client receives this request, it re-sends the user's account information, and the server can re-authenticate it. He figured that forcing a re-login was the simplest way to handle broken and reestablished connections. And it also handled the problem invisibly to the user. **[Solve Problems; Don't Complain or Pass the Buck]**

What he didn't anticipate was how often this "edge case" would occur. Once people started using Hubbub, we discovered that there were many cases when people lost and regained connections even when they were on PC clients. For example, many of our users worked from home and connected to their corporate network through a Virtual Private Network (VPN). When they connected this way, the IP address of their PC changed, which made their client look like an entirely new client to the Hubbub server. Since the server sent a re-login request, the client logged in again and the user reconnected transparently— they never saw a discontinuation of service. Other times the network or firewall went down for a minute or two, and everyone lost their connection to the server. But once the network recovered, all the clients automatically logged back in without disrupting users with error messages or requests that they log in again. Alan's attempt to smoothly handle an error condition saved users from being bothered repeatedly with the message, "Something's wrong with your connection, but I have no idea what. Should I try to connect again?" (As uncooperative as that is, we showed in Chapter 4 how AOL's instant messenger pops up a message that essentially says just that.)

We were also able to use the re-login request much later when we focused on scaling. We realized that when a client asks to log in, the server could respond with, "I'm too busy, try the server at this other address." So if the server notes that it's getting bogged down, it can ask clients to log in again, and when they do, it can redirect them to an alternate machine. **[Solve Problems; Don't Complain or Pass the Buck]** Again, this mechanism improves the user experience because service can continue uninterrupted even when the load is high without users being made aware of the problem.

The point here is that Alan's concern for gracefully handling a technical issue made Hubbub much more pleasant to use because he found a way to fix the problem without bothering the user. It turned out that this edge case occurred much more frequently than we'd anticipated, which meant that his defensive programming practices paid off generously.

Unanticipated Requirements

In every project we've worked on, requirements have changed in midstream. Often management or the marketing department decides that they want a feature they hadn't anticipated. Maybe it has become a popular feature in a competitor's product, maybe an important account has asked for it, maybe they simply didn't think of it earlier. Let's assume you can provide the feature with minimal impact on the UI design and architecture—let's say it's just more work. Here's when a prioritized Feature List helps because it forces you to decide where the new feature goes. It becomes clear to everyone that you have to either slip the schedule or bump a feature. As we've been saying, it's all a matter of tradeoffs.

Sometimes, though, you can have a collaborative interaction of the type we've been describing to figure out a way to satisfy the person who wants the new requirement without overburdening the rest of the team. Here is an example of how we were able to handle such a request from our management.

Example: Collaborating with Management

While we were still working on Important features, our manager wanted us to add the ability to e-mail a bub when they were offline. (An earlier example mentioned this feature.) This feature was on the Nice to Have list, but he was asking for it now. We asked him why he needed it, and it turned out that he mainly needed to be able to promise the feature, he didn't need it immediately. We weren't certain we would be able to support it at that point, so we agreed to do enough work to establish that we could include it, without completing the feature. He agreed that that would be sufficient. Alan spent a few hours putting in enough support to prove that we could offer the feature, and then we postponed the rest of the work until later. It isn't always possible to handle such a request so smoothly, but it helps if you can have a similar collaborative environment where everyone tries to find a solution that meets everyone's needs.

You probably noticed that there are a lot of judgment calls being made throughout this process. How much is too much time or effort for the value of the feature? Which part of the feature is critical to the user experience and which is just a nice aspect? There are no strict rules for making these decisions. Good judgment comes with experience, and even when you are experienced, you'll still make some mistakes. But you can greatly improve your record by doing two things. First, treat everyone's concerns with respect, trying your best to accommodate while representing your concerns responsibly. It's amazing how adjusting your position a little encourages others to adjust as well. Second, each time you build a technology, find out how your decisions pan out. If you build it, ship it, and move on, you won't develop a sense of which aspects of the user experience turn out to be important in real use. In the next chapter, we'll discuss in detail how to get that usage feedback and we hope you'll see how valuable it is.

Designer Activity

Although we've focused on the team's interaction during the Initial Development phase, the engineers are for the most part intensely focused on writing code as fast as they can while the designer checks in regularly to see whether any issues have come up. Given that, people sometimes ask whether you need a full-time designer on a project. If you do the UI up front, what does the designer do during the development phase? If you simply implement and ship the initial design, the interaction designer doesn't have much more to do after the design phase. But if your development process includes mechanisms to collect and incorporate feedback from users, as we're suggesting, then the designer still has a lot more work to do. As soon as development begins, they need to prepare for usability testing or a usage study, which will begin shortly after you've finished the Core features. In some cases, the designer may have delayed designing certain elements of the application that won't affect the implementation just so they can provide a UI Spec to the engineering team as quickly as possible. For example, if the interaction designer is also a graphic designer, they might design icons and logos after designing the interaction; if not, they might give input to a graphic designer during this phase. This is not to say that the UI designer can't work on any other projects during this phase, but it's difficult to have more than one major project if you're practicing user-centered design.

In the case of Hubbub, after designing the UI Spec, Ellen created the sounds. The engineers could proceed without the sound files—they just needed to build in support to play small MIDI files. Since sounds were such an important part of the system, we wanted to do everything we could to make sure people could learn them. During the time that Alan and Dipti were busily implementing features, Ellen did some "quick-and-dirty" usability testing, to help design the sounds. Ellen briefly describes how she conducted these tests as an example of how you can conduct usability tests on just a portion of your system to get very early feedback.

Quick-and-Dirty Usability Testing

To design the first draft of the sounds, I worked with a professional musician who had recently been involved with creating sounds for Web applications. I also read a number of papers about sound design and discovered a wonderful Web site with concrete guidelines.[1] We had a list of 14 sound messages we wanted to create, and we did our best to express the attitude or emotion behind each sound with a few notes. For example, "hi" is bright and cheery, "bye" has a sense of closure, and "OK" is quick and light.

Once we had designed an initial set, I conducted a series of tests with people around the office who were not involved with our project. Some were musically talented and some couldn't carry a tune, but most were somewhere in the middle. Some were young, some were older; some were women, some were men. By this time, Alan had already created a Palm screen that would play the 14 sounds, so I used it to test. I tried

---

[1] www.dcs.gla.ac.uk/~stephen/earcon_guidelines.shtml

two methods. At first, I gave the Palm to one person and asked them to play the sounds as much as they wanted until they felt they'd learned the sounds, usually about 10–15 minutes. Then I took the Palm back, played the sounds in a random order, and asked them to name the sounds. Later, I gave two Palms to a pair of colleagues and asked them to learn them together, figuring that learning them in pairs would be more fun. Each pair took a different approach, but they generally spent about 20–30 minutes learning the sounds. Then I tested each person separately. With each test, I noted which sounds were not remembered. After a few tests, I revised the ones that most people found difficult, and tried again with new people. I did this with about 15 people until most of the sounds were remembered reasonably well. I stopped when, after about 20 minutes of practice, people learned about 10 of the 14 sounds, and no one sound was consistently difficult to learn. (The results didn't vary systematically between those who learned the sounds alone and those who learned them with a friend.)

This was not a classic usability test because it focused on a single aspect of the design. Typically during usability testing, people are asked to carry out a range of tasks using the technology and to think aloud while they do their tasks. Still, testing just a single element of a design is another valid form of testing. In our case, testing the sounds allowed me to iterate this one important component of the design many times before building it into the system.

Changes Based on Development Issues

After Initial Development of the planned features, Hubbub had changed somewhat as we worked around development issues. Figure 9.6 shows the list of things we changed, added, and removed because of issues resolved during Initial Development. You don't need to understand the details of all the modifications, just skim the list to get a sense of the number of changes we made and their scope. In all, about 15% of the items in the original Functional Requirements were changed or removed at this point, and the new items made up 2% of the new set of requirements. (This is only a rough estimate of the overall amount of change, since changes varied in magnitude and multiple changes sometimes affected a single requirement. Still, we think it's a good approximation.) In the next chapter, we'll show how Hubbub changed at other phases of development, and you'll see how the changes shown here compare with those that we made based on our own usage and those that were based on feedback from others using Hubbub during the usage study.

9.6

Aspects of Hubbub that changed based on issues that arose during Initial Development. In all, we removed or changed the design of 15% of the initial functional requirements and added 2% more.

Changes After Initial Development

Changed

PC Client

Self entry in bub list moved from bottom pane to top of list

Changed bub selection to highlight just the name, not the entire line (this was easier to implement and matched the PC convention—i.e., we fixed a design error)

Made SIM icons black and white on Main screen to reduce visual overload

Adjusted Text Window footers to explain other person's activity in that window

Palm Client

Limited the number of messages saved per conversation

Alphabetized the menu of active text messages

Both Clients

Changed location to 4 characters instead of 2 on Palm and 6 on PC

Decided we would save Mute state of each bub per client rather than across clients, unless usage study shows we need to save across clients

Decided not to show when the other person closes their text window, and instead just show three states: typing, focus in window, no focus in window

Changed which sound messages we provided

Added fourth state to activity meter (Not Active in addition to Low, Medium, and High)

Added

PC Client

Added a footer to indicate whether Hubbub is connected, connecting, or not connected

Palm Client

Added dynamic multiline pop-up window for entering text

Removed

Both Clients

Decided against showing who's messaging with whom

Removed sounds for log in or log off, since the implications are similar to becoming active or idle

Removed playing a sound to indicate on which device a bub became active/idle, to reduce number of sounds

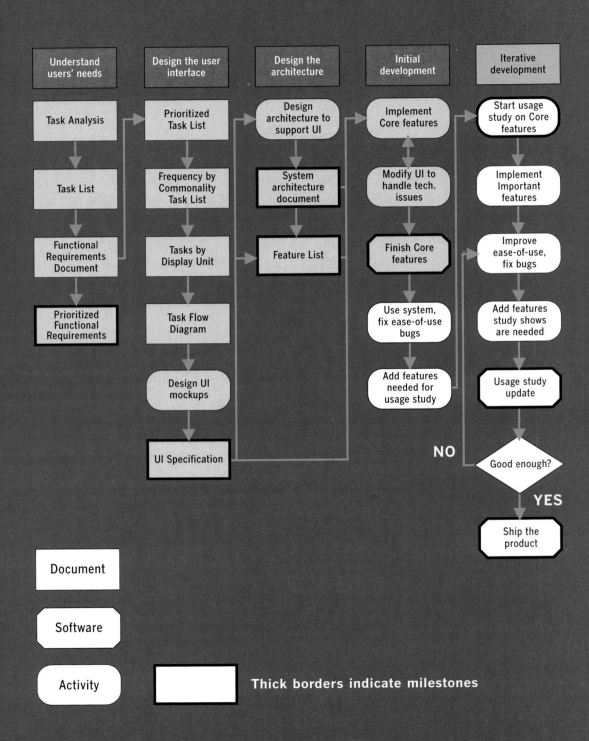

Understand users' needs	Design the user interface	Design the architecture	Initial development	Iterative development

Task Analysis

Prioritized Task List

Design architecture to support UI

Implement Core features

Start usage study on Core features

Task List

Frequency by Commonality Task List

System architecture document

Modify UI to handle tech. issues

Implement Important features

Functional Requirements Document

Tasks by Display Unit

Feature List

Finish Core features

Improve ease-of-use, fix bugs

Prioritized Functional Requirements

Task Flow Diagram

Use system, fix ease-of-use bugs

Add features study shows are needed

Design UI mockups

Add features needed for usage study

Usage study update

UI Specification

NO

Good enough?

YES

Ship the product

Document

Software

Activity

Thick borders indicate milestones

CHAPTER 10
Iterative Development: Observing Use

Once you've built the Core features, it's time to find out how easy it is to use the system in its current state. If you've kept your User Interface Specification up to date, your testing team can find ways in which the technology is not behaving as designed. But you still need to find out whether the specified design is usable in the first place, and that requires using the technology to do real tasks. Start by using the technology yourself, partly so you can find some of the obvious ease-of-use problems, and partly so you can figure out what else you need to build before giving the system to others. Using your own system does not tell you whether it is easy to use; it just gives you a head start on finding and fixing problems. Once you build the additional features, you must observe other people who are not involved with the project using the system. This is how you'll discover many of the ways in which your technology is not behaving like a butler.

This chapter has two parts. First, we describe the value of using your own technology, illustrating with some examples of what we learned by using Hubbub ourselves. Then we walk through the process of setting up a usage study, collecting feedback, interpreting it, and changing the design to address the problems you find. We describe the Hubbub usage study in detail so you can understand the process and observe the dramatic effect it had on the design of the system.

Using Your Own Technology

One reason to use your technology yourself is to find problems that appear when you're not focusing on testing it but instead treating it like any other application. You expect it to *just work*, so you notice when it doesn't. You also see it under realistic conditions—such as when you're doing three other things and someone's talking to you and you need to get something done quickly. Of course, you can also poke around a little and see whether you can find problems with the user experience.

Good things to notice are whether menus offer features that are not available, whether windows stay where you put them, whether the application remembers your choices when you return to a screen, and so on. (Part I of this book mentions many issues to look for.) You can also ask your testing team to look for problems that make the application clumsy, surprising, or annoying. The technical writers can be especially helpful in giving you early feedback on the usability of the system. If they find it difficult to explain how to do a task, that's a good sign that the task may be difficult to use. Or if they find themselves explaining how to handle multiple error cases, maybe you can find a way to avoid those errors in the first place.

Some systems are easier than others to use yourself, and some may just be too difficult. If your system is designed for end users who have roughly the same background knowledge as you, then you should be able to use it yourself. If you've got a standalone application that supports tasks that you happen to do on a regular basis, you're in luck. But usually it won't be that easy. Maybe you're building a Web-based system that depends on content that won't be available for a while. Maybe it will run on hardware that is still under development. Or maybe it supports tasks that are specific to another industry and are not relevant to what you do. These are obstacles, but if you're creative you can find ways around them. If you depend on specific data, try to feed the system with a sample of realistic data. If you depend on certain hardware, you may have a simulator that you can use until prototypes of the hardware become available. If you're building technology to support tasks you don't do, at least try running those tasks as if you really had to do them. It may be difficult, but using the application yourself is valuable if you want to build usable technology. We once designed and built a video-based collaborative system that required a group of people to use it, so we set up everyone on our team with cameras and microphones and used the system to communicate about the project.

Frequently you'll find that you have to jury-rig the technology a little to get started. For example, with Hubbub, we hard-coded our account information since the account administration features weren't implemented. We also set the maximum number of bubs to nine because the Palm Main screen wasn't scrolling yet. On the PC client, we had planned a separate pop-up window to specify your location, but that wasn't ready, so Dipti put a temporary text field on the Login screen so we could enter a location. That meant you'd have to log out and back in again just to change your location, which is silly, but this was the simplest way to enable the location feature. Normally, we would not hack together a solution and fix it later, but it was worth doing in a few cases so we could start to use the system, given that the changes were minor and not structural.

If your system is designed for people with a very different skill set than you have, it may be difficult to get meaningful information from using the system yourself. In that case, try to get started on a usage study as soon as possible. Even if you did an extensive task analysis early on, your intuition about users' behavior is less likely to be accurate than it is for tasks you're familiar with. In this case, a usage study is especially important because you need to base your decisions on hard data about real users' behavior. You want the system to feel like a butler trained to respond to their needs, not your impression of their needs. Again, you can rely on the technical writers before the study begins to find tasks that are difficult to explain and problems that should be fixed before the test users see the system. You might also get some help from a user representative who can help you determine when there is enough functionality to give it to users.

Development Guideline
When using your own technology, notice when your flow is broken, even for a split second. Pop out of your task to figure out what caused the break and write it down before moving on. You might have to accumulate several related problems before you can figure out how to improve the design.

Assuming you can use your own technology, as soon as you do so you'll find some obvious bugs to fix, but you especially want to keep an eye out for smaller bobbles that break your flow. The natural thing is to adjust and keep going since you're trying to do a task. But as soon as you notice yourself thinking "huh?" for even a split second, pop out of your task and think about what caused the double take. Write it down and keep track of it. You might not figure out how to solve the problem right away, which is fine. Later you might see patterns of problems and figure out a general solution. As before, you'll also have to balance ease-of-use considerations with the engineering cost of potential solutions. The following sections explain some of the problems we found when we started using Hubbub and how we handled them.

Fixing Ease-of-Use Problems

Once we started using Hubbub, a few problems popped out immediately. In some cases, we had even debated the design decision earlier, but as soon as we started using it the right answer became obvious. In many cases, it was relatively quick and easy to fix the problem.

For example, we had previously discussed whether sound messages should play when you *send* them in addition to when you receive them. On the one hand, hearing them would provide feedback that you sent them, **[Give Feedback]** but on the other hand it might overwhelm you with sounds. **[Don't Impose]** As soon as we used Hubbub ourselves, it became obvious that the sound should play when sent. If you just saw the sound message appear in the conversation, you stopped for a split second to wonder whether the other person had heard it, which broke your flow. Also, it was important to share the experience of hearing the sound, especially if someone commented on the sound itself.

Other problems were hard to anticipate but easy to fix. For example, Alan initially implemented the sound message buttons on the Palm as icons because it wasn't obvious how to create graphical buttons (see Figure 10.1). When we tapped them, we noticed right away that they didn't flash or make a clicking sound, so we weren't sure whether we'd hit the target. **[Give Feedback]** Not only was this disconcerting, but our natural reaction was to try tapping them again, which meant that we'd send several sound messages in a row. The UI Spec had not indicated that the buttons should click and flash when selected because buttons normally do so by default. Once we realized that we had to add it ourselves, Alan figured out that the trick for making icons behave like standard buttons is to hide real buttons underneath the icons.

10.1

The sound message buttons on the Palm's Bub screen were originally implemented as icons and not buttons, so there was no feedback when you successfully tapped them. Once we realized that this was a problem, Alan learned that you can hide buttons behind the icons to make them flash and click when tapped.

In other cases, the solution to a problem was not as obvious or quick to implement. When this happened, we'd often find an easy-to-implement alternative UI that worked around the problem for the time being. Since so many things change as you implement the technology, and since you learn as you go, it's common to find a technical solution to the problem later on. But you never know which ones you will be able to fix later, so it's good to implement an acceptable solution in case you have to ship without the ideal solution.

For example, once we started using Hubbub on our PCs, we discovered that the sound icons did not appear in the conversation window if you ran Hubbub on Windows NT, but they did if you were using Windows 98. The same code running on different versions of Windows resulted in different behavior. This type of inconsistency across different versions of an operating system drives application developers crazy. **[Be Predictable]** We did not have a solution at the time, so we made the simple change of putting curly braces around the sound message labels. For example, if Ellen sent Alan the sound message "Cool," here's what it looked like before and after we made this adjustment.

	Before adjustment	**After adjustment**
Windows 98	Ellen: 🔲 Cool	Ellen: 🔲 {Cool}
Windows NT	Ellen: Cool	Ellen: {Cool}

This design at least allowed those on NT to distinguish a sound message from a text message after the sound had played. Later, we discovered more problems with the text pane, so Dipti dug around and discovered the root cause of the problem and was able to get sound icons to display on NT. (Still, we kept the curly braces in case other similar bugs emerged.)

Development Guideline
If you find ease-of-use problems that are complicated to fix properly, don't just file a bug report and move on. Find a way to adjust the UI that is relatively easy to implement, in case you never find a better solution or the time to fix the problem.

We saw another difficult-to-fix problem on the Palm client. Early on, it took some time to disconnect from the network when the user exited Hubbub, and during that time the UI froze. Of course it would have been better if Alan had found a way to make Hubbub disconnect and exit instantly, but he was still learning. Instead, we added a Hubbub Is Exiting screen to let the user know what was going on. **[Show Signs of Progress]** Later, as Alan learned more, he found a way to make Hubbub disconnect quickly enough that the exiting screen is rarely seen. If he hadn't found the fix and we were scrambling to meet a deadline, at least we wouldn't have had to ship with a rude exit process.

Polishing Features

We probably would have found many of these problems with some quick usability testing since they were so prominent. But there were other issues that we didn't notice until we'd used Hubbub under ordinary conditions for a while. Finding and fixing these types of problems allowed us to start polishing the design.

For example, we had to decide how much time should pass before someone would be considered "idle." People aren't using their computers continually even when they're actively working on them, but how long after they have stopped working is it reasonable to consider them idle? We started with the guess of one minute. But after using Hubbub for a little while, we were surprised at how frequently we were going idle and active. Apparently, it's much more common than we thought to stop clicking, typing, or tapping for a minute. So we adjusted the time to five minutes, which worked much better. **[Respect Mental Effort]** We heard each other's activity sounds frequently enough to stay aware of one another but not so frequently that everyone seemed to have attention deficit disorder!

Here's another problem that took real use to discover. When you first start up Hubbub, usually several of your bubs are already active. Since this is the first time they are reporting their active state to your client, Hubbub played the active sound followed by the Sound ID for each of the active bubs, thus bombarding you with songs. On the PC, it's common to start up an instant messenger and keep it running all day or even several days at a time, so it might not seem like a big issue. But we realized it was a problem when Ellen went to a meeting where she started Hubbub on the Palm. All she could do was smile apologetically when everyone turned to find out what the odd chorus of sounds was about. **[Don't Impose]** We quickly made sure that when Hubbub starts up it does not play the active bubs' sounds.

Using your own technology can be very helpful, but you also have to be careful about interpreting your own reactions. You know a lot more about your system than your users will, so it's hard for you to tell which features will seem unclear to others. A fair generalization is that by using your own technology, you can find problems in the design but you cannot determine whether a design is easy to use.

Here's an example of a case where we knew too much to judge whether a feature was working. We wanted to provide feedback in the Message window to let people know what their conversation partner was doing.

While using other instant messengers, we didn't like the experience of sending a message, waiting for what seemed like a reasonable amount of time and getting no response. We would wonder, "Is the other person writing a longer message than I expected? Are they a slow typist? Did they get distracted and start doing something else? Are they waiting for me to say more? Should I give up and start doing something else?" We thought we could do a better job of letting people know whether the other person is typing in the window, has input focus in that window, has focus in another window, or has closed the window. **[Offer Sufficient Information Early and in Context]** The question was how to convey this information.

We decided to use the footer of the Message window to provide the information because it's easily visible on a small window and it's near the input area where the user's eyes are focused. Since the activity meter on the main window already shows how actively that bub is typing, clicking, or tapping, we decided to replicate that bub's activity meter in the footer. Then all you'd need to know is whether they're focused in that Message window. If they have focus in the window and the meter is high, they're typing a response. If they have focus in the window and the meter is empty, they're waiting for you. If they don't have focus in the Message window but the activity meter is high, they're busy doing something else. And if they don't have focus in the Message window but the activity meter is empty, they're probably not paying attention to their computer. So we added text next to the activity meter indicating whether or not they had focus in the window. Figure 10.2 shows what this looked like.

10.2

Mock-up of the original design for indicating a conversation partner's status in a Message window. The activity meter indicates how actively the person is typing, and the text message indicates whether that activity is focused in this window. Although we loved the feature, we discovered that others could not interpret the information easily, so we changed the design (shown in Figure 10.8).

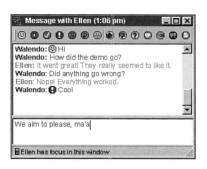

Development Guideline
Using your own techno-
logy can help you find
problems, but it will not
tell you whether your
customer will find the
technology easy to use.
You simply know too
much about the design
to tell whether others
will understand it.

As we used Hubbub, we loved this feature because it told us just what we wanted to know. We already understood the meaning of the activity meter, so it was easy to put together the two pieces of information (the activity meter and the text information about focus) to draw conclusions about the other person's activity. Most likely as you read this, you're rolling your eyes at how silly we were to think this was obvious. As soon as we gave Hubbub to "real people" to use, we found that they didn't understand this design at all. Later in this chapter we'll explain how we revised the design based on their feedback. That feature has become one of the most appreciated features in Hubbub, and we wouldn't have gotten it right if we had tried it ourselves and gone with the original design.

Changes Based on Our Use

These are just a few examples of the features we modified based on our own use. Figure 10.3 shows the list of all the things we changed at this stage. As before, it's not important that you understand all the details. The point is that we made a moderate number of changes, about the same number as we made based on Initial Development issues, and those changes tended to fix problems. Using the same approximate measure of the amount of change as before, the changes based on our use affected only about 11% of the items in the Functional Requirements. We didn't add any features and we removed one.

10.3

The changes we made to Hubbub after we used it ourselves but before we gave it to others to use. Mostly we fixed ease-of-use problems and adjusted a few sound-related features to get the effect we had in mind. We experimented briefly with one feature (a "sound logo" on startup), but didn't like the result, so we removed it.

Changes After Using Hubbub Ourselves

Changed

PC Client

Put curly braces around SIM labels so that when the icon doesn't appear people can tell it was a sound, not just the person typing that text

Palm Client

Made sure the sound message button flashes when you tap it so you know you hit the target

Extended the timeout period when starting up Hubbub

Removed leading 0 from hours active/idle to save room

Don't auto-capitalize e-mail field when logging in

Both Clients

Changed active time from 1 minute to 5 minutes

Realized the sound message must play when sent in addition to when received

Realized we must show the SIM labels next to the sound messages in a conversation (we had considered just showing the icon without the label to make the messages more flexible, but realized you needed to see the label to interpret the message—that was just a bad idea)

Decided not to play a Sound ID each time a message arrives, only if you haven't gotten a Sound ID for 5 minutes and you haven't received a text message—from someone else in between

Added

None

Removed

Both Clients

Tried playing a "sound logo" when Hubbub starts up, but we found it more confusing than helpful, so we dropped it

Observing Others Using Your Technology

Finally we come to what we believe is the most satisfying and exciting part of developing technology—watching people use your technology and iterating on it until it is easy for people to use. This may also be the most painful part of the process, since you'll find that after all the work you've done to design and implement the system, people won't understand how to use some of the features. You'll want to grab them by the shoulders and explain to them why it really is obvious, but of course, *if it ain't obvious to them, it ain't obvious*. Instead, treat it as a challenge, a problem-solving exercise that you can use to find a better way to communicate the features.

Testing a product for its ease of use is similar in purpose to testing a product's functionality. Both forms of testing give you quick and early feedback on your work so you can fix your mistakes before they are exposed to thousands or maybe even millions of people. Just as you wouldn't ship code without testing to make sure that it runs properly, you shouldn't ship software without testing to see whether people can use it. Just as it can be frustrating and embarrassing when a test engineer points out bugs in your code, it can be annoying to find that people stumble over tasks that seemed straightforward. But just as it's exhilarating when you finally get some functionality to work, it's wonderful to watch people glide easily through their tasks, using technology you created for them.

Usability testing is by far the most widely used testing technique, and quite a bit has been written about it. In this book we focus instead on usage studies—partly because they're less understood but mainly because we think they provide a broader and deeper range of feedback that can have a bigger impact on your product. Still, if you can't run a usage study, do run multiple rounds of usability tests. Before getting into the details of conducting a usage study, we quickly explain usability testing so that you can understand the difference between the two methods. We encourage you to check the materials listed in the Recommended Readings (Appendix B) to find out more about this method.

Comparing Usability Testing with Usage Studies

Typically, usability testing is done in a lab, though it may be done anywhere. Participants are representative of target users; they may use similar products or earlier versions of your product. Six or so participants are brought into the lab, usually one at a time for an hour or two. They are asked to imagine that they are in a certain situation with a certain goal and to carry out a set of tasks that accomplish that goal. Sometimes they are also asked to explore on their own. Either way, they are usually asked to "think aloud" so those observing the test can understand what assumptions they're making and why they might be having trouble. The person running the test (often called a usability specialist or usability engineer) collects qualitative data about what users did, paying special attention to features that confused them and tasks they could not complete correctly, and often interviewing them afterward to get their subjective reactions. They also collect quantitative data, such as the time it took users to do the tasks, the number of errors (if they can be meaningfully defined), the outcome of the tasks, and sometimes people's ratings of the system. After analyzing the results, the specialist writes up a report and/or gives a presentation summarizing the main problem areas of the technology, providing specific examples. Sometimes they make a video "highlights tape" to illustrate people having trouble with the software. In some organizations, those on the team can watch testing in progress from another room through a one-way mirror or via a monitor showing what the user is seeing. There's nothing more compelling than watching someone struggle with your technology to get you to see it from their point of view. You might be tempted to write them off as a novice or even a person who is clueless about technology, or you may want to run into the room and show them how to do it. Resist both of those urges. Treat the information as valid input that will help you figure out how to make the tasks clear and simple for other people, not just for yourself and your tech-savvy friends.

Usability testing turns up most of the big, obvious problems with a technology, the kinds of things that most users stumble over and that seem obviously wrong in hindsight. It also turns up a lot of smaller issues that can help make the system behave more like a butler. Usability tests are also effective for finding out whether your system meets certain benchmarks and for comparing multiple designs. However, there are a few important limitations of usability testing. One is that you find problems only in the areas you explore, so if you don't test every feature and every common scenario, you could miss big problems. A second limitation is that people carry out the tasks in an artificial setting *as if* they were really doing them. They do not have as much invested in the outcome as they would if it were their real work, which may affect their behavior. It's difficult to find out which tasks people do naturally, in what order, and under what circumstances. They also do the tasks with no other distractions around, no interruptions, and no responsibilities other than to test your software, which is probably not representative of how they would use it. If you're working with a technology that people use outside an office setting, it's even harder to re-create a realistic scenario. Third, usability tests primarily tell you about the "learnability" of your system rather than about its ease of use because most tests observe people using the system for the first time. It's hard for usability testing to evaluate how the system will stand up under frequent use.

Usage Study Guideline
It is critical to start usage studies *very early* when you have just enough functionality working to make it possible to do a basic set of meaningful tasks. Give people the system to use for just those tasks in their real settings, and then continue to build the rest of the system, incorporating feedback as you go. Each new "release" should include many revisions of existing features and a few new features until you stop adding new features and have polished all the existing ones.

Usage studies are designed to give you an understanding of how real customers will use the technology in practice. You can't guarantee that every person will do every task, but you can find out which tasks people ordinarily do under realistic conditions and which features they don't need. You also find out how they carry out the tasks, what problems they have, and whether important features are missing. Here's how it works. You start by giving a primitive version of the technology to a group of representative users who have volunteered to use it to do real activities in their real setting. You automatically log their actions so that you know which features they use and how, and you periodically observe them or put a camera in their setting and let it capture realistic use. You also collect their feedback in a variety of ways: by sending out surveys, interviewing them, chatting with them informally, and making it easy for them to send you their ideas sponta- neously. As you continue with development, you incorporate feedback from these multiple sources, and then you release new versions to this small group on a regular basis, each one including changes to the existing features to address the problems you uncovered plus a few new features. You find out how the new version fares and continue the process until you have enough features to make the product useful and you've refined them enough that they are usable, at which point you release the technology as a product. The downside to usage studies is that they can take more effort from a tester over a longer period of time than usability testing (which in itself isn't trivial to do), and they require you to spend more time getting early releases ready. Usage studies are similar to beta tests, except that they are conducted *much* earlier and you collect far more information about ease-of-use problems, not just functionality bugs.

Usage Study Guideline
Usability testing is more effective for studying technology people use on an occasional basis for tasks they complete in one session. Usage studies are more effective for studying technology that people use on a regular basis to complete tasks that take time and that evolve over time.

In general, usability testing is more effective for studying systems that people typically use on their own on an occasional basis to do tasks they can complete in one session. Some examples include getting information from a Web page, using an information kiosk at an airport or museum, or using an automatic teller machine at a bank. In those situations, the lab is simulating a similar experience to the one real users will have. Usage studies are better for studying systems that people use on a regular basis, sometimes in collaboration with others, to complete tasks that take time and that evolve over time. In those cases, it's very hard to simulate users' environments, so you need to take a naturalistic approach to observing use.

Running a Usage Study

To run a usage study, you need a person assigned to find an appropriate user group, set up the study, collect the data, and work with the team to interpret the findings and figure out how to incorporate changes into the design. We'll call this person the *usage tester*. The usage tester should have skills in observational techniques (that is, in collecting different types of observational information and interpreting it without bias). It is also critical that the usage tester stay open-minded about the system being studied. Their job is to find as many potential problems as possible as early as possible, not to defend the system as it stands. If they try to explain to users why the system is good the way it is, they should be prepared to do a lot of explaining to a lot of customers as well. This is not to say that you need to change the design every time someone pauses when doing a task, but the reason for that pause should be taken as one piece of evidence that the design is flawed. Ideally, the usage tester will also have a thorough understanding of the system so that they can pick up problems that may be caused by seemingly unrelated design decisions. It's often the case that people have problems with one feature because of a decision associated with a different feature, so if you fix the symptom you may cause problems in other features. The more the usage tester understands the reasoning that went into each design decision, the better they'll be able to diagnose the root cause of a problem and assess whether potential solutions will address it. If the usage tester does not have this background, they should focus on characterizing problems in as much detail as possible without offering potential solutions. Then the design and engineering team can work with them to figure out the underlying cause of the problem and consider ways to address it.

Usage Study Guideline
The usage tester must be (a) trained in observational techniques, (b) open-minded and eager to find problems rather than trying to defend the system, and ideally, (c) deeply knowledgeable about the system so they can decipher the underlying causes of problems.

In the usage studies we've seen, the designers happened to have advanced skills in observational techniques[1] and so they ran the study, but someone else familiar with the technology could run it as well. Certainly a usability specialist could do it, as could a project manager or a technical writer who is interested in the user experience (assuming they aren't also trying to do their other job full time).[2]

Some projects are more straightforward than others for running a usage study, but if you plan to do one from the start you can usually find a way to manage it. If you're writing desktop software that allows people to create certain kinds of documents, it probably won't be hard to find people willing to use it when they create new documents. If you're working on interactive TV technology, you can set people up with hardware in their homes and ask them to use it to watch the shows they normally watch. If you're working on a handheld GPS, you can give people early prototypes and ask them to use it any time they're going somewhere unfamiliar instead of using a map or getting directions (though they might want to have the maps or directions for backup). If you're working on an enterprise workflow application, it might be more challenging to run a usage study, but it's still possible. If, for example, you're creating an online business expense reimbursement process, you'll want to ask people who really are filing their expenses to use it. Since you want to study the system long before it's all done, focus on one part of the process, perhaps on entering the expenses, and then find a way to hook into the existing process, even if that means spitting out paper forms that you can send to the accounting department. Then as you build more components, have

---

[1] In one case, the designer had a Ph.D. in ethnographic methods, and Ellen has a Ph.D. in experimental psychology. Both had learned objective methods for observing and analyzing data.

[2] Many people believe that a designer cannot test their own system because they are too biased. We believe that if the designer is trained in observational techniques and is motivated to improve the design, they can do a good job. An outside tester has fewer biases, but they also have less knowledge about the system, and they sometimes focus too much on surface issues rather than deeper interaction problems. As long as the usage tester has skills in observational techniques and an open mind, they can do a high quality study, regardless of their relationship to the project.

people use them and keep hooking into the real process until they can use your system all the way through. We've mainly done usage studies on applications that require collaboration among several people in distributed locations, so we've had to find groups of people who work together from a distance and set them all up on the system. As we explain the steps involved in our Hubbub usage study, you should get an idea of what might be appropriate for your project.

Running a usage study while developing technology is a departure from the standard software development process. You start doing "practice releases" much earlier than you're used to on software that is nowhere near feature-complete, and you spend a lot more time polishing features than doing new features. The benefit is that by the time you ship, you will have focused your energy on the features people really use and you will have caught most of the glitches that break people's flow. As we've mentioned throughout this book, you do fewer features but you do them well.

In the rest of this chapter, we walk through the process of conducting a usage study, using many examples from Hubbub. We go into a lot of detail because we want to show you how a usage study is done, and because we hope to convince you that the adjustment to the development process is well worth the effort. To do that, we have to show you the type of problems we found, large and small, and how we used an iterative process to adjust the features until they were smooth. We ran the Hubbub usage study for just over five months, during which time we released five iterations. The second release came just one week after the first to fix a major problem, but then we released a new version about once every five weeks. That pace allowed us to get timely feedback while still giving us enough time to modify and add features. Most of our effort was spent polishing existing features and adding ones we discovered were needed, and relatively little was spent implementing features we had planned to provide from the start. Occasionally we even discovered features we could remove from the Feature List entirely.

To run a usage study, you need the following:

- Willing participants
- Technology with a minimally useful set of features that is acceptably stable and causes no damage

- A way to make the technology available to participants and to update it on a regular basis
- Many mechanisms for collecting data about participants' use of the technology and their feedback about it
- A process for interpreting feedback and incorporating it into development

Finding Usage Study Participants

The first thing you'll need to do is find a group of people representative of your target customers who are willing to use very preliminary technology. These people must understand that they will be using the technology well before all the features are available, and that it will have bugs that they wouldn't expect to see in product-quality software. The incentive for them is that they get to try out new technology early and they have a big effect on its design and quality. (Of course, thank-you gifts are always a good idea.) In many cases, you can find a group of people inside your company who are not associated with your team but are similar to the target market. Other times, you can network through friends and colleagues to find interested people. It's best to choose people who are not connected with your project and don't know much about it, but are potential users of it. The number of participants needed varies depending on how your technology is used, but we recommend including roughly 5–15 people. It also helps to include a range of people whose characteristics vary along dimensions relevant to the technology.

In the case of Hubbub, we had to find a distributed group to use it, since those who work near one another don't need Hubbub's awareness features. We did our usage study with a group of about 25–30 people in our department who are distributed across two campuses in New Jersey and one in California. Not everyone worked together with everyone else, but we tried to make sure that everyone had at least one other person to interact with. (After the study got started, some people asked if we could add one or two other colleagues, which we did.) We included researchers, engineers, administrative assistants, and managers, and we made sure to find people who worked from multiple locations, worked entirely from home, and/or traveled frequently. Most of the people in the study had no connection to our project, although we did interact occasionally with a few of the participants on other projects or administrative matters.

It's very important for the participants to be fully aware that you will be tracking all of their activity with the technology during the study before they agree to participate. Make sure that they know who will see the data and how the information will be used—usually you can assure them that only your team will view it and that it will be used solely to improve the technology, but if you know that you have other goals in mind, make that clear. Sometimes you discover another use for the data later on, in which case you must go back to the participants and ask permission.[3] Certainly if you ever want to use the data for marketing purposes, be sure to show the material to the participants and get their consent.

Usage Study Guideline
Take care to protect study participants' privacy. Make sure that they understand what data you will collect and how the information will be used before agreeing to participate. If you later want to use the data for another purpose, go back and get their consent.

Also tell participants that they can always ask you to delete certain data (such as portions of logs or sections of videotapes) if they realize they've done something they don't want recorded. In practice, this rarely happens, but it's a comfort for people to know that they have this option. (We were asked to expunge one conversation from the logs, which we did without question.) If you're dealing with a system for the home, get agreement from other family members who might be affected, especially parents if you're working with teenagers or younger children. Also be sure to protect the data so that others cannot find it and use it for other purposes. Respecting the participants' privacy is critical in a usage study (as it is with usability testing).

As you're looking for suitable people for the study, you'll need to interview them, if only informally, to find out whether they have the right characteristics. Once you choose your participants, have follow-up conversations to find out more information for the study. If you don't know already, you'll want to find out how much experience they have performing the tasks your technology supports and how they typically carry them out. Also find out what their physical environment is like, what type of equipment they have, and so on. If you understand their conditions, it will be easier to prepare your technology for the study because you won't need to build in support for scenarios that aren't relevant to this particular group. For the Hubbub study, we asked our participants whether they had used an instant messenger before (only a few had), whom they interacted with, what type of work they

---

[3] We got participants' permission to show the real Hubbub screenshots and conversations included in this chapter.

did, how many locations they worked from, what version of Windows they used on which machines, whether they had laptop or desktop machines, what type of Palm they had, and so on.

Preparing the Technology

We've already mentioned the importance of starting a usage study as early as possible in the development process so that you have more time to get and incorporate feedback. Once you've started to use the technology yourself, you'll know whether it has enough features to let others use it meaningfully. If it doesn't, add just the necessary features and no more. Not everything has to be working, as long as you have a way to get people started with the system. With Hubbub, we didn't have any account administration features working when we gave it out. Instead, we manually created accounts for the study participants and gave each of them all the other study participants as their bubs. This is a little artificial, since not everyone in the study collaborated with everyone else, but it gave everyone a good sized bub list to work with. We realized we had to implement logging in and out (which was on the Important list), but we didn't handle all possible cases. For example, it probably would have broken if someone had borrowed another person's machine and logged in as themselves, or if two users had shared a machine, but we knew from our earlier interviews that everyone had their own machines and that people rarely borrowed machines for any period of time.

Once you have a good working set of features, stop adding features and turn your attention to testing and debugging the system so that it's reasonably stable and won't cause damage. This should feel like a little practice run for preparing to ship. This may seem like a bit of a distraction at this stage, but the value of the usage study should greatly outweigh this effort, and besides, it's not a bad thing to make sure you can put together a working system halfway through development. Your system doesn't need to be nearly as solid as it would to ship, but it shouldn't crash people's machines or lose their data.

Before you give the system to users, you should include a mechanism to log participants' actions if at all possible (with their permission, of course). This type of data is the most important for learning which features people really use and how. If the system runs on a network, you can have it send logs to a server on a regular basis. If it runs as a standalone application, have it create a log file and then ask people to e-mail it to you periodically. You may even need to visit them to collect the data. In our case, the Hubbub server logged all text and sound messages sent from one person to another as the messages passed through the server, the clients sent a message to the server each time users carried out certain commands, and the Web site kept a separate log indicating each time users went to any page or made changes to their account.

Usage Study Guideline
Before giving out the technology, include a mechanism to log all important user actions. This information is critical for learning which features people use, how often, and in what ways. There is no other good way to collect this information accurately.

The designer needs to specify which user actions should be logged. Typically you want to know any time people issue a command but not necessarily when they take intermediary actions such as scrolling or moving the mouse or cursor. Still, on a cell phone application, you may want to know intermediate states such as the order in which they navigate through the menus in addition to the commands they eventually choose. On a Web application, you may need to know the order in which they visit the screens, not just which pages they view. On a desktop application, you may want to record where they place the windows, whether they resize them and how. Whatever you decide, it must be determined up front so the engineers can write the appropriate logging code. (And since this part of the process is iterative as well, you may discover that you need to add new logging code after you observe some use and realize that you can't track something of interest.)

You'll also need to plan a way to distribute updates during the study. You might need to visit each person and manually install the updates, or you might make it possible for people to install updates themselves. With Hubbub, we asked the users to install the updates, providing explicit instructions on a Web page. Most could do it, but we had to walk some people through it over the phone or do it for them. We also quickly learned to embed a protocol version in every Hubbub message, which allowed us to force our small group of users to update. When a client tried to send a message with the wrong protocol version, a window popped up explaining that the version of Hubbub that they were using would no longer work and providing the URL of the Web page where they could get the update. It would have been even nicer to do the update automatically for them (at least on the PC), but that took more time than we wanted to spend and the manual updates worked well enough.

Finally, in our case, we were running a live service, so we took steps to help us track status and keep the service running. Alan added a mechanism that allowed us to view a Web page showing server status without logging into the live server machine. He did this so he could make sure everything was running properly at any time and debug if it wasn't. An added benefit was that Ellen could look at that day's logs at any time, without having to wait for the end of the day when the information was saved to a daily log file. Alan also wrote a process to check the server once a minute, and to page him if it got no response. If it later noticed that the server was back up, it sent another page indicating that all was well again. Finally, when we started using proxy servers later on (to handle some firewall issues), Alan created a process to monitor the status of the proxies and to restart them if they weren't running. These mechanisms are similar to those used in real services. If you prepare them early for the usage study, you get to test your procedures for monitoring and maintaining the service well before you have a larger population of users to support. Of course, your technology is different and may not require these types of features, but you should include utilities that enable you to address problems quickly.

Installing the Technology

Once you're ready to give out the technology, you may need to go to each person's location and set it up for them. Even if people can get access to the technology themselves (if you're studying a Web site, for example), it's helpful to pay them a visit to explain how to get started, what to do if a problem emerges, and what they can expect during the usage study. Remind them that many features are not complete. Also be sure that they understand what data you're collecting and how often you will be asking for their feedback. During the setup visit, refrain from explaining how to use the technology. If you give them a personal tutorial, you won't learn what your real customers will experience when they start using it (unless you plan to give a personal tutorial to all of your customers).

With Hubbub, we also created a Web site for the study, a place where people could go to get answers to simple questions. It included a list of available features along with some preliminary help pages. We also set up an e-mail address where people could send feedback and listed it on the Web site. When we initially installed the software, we made a bookmark on each person's browser to make it easy for them to get to the Web site. Each time we sent out a new release, we updated the Web site with a list of the new features and known bugs. Then, when we announced the new release via e-mail, we gave a quick summary of new features and pointed people to the Web site to get more details. As we got questions, we created an FAQ (frequently asked questions) section on the Web site to address them. All of this helped us build and test our help materials early.

Collecting and Interpreting the Data

Once people are finally using the technology, the data collection begins. This is when you get your first glimpse into how well you've designed and built the technology. There are many techniques for collecting data, including log data, observation, surveys, interviews, and user comments and suggestions. In this section, we walk through each of them, explaining what type of information they yield, and how to interpret the information to improve the design. Each method has its pros and cons, and your job is to combine data from multiple sources to get as accurate a picture as you can about the usability of your technology.

Logging User Activity

Let's start with logging. Logs are critical for learning about the complexities of real use. There is no better way to collect accurate data about how often people used certain features. (Humans are just plain bad at recollecting this type of information, so you can't rely on self-reports, and coding videotapes is much too labor-intensive for large amounts of data.) By analyzing log data, you get a richly textured feel for people's use of the system. You learn about scenarios of use that you hadn't anticipated, and sometimes you can determine that it is safe to remove a feature or drop plans for extending it if few people are using it.

Once you start to receive the raw data, you'll probably need to write scripts to help you parse the information in a way that is meaningful for analysis. For example, you may wind up with huge files that list certain events occurring in chronological order. In some cases, all you want to know is how often an individual command was used, so it's easy to search or sort the data to find out. But other times it's important to know the order in which commands were used, or how a set of commands were used together, or how frequently something happened given that something else had happened, and so on. You need scripts to answer these questions. Once you have them, the usage tester should pore over the data to learn how the system is being used, to find problem areas, and to figure out what else should be logged in the next round.

We did a lot of processing of the Hubbub server logs to get an overall picture of usage and to help us refine the design. The raw logs were hard to interpret because they interleaved conversations among different pairs, they referred to bubs by ID number rather than name, and they represented sound messages as ugly 32-character resource IDs. So we wrote a script to break into separate files the set of messages sent between any given pair of bubs per day and to show bubs and sound messages by name. (Figure 10.4 shows a portion of a raw log, and 10.5 shows how it looked once processed.) We also wrote scripts to find out who logged in each day, how much time people spent active, idle, and offline per day, and so on. We used this information to find out how well Hubbub supported some of the activities we had set out to provide. For example, we were especially interested to know how well Hubbub supported opportunistic conversations (those that were triggered by hearing someone become active). So we looked at the percentage of conversations that were initiated within two minutes of the recipient becoming active (not a perfect measure, but a good approximation). We found that over the course of the usage study, 24% of the conversations were opportunistic, which was encouraging. If people were using only the visual cues, you would expect conversations to be initiated fairly evenly across the span of time during which people were active, which was not the case. So this was one piece of evidence that the awareness sounds were effective.

10.4

A raw log from just over one minute of activity during which Walendo and Ellen have a conversation. Most of the messages are from clients reporting in about their activity level. Users are referred to by ID number, and the sounds are listed as 32-character resource IDs. The log is very difficult to read if you want to understand how people are using the application.

Raw Hubbub Log

CLE: Client Log Entry
IM_TEXT: Text Instant Message
IM_SOUND: Sound Instant Message
CLIENT_AI: Client Activity Information
ACK: Client acknowledgment
TIM: Text Instant Message window

Note: Bold items indicate messages that appear in the processed logs. They do not appear in bold in the real logs. IP addresses have been masked.

[2000-1214-19:07:44]: CLIENT_AI: [3 @ yyy.yyy.yyy.yyy:5678] : 1
[2000-1214-19:07:44]: CLIENT_AI: [1 @ xxx.xxx.xxx.xxx:1234] : 0
[2000-1214-19:07:54]: ACTIVITY [1] from: xxx.xxx.xxx.xxx:1234 for UID 3
[2000-1214-19:07:54]: CLE [1 @ xxx.xxx.xxx.xxx:1234] : [0] focus in TIM [03]
[2000-1214-19:07:54]: Sent ACTIVITY to: yyy.yyy.yyy.yyy:5678
[2000-1214-19:07:55]: ACTIVITY [2] from: xxx.xxx.xxx.xxx:1234 for UID 3
[2000-1214-19:07:55]: Sent ACTIVITY to: yyy.yyy.yyy.yyy:5678
[2000-1214-19:07:59]: CLIENT_AI: [3 @ yyy.yyy.yyy.yyy:5678] : 1
[2000-1214-19:08:00]: CLIENT_AI: [1 @ xxx.xxx.xxx.xxx:1234] : 3
[2000-1214-19:08:01]: Recvd IM_TEXT [**dubious has been up for 367 days!**] from: xxx.xxx.xxx.xxx:1234 for UID 3
[2000-1214-19:08:01]: ACTIVITY [1] from: xxx.xxx.xxx.xxx:1234 for UID 3
[2000-1214-19:08:02]: Sent ACTIVITY to: yyy.yyy.yyy.yyy:5678
[2000-1214-19:08:02]: Sent IM_TEXT [dubious has been up for 367 days!] to: yyy.yyy.yyy.yyy:5678
[2000-1214-19:08:02]: Recvd ACK (seq# 53174) from: yyy.yyy.yyy.yyy:5678, destined for UID 1
[2000-1214-19:08:02]: Sent ACK to: xxx.xxx.xxx.xxx:1234
[2000-1214-19:08:02]: CLE [3 @ yyy.yyy.yyy.yyy:5678] : [0] ..
[2000-1214-19:08:08]: CLE [3 @ yyy.yyy.yyy.yyy:5678] : [0] SIM 139b6177f95fce2a251a0bba3c474193 from TIM

[2000-1214-19:08:08]: Recvd IM_SOUND [**139b6177f95fce2a251a0bba3c474193**] from: yyy.yyy.yyy.yyy:5678 for UID 1

[2000-1214-19:08:08]: Sent IM_SOUND [139b6177f95fce2a251a0bba3c474193] to: xxx.xxx.xxx.xxx:1234

[2000-1214-19:08:08]: Recvd ACK (seq# 811) from: xxx.xxx.xxx.xxx:1234, destined for UID 3

[2000-1214-19:08:08]: Sent ACK to: yyy.yyy.yyy.yyy:5678

[2000-1214-19:08:10]: ACTIVITY [2] from: yyy.yyy.yyy.yyy:5678 for UID 1

[2000-1214-19:08:10]: Sent ACTIVITY to: xxx.xxx.xxx.xxx:1234

[2000-1214-19:08:11]: Recvd IM_TEXT [**congrats**] from: yyy.yyy.yyy.yyy:5678 for UID 1

[2000-1214-19:08:11]: ACTIVITY [1] from: yyy.yyy.yyy.yyy:5678 for UID 1

[2000-1214-19:08:11]: Sent ACTIVITY to: xxx.xxx.xxx.xxx:1234

[2000-1214-19:08:11]: Sent IM_TEXT [congrats] to: xxx.xxx.xxx.xxx:1234

[2000-1214-19:08:11]: Recvd ACK (seq# 813) from: xxx.xxx.xxx.xxx:1234, destined for UID 3

[2000-1214-19:08:11]: Sent ACK to: yyy.yyy.yyy.yyy:5678

[2000-1214-19:08:14]: CLE [1 @ xxx.xxx.xxx.xxx:1234] : [0] SIM fc16d4e876756702f78af580c377c875 from TIM

[2000-1214-19:08:14]: Recvd IM_SOUND [fc16d4e876756702f78af580c377c875] from: xxx.xxx.xxx.xxx:1234 for UID 3

[2000-1214-19:08:14]: Sent IM_SOUND [fc16d4e876756702f78af580c377c875] to: yyy.yyy.yyy.yyy:5678

[2000-1214-19:08:14]: Recvd ACK (seq# 53179) from: yyy.yyy.yyy.yyy:5678, destined for UID 1

[2000-1214-19:08:14]: CLIENT_AI: [3 @ yyy.yyy.yyy.yyy:5678] : 3

[2000-1214-19:08:14]: Sent ACK to: xxx.xxx.xxx.xxx:1234

[2000-1214-19:08:15]: CLIENT_AI: [1 @ xxx.xxx.xxx.xxx:1234] : 2

[2000-1214-19:08:17]: ACTIVITY [2] from: yyy.yyy.yyy.yyy:5678 for UID 1

[2000-1214-19:08:17]: Sent ACTIVITY to: xxx.xxx.xxx.xxx:1234

[2000-1214-19:08:19]: ACTIVITY [2] from: xxx.xxx.xxx.xxx:1234 for UID 3

[2000-1214-19:08:20]: Sent ACTIVITY to: yyy.yyy.yyy.yyy:5678

[2000-1214-19:08:24]: Recvd IM_TEXT [**groan... icons are missing**] from: yyy.yyy.yyy.yyy:5678 for UID 1

[2000-1214-19:08:24]: Sent IM_TEXT [groan... icons are missing] to: xxx.xxx.xxx.xxx:1234

[2000-1214-19:08:24]: Recvd ACK (seq# 818) from: xxx.xxx.xxx.xxx:1234, destined for UID 3

[2000-1214-19:08:24]: Sent ACK to: yyy.yyy.yyy.yyy:5678

[2000-1214-19:08:27]: Recvd IM_TEXT [**and this is the new version**] from: yyy.yyy.yyy.yyy:5678 for UID 1

[2000-1214-19:08:27]: Sent IM_TEXT [and this is the new version] to: xxx.xxx.xxx.xxx:1234

[2000-1214-19:08:27]: Recvd ACK (seq# 819) from: xxx.xxx.xxx.xxx:1234, destined for UID 3

[2000-1214-19:08:27]: Sent ACK to: yyy.yyy.yyy.yyy:5678

[2000-1214-19:08:29]: CLIENT_AI: [3 @ yyy.yyy.yyy.yyy:5678] : 3

[2000-1214-19:08:30]: CLIENT_AI: [1 @ xxx.xxx.xxx.xxx:1234] : 3

[2000-1214-19:08:31]: Recvd IM_TEXT [**we need an "I have no response to that" button.**] from: xxx.xxx.xxx.xxx:1234 for UID

10.5

A processed log that shows only the messages relevant to one conversation between Walendo and Ellen. The script calculates when each person went idle by determining when five minutes have passed without activity information. This log makes it much easier to interpret the conversation and each user's activity during it.

Processed Hubbub Log

SIM: Sound Instant Message (Message displayed in quotes)
CLE: Client Log Entry
TIM: Text Instant Message (Message displayed in square brackets)

The text following the @ is that person's location at the time they sent the message

[19:08:01] TEXT: [Walendo @ [MP, x7753] => Ellen] [dubious has been up for 367 days!]

[19:08:08] SIM: [Ellen @ [Work (MP)] => Walendo] "Cool"

[19:08:11] TEXT: [Ellen @ [Work (MP)] => Walendo] [congrats]

[19:08:14] SIM: [Walendo @ [MP, x7753] => Ellen] "Thanks"

[19:08:24] TEXT: [Ellen @ [Work (MP)] => Walendo] [groan... icons are missing]

[19:08:27] TEXT: [Ellen @ [Work (MP)] => Walendo] [and this is the new version]

[19:08:31] TEXT: [Walendo @ [MP, x7753] => Ellen] [we need an "I have no response to that" button.]

[19:08:33] TEXT: [Ellen @ [Work (MP)] => Walendo] [sigh]

[19:08:40] TEXT: [Walendo @ [MP, x7753] => Ellen] [You sure it's the new one?]

[19:08:42] CLE: [Walendo @ [MP, x7753]] moved focus out of TIM with Ellen

[19:08:43] TEXT: [Ellen @ [Work (MP)] => Walendo] [8.2]

[19:08:45] CLE: [Walendo @ [MP, x7753]] moved focus into TIM with Ellen

[19:08:49] TEXT: [Walendo @ [MP, x7753] => Ellen] [that'd be it]

[19:08:52] CLE: [Walendo @ [MP, x7753]] closed TIM with Ellen

[19:08:52] CLE: [Walendo @ [MP, x7753]] moved focus out of TIM with Ellen

[19:08:52] SIM: [Ellen @ [Work (MP)] => Walendo] "Bummer"

[19:09:03] CLE: [Ellen @ [Work (MP)]] closed TIM with Walendo

[19:09:03] CLE: [Ellen @ [Work (MP)]] moved focus out of TIM with Walendo

[19:27:47] IDLE: Ellen

[19:30:45] IDLE: Walendo

We also used the logs to make many design improvements. Here's an example of a problem we were especially glad to catch. One manager (call her Cindy) typically kept Hubbub running all the time from work, and then she dialed up from home periodically and connected from the Palm when on the road or in a meeting. Once while on a trip, she connected through her Palm and sent a note to her administrative assistant (Maya) asking her to make an appointment. Maya wasn't at her desk, but later she saw the message. She ran into a problem making the appointment, so she sent a message back to Cindy, but by this time Cindy had logged off her Palm. Since she had kept Hubbub running at work, Maya's message went to Cindy's desktop. This meant that Cindy would not see the message until she came back from her trip, even though she checked in again from her Palm. Figure 10.6 shows the log of the interaction. This was a serious problem because Maya thought she had successfully sent a message, but Cindy had not received it. **[Don't Mislead]** This only needs to happen once or twice for people to lose confidence in the system. A butler would make sure the other person got the message. Even though we spent a lot of time imagining possible situations, this was a scenario we hadn't thought of.

10.6

The log of Cindy and Maya's conversations, which made us realize that it was possible for recipients to miss messages that the sender would think were received. Cindy sends Maya a request from her Palm in Vancouver, but Maya sends her reply when Cindy is not connected from her Palm, so the message goes to her work computer and Cindy doesn't see it when she connects again from her Palm later in the day, at 13:28:13. (This conversation also revealed a problem with Message windows not popping to the top, discussed later.)

SIM=Sound Instant Message
Gaps indicate more than five minutes have elapsed

[08:32:44] ACTIVE: Maya

[08:47:54] ACTIVE: Cindy

[08:48:46] TEXT: [Cindy @ Palm => Maya] [Hi]

[08:49:12] TEXT: [Cindy @ Palm => Maya] [I'm at the airport in vancouver]

[08:51:30] TEXT: [Cindy @ Palm => Maya] [Would you please call medical in basking ridge and find out if they give typhoid and polio booster shots? I think ian was going to get his shots for hong kong there.]

[08:52:20] TEXT: [Cindy @ Palm => Maya] [If they do,then please make an appt for me sometime ne]

[08:52:26] TEXT: [Cindy @ Palm => Maya] []

[08:52:44] TEXT: [Cindy @ Palm => Maya] [Xt week. Thanks]

[08:52:54] SIM: [Cindy @ Palm => Maya] "Hi"

[08:59:05] IDLE: Cindy

[09:02:29] IDLE: Maya

[09:04:44] ACTIVE: Cindy

[09:05:14] ACTIVE: Maya

[09:05:33] SIM: [Cindy @ Palm => Maya] "Hi"

[09:06:30] TEXT: [Cindy @ Palm => Maya] [Did you see my previous message?]

[09:09:23] SIM: [Cindy @ Palm => Maya] "Hi"

[09:09:28] SIM: [Cindy @ Palm => Maya] "Hi"

[09:13:44] IDLE: Maya

[09:14:46] IDLE: Cindy

[09:21:14] ACTIVE: Maya

[09:29:45] TEXT: [Maya @ work => Cindy] [I will call. My msgs. do not pop out on the screen. That would make me more alert to them.]

[09:37:46] TEXT: [Maya @ work => Cindy] [Left voicemail with the nurse. Will let you know the outcome]

[09:43:00] IDLE: Maya
[09:45:00] ACTIVE: Maya

[10:01:05] TEXT: [Maya @ work => Cindy] [You have appt. Tues, 9/19, 9:15 a.m.-will take 1/2 hr. Nurse Kate O'Leary checking your records and will give you what you need]
[10:01:42] TEXT: [Maya @ work => Cindy] [(She knows you requested typhoid and polio booster)]

[10:07:15] IDLE: Maya

[13:28:13] ACTIVE: Cindy

[13:34:52] IDLE: Cindy

We came up with an idea that has greatly increased Hubbub's support for mobility. Remember that the Hubbub server sends messages to the Last Active Client if one is active, or all clients if all are idle. We added a third case. If a bub receives a message and their next reported activity comes from a new client that did not receive the message, the server resends the message to the newly active client. With this change, the next time Cindy checked in with her Palm, the message would have been re-sent to her there. After we implemented this, we found other cases when it was helpful. For example, Ellen uses a desktop machine at home connected via a cable modem, but her work machine is a laptop, which she brings home with her every evening. If she receives a message on her desktop while traveling to work, she sees it when she boots up her laptop at work. **[Look for "Widgetless Features"]** Once we made this change, messages appeared to "follow you" wherever you went, which was the effect we wanted.

Usage Study Guideline
Log information is ideal for learning how frequently people use certain features and in what combination. It also reveals scenarios of use that you may not have imagined, and it can help you decide to remove features or not expand on them if they are rarely being used.

Other problems were easier to spot in the logs. We noticed a few cases when someone muted every person in their bub list one at a time. We had forgotten our own rule about making it easy to take the same action multiple times. So we added a way to mute all activity sounds at once. **[Treat Clicks as Sacred]** We also used the logs to confirm that we could safely remove a feature. During the initial design phase, we were concerned that people would hear some sounds but not know what they meant, so we provided a Last Sounds window/screen listing the last 10 sounds that had played. But on the PC client, we made other minor changes along the way that helped people identify the sounds as they arrived, so this window no longer seemed necessary. We checked the logs and indeed, few people had opened it more than once (presumably to see what it was), so we removed it. **[Use Visual Elements Sparingly]** What a nice feeling it was to be able to trim a feature with confidence before we shipped.

Formal Observation and Videotaping

Logs are invaluable for learning about frequency of use and for uncovering patterns across a broad range of use. But they don't give you a picture of what's going on in the world while the technology is being used. To learn that, you have to watch people. You can do this both formally and informally.

Depending on the technology, you might be able to arrange to have people use it while you're there (perhaps before you give them an update or conduct an interview). If your system runs on a desktop, it's usually easy to arrange to meet people at their workplace or home. For other types of devices, you might arrange to go for a drive with people who are using your car-based technology, attend an event with someone using your camera, watch TV with a family using your interactive TV device, and so on. While observing, it's critical that you fade into the background so you can see how people normally do things. Don't interrupt, just observe and make note of problems as well as tasks that go smoothly. (If the technology breaks down, you can fix it for them so that they can continue.) If the participants are willing, you might also videotape the event so you can look for subtler clues that you may not have noticed initially and so you can share the experience with other team members.

In other cases, you can't plan when study participants will use the tool, so you need to find a way to capture spontaneous use. This was our situation with Hubbub, which is intended to support background awareness and allow for opportunistic interactions. How can you arrange to observe that? In this case, you can arrange to have a video camera set up and let it run for a period of time when you're likely to capture use. (You'll probably need to drop by and change the tapes from time to time, or you can ask the participants to do it.) If they're in an area where others may enter, put up a sign indicating that the activity in that area is being videotaped and offer to delete parts of the tape if someone requests it. Some of your study participants may not want you to tape their activities, but usually you can find at least a few who are willing to let you do so. Once you collect the tapes, the usage tester reviews them and locates key instances when something went wrong or when someone did something interesting. These tapes can be very powerful because they allow the team to see realistic use and then solve problems with a rich (and shared) set of assumptions.

During the Hubbub study, we observed most people as part of an interview (described later), and we videotaped one person over a two-day period. We set up two video cameras in her office—one pointed at the screen and the other at her work area—which enabled us to capture eight conversations. We also saw cases where the awareness sounds had an effect. When an awareness sound played while someone was in her office, we got to see how she handled the interruption. These observations led to some important changes. One was in relation to the sound design. We had designed Hubbub so that if someone sent you a sound message, you would hear it and know what it meant with no effort, or you could glance at the window footer (shown in Figure 10.7) to see what it meant.

10.7

The original design called for a footer to appear when a sound message arrived, indicating its meaning so that we did not have to pop up a Message window when a conversation started with a sound. In use, we discovered that people did not always notice the sounds, so we popped up a Message window when either sound or text messages arrived, which worked better.

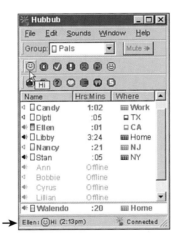

We liked this design, because it meant we could "say hi" to each other by using just the sounds, without having a window pop up on the screen. **[Use Visual Elements Sparingly]** But when we watched people, we saw that they didn't always discriminate between messages and activity sounds. We saw cases when someone started a conversation with the "Hi" or "Talk?" sound messages, but backed off when they got

Usage Study Guideline
Formal observations allow you to understand the context in which people use the technology, giving you a rich understanding of how people use the system for real tasks. They are especially helpful for finding subtle ways in which the design causes important usage problems.

no response, figuring the person was busy. But sometimes that person was on the phone or otherwise distracted (talking to us in an interview, for instance), so they didn't notice the sound. **[Make Common Tasks Visible]** That's fine for awareness sounds, but not for messages. Even though we as expert users weren't as happy about this, we decided to pop up the Message window (and open the Message screen on the Palm) displaying the sound message, just as we would if a conversation were started with a text message, making it easier for the recipient to respond. We decided not to make this behavior a preference because we didn't think people would look for a way to play the sounds without popping up a window. **[Keep Preferences to a Minimum]** Upon follow-up, we found that this design reduced the number of cases in which people missed messages.

Informal Observation and Conversation

In addition to observing with formal methods, it's helpful to drop by to chat with participants and informally observe them using the technology where possible. Often in this situation, people tell you interesting stories about using your technology. You might uncover problems, hear about successes, or even discover unexpected uses. All of that is precious information. If you notice interesting behavior in the logs, chat with the person responsible to get a better understanding of the situation and why they did what they did. You might follow up with someone who added comments to a survey (discussed in the next section) to find out more—and to convey that you really do read and value their survey input. We frequently saw people using Hubbub in California when we happened to be in or walking by someone's office. We also made periodic trips to New Jersey to observe use (and to track down bugs that showed up only on certain people's machines). In addition to interviewing participants there, we visited people and wandered the halls near people who used Hubbub to catch a glimpse of it in action.

We refined many features using this technique, including two that became quite popular. One was the Message window footer. You may recall that earlier we explained our misguided approach to showing the other person's status while in a conversation. The footer of the Message window showed their activity meter and text indicating where they had focus. By talking to people, we learned that they didn't understand how to combine the activity meter with the text information, and that they didn't realize that the term "have focus" indicated which window was selected. **[Explain in Plain Language]** One person suggested that we make the color of the window fade darker and lighter depending on whether the other person was focused in it and whether they were typing. We liked that this would be an instinctive, visual cue, since intensity maps nicely to level of interest. But it also seemed too abstract. So we stepped back and thought about what states we wanted people to know about. It came down to three: whether their bub was typing in the window, had focus in the window, or did not have focus in the window. We created three icons that visualized the status of the other person's window, so you get a gut-level interpretation of the meaning (see Figure 10.8). We also changed the wording of the text from "has focus in" to "is focused in," which seemed more like real English. (Not everyone likes that terminology, but we haven't come up with a clearly better way to phrase it. Any suggestions?)

10.8

We revised the design of the Message window footer after learning that people did not understand the one in the first version. The icons visually represent the status of the other person's window, which is reinforced by the text explanation on the PC (above). On the Palm (below) we had room for only the icons. People found this design much easier to understand and generally loved the feature.

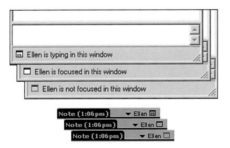

Another slight improvement to this feature occurred to us when we saw someone on the PC talking to a colleague on a Palm. Although the Main window indicates which device they're using, you don't notice that information when you're looking at the Message window. It is more difficult to enter text on a Palm than it is to type on a keyboard, so it helps to have a constant reminder of their status so that you appropriately interpret the lag and their "sloppiness." So we created three more icons to show the three levels of focus on the Palm (shown in Figure 10.9). **[Offer Sufficient Information Early and in Context]** (Later, when one of us switched from a Palm to a PC in mid-conversation, we realized that the icon on the other person's Message window needed to update as well.)

10.9

The icon in the Message window indicates which device the other person is on. This visual indicator is especially helpful when the other person is on a Palm because it reminds you that they cannot type as quickly and will probably make more typos.

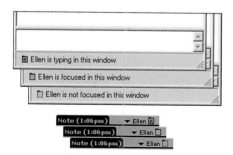

Finally, we discovered a much subtler problem that had interpersonal implications. When you send someone a message, the window pops up on their screen and takes focus,[4] so the footer indicates that they are focused in the window. However, in informal conversations, participants told us that when the recipient wasn't physically at their PC, they found it misleading to be informed that the person was focusing in their window. **[Don't Mislead]** It felt as though the person saw the message but wasn't responding, which made them feel subtly ignored. Even though this feeling came from a flaw in the design, people unconsciously attributed it to the other person. So we adjusted the feature to provide information about the other person's focus only after that person had clicked in the window. Until then, it indicates how long that person has been active or idle (see Figure 10.10), which might give people a sense of whether the person is likely to respond quickly. **[Request and Offer Only Relevant Information]** This tiny adjustment smoothed out the social dynamics of using Hubbub.

10.10

When you initiate a message with someone, the PC Message window footer indicates their active or idle status until they click in the window. We added this case to avoid leading people to believe that the other person was focused in the window when they were not even there.

---

[4]Despite many attempts, we have not been able to get the window to pop up without stealing focus, at least not consistently.

We would never have discovered these issues and refined the design to this level if we had not observed Hubbub over a long period of time in real use. If we had shipped with our original design, the window footer would have been a confusing feature. Instead, it has become one of Hubbub's most appreciated features. People frequently mention how helpful it is right away, and some have told us that they feel "blind" when interacting with someone through other instant messengers.

Another feature that underwent important changes based on informal observations is the location field.

During the design phase, we provided only four characters for location so that people could indicate their context (Home, Work, Mtg, and so on). Some colleagues had initially suggested providing more room to let people indicate things such as "Not available" or "Do not disturb," but we didn't think this was necessary. From our use of other instant messengers and some articles about other relevant systems, we knew that people hardly ever specified their status. Although it seems like a nice idea, most people don't think to update their instant messenger when they start a task and don't want to be interrupted. Besides, your willingness to be disturbed depends on who the person is, what they want to talk about, how much time it will take, and so on. Plus, the Palm screen allowed us only so much room for the location. For all these reasons, we went with a short location field.

In the first month or two of the study, one of our participants regularly entered interesting four-letter words in his location rather than using it to indicate his location. He set it to "rain" when it was raining, "farm" when he was working from his rural home, and "Mars" and "Moon" for reasons we don't know. What's more, people started talking about it. "Hey, did you see Josh's location yesterday? What did he mean by that?" People sent him messages to ask him about his location, which increased their contact with him. He told us he was frustrated that he had only four characters and he wanted more, and others concurred. Despite all our earlier reservations, we decided to increase the number of characters. Figures 10.11A and 10.11B show what the new main screens look like on the Palm and the PC. This was a significant change because it meant adjusting the protocol, and it meant that Palm users would see only the beginning of the location. We had to adjust the Palm design so that you'd see the rest of the location when you tapped on someone's name (see Figure 10.11C).

10.11

Once we extended the location field, people used it to post information about the weather or their status, or to send friendly messages ("have a nice weekend," for example) (A). A long location didn't work as well on the Palm (B), which cut off much of the message, forcing you to tap the name to see the full location (C). However, since more people used the PC version and even those who used the Palm spent more time on the PC, the tradeoff seemed worthwhile.

A

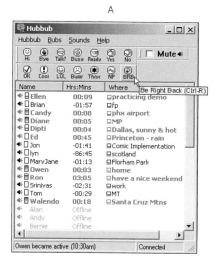

B

C

Usage Study Guideline
Try to chat with participants and observe their use informally, if possible. You may uncover problems, suggestions, or interesting new uses. It's helpful to check in with people informally to follow up on data from other sources, such as logs or surveys.

Once we extended the location field, it started to become a kind of "bulletin board" where people posted interesting information. People frequently indicated the weather in their part of the country, especially when it was unusual ("dreary, drippy"). When a blizzard hit the East Coast, some people used it to report how many inches of snow had accumulated ("19" of snow so far"), while those in California reported on the status of predicted power failures ("still no blackout!"). Some people made announcements ("UCLA by 8 at the half"), and others used it to amuse people ("in my coding jammies," from a programmer who worked at home). And of course people used it to provide information about their location ("Seattle hotel," "København," "phx airport") or status ("conf call--mute," "acl deadline"). It became a real community-building feature. In retrospect, we believe that the Hubbub location field was used more during the study than we'd seen it used on other IMs because it is visible all the time for every bub. You don't have to select each person one at a time and view the footer or pop up a window, you can just glance at the screen. You're also aware that everyone can see your location all the time, so it's more fun to post something interesting for people to see. Here was a feature we had not planned to provide, but watching real use over time convinced us to facilitate a naturally occurring behavior, making Hubbub more fun to use.

You can learn a lot from what people do, but you need to combine those observations with people's opinions, complaints, and suggestions. There are several methods for doing this, including surveys, interviews, and spontaneous suggestions.

Surveys

Surveys are useful for getting quantitative data about people's subjective reactions to each feature. They allow you to collect numerical ratings of each feature, which you can compare across features, across users, and across time if you administer the survey at different times during the project. In a survey or questionnaire, you ask people to rate or rank certain features along different dimensions, offer suggestions for improving them, and tell you about problems. Surveys are mostly multiple-choice, which are easier for people to complete, but it's good to include a few open-ended questions that give people a chance to say what they like and don't like. The multiple-choice questions should be designed to give you a quick sense of how people are reacting to the features, and the open-ended questions should help you understand why. We also like to offer a "Comments" area after each multiple-choice question just in case people want to say more. Your goal with the survey is not to get a large set of data and run statistics on it. It's to get feedback from your small sample of people in a way that's easy for them to provide and meaningful for you to analyze.

Figure 10.12 shows the survey we created for Hubbub. We sent it to everyone after they had been using Hubbub for one week and then again after either two months or four months of use so we could track progress over time without bothering people too many times. For the most part, we asked people to rate how useful they found each feature to be and gave them the opportunity to explain why. We were especially concerned that the sounds would annoy people, so we included two questions about it. We also asked for suggestions of new sound messages to create, since we weren't sure we had the right set. We asked what people liked most and least, and then gave them a place to tell us stories or give general feedback. We focused on collecting information we couldn't get from usage logs or observation. We also wanted to hear from people who used Hubbub rarely or had stopped using it so that we could learn why. Although some people may simply not have a need for a product, you can find out about important problems by questioning these users. (But do it only once so that you don't annoy them by asking for information that has not changed.) Most people filled out all of the multiple-choice questions and added comments on two or three of them, and about half of the people addressed the open-ended questions. While we would have loved more free-form input, it's quicker and easier for people to respond to multiple-choice questions, so make sure you can get meaningful answers from just those.

10.12

The survey sent to each Hubbub study participant after one week and then again after either two or four months. Each multiple-choice question includes a "Comments" area and the open-ended questions were filled out by about half of the people. We used the quantitative data to assess the effectiveness of the features and the qualitative data to guide our thinking on how to resolve problems.

Hubbub Survey

1. To what extent have you used Hubbub (had it running on your computer)?

    It's running all the time   5   4   3   2   1   I've barely used it

    If you answered 1 or 2, please explain why:

2. Hubbub plays "activity sounds" when people become active and idle on their computer, and you can choose whose activity sounds you hear.

    After using Hubbub for <about a week, a few months>, how many people's "activity sounds" do you have turned on (unmuted)? ____
    Do you listen to your own activity sounds? Yes   No

    Comments:

3. How many people's Sound IDs have you learned?

    I've learned [ ] people's Sound IDs with about 75% accuracy. Please name them:
    I've learned [ ] people's Sound IDs with 100% accuracy. Please name them:
    I've learned my own Sound ID with [ ] % accuracy

    Comments:

4a. How useful is it to hear people as they go active or idle?

    Very useful   5   4   3   2   1   Not at all useful
    0 = I don't listen to anyone's activity sounds

    Comments:

4b. How annoying is it to hear people as they go active or idle?

    Very annoying   5   4   3   2   1   Not at all annoying
    0 = I don't listen to anyone's activity sounds

    Comments:

5. How useful has it been to see who's active or idle (name in bold vs. regular type) on the main Hubbub window?

    Very useful   5   4   3   2   1   Not at all useful
    0 = I haven't used/noticed this feature

    Comments:

6. How useful has it been to see how many minutes people have been active or idle?

    Very useful   5   4   3   2   1   Not at all useful
    0 = I haven't used/noticed this feature

    Comments:

7. How useful has it been to see what device the person is on (Palm or PC) and where (Home, Work, etc.)?

    Very useful   5   4   3   2   1   Not at all useful
    0 = I haven't used/noticed this feature

    Comments:

8. How useful has it been to see how active each person has been over the past 15 seconds (using the activity meter)?

    Very useful   5   4   3   2   1   Not at all useful
    0 = I haven't used/noticed this feature

    Comments:

9a. How useful has it been to send and receive sound messages (i.e., the icons that send sounds to mean things like Hi, OK, LOL)?

    Very useful   5   4   3   2   1   Not at all useful
    0 = I haven't used/noticed this feature

    Comments:

9b. How annoying has it been to send and receive sound messages?

      Very annoying   5 4 3 2 1   Not at all annoying
      0 = I haven't used/noticed this feature

      Comments:

10. How many of the 14 sound messages do you think you've learned (just by hearing them) with about 75% accuracy? _____

      Which ones have you learned?

      Comments:

11. Were there any sound messages you wanted to send that were unavailable? If so, what were they?

12. How useful has it been to be able to communicate with people who are on a Palm?

      Very useful   5 4 3 2 1   Not at all useful
      0 = never did it

      Comments:

13. If you have Palm Hubbub, how useful has it been to be able to communicate with people when you are on the Palm?

      Very useful   5 4 3 2 1   Not at all useful
      0 = don't have a Palm

      Comments:

14. If you did interact with someone on a Palm or from a Palm, did you experience any problems or surprises? Please explain.

15. What aspect of Hubbub do you like best?

16. What aspect of Hubbub do you like least? How would you change or fix it?

17. Any stories you can tell us about good or bad experiences you've had so far?

18. Is there anyone you'd like us to add in our next round of expanding Hubbub usage?

Usage Study Guideline
Surveys can give you a systematic overview of participants' opinions of each feature, as well as their complaints and suggestions. It's good to follow up surveys with other information-gathering techniques to get a deeper understanding of any issues.

We found several interesting things from this survey when we administered it after one week of use. One of the major findings was that Hubbub had too many sounds. Several people mentioned that the sounds were overwhelming, but that didn't tell us how to address the problem. Two people said that it was frustrating to hear when someone went idle because it sometimes reminded them of something they wanted to say to that person just at a time when they were no longer available. **[Request and Offer Only Relevant Information]** They didn't understand why it would be useful to know when someone went away. We had hoped to simulate a real work setting where you might hear someone leave the area, letting you know that if you want to interact with them, you need to wait for them to come back or contact them in another way. Obviously it wasn't having that effect. We realized that if we removed the sounds that play when a bub goes idle, we would reduce the number of ambient sounds by about half and address the problem of too many sounds. It might even help people learn the other sounds more easily because there would be fewer to learn. So we removed them for the next release, a month later. We then followed up by asking people informally whether it was an improvement and nearly everyone said that it was. Only one person complained that he had liked hearing all the activity and now there was "less of a hubbub!"

Interviews

It's important to interview people during the study so that you can get a richer idea of their reactions than you can pick up from a survey. Do it periodically throughout the study, perhaps a few weeks after they've been using it, midway through the study, and then at the end. If you need to manually install each update, it makes sense to combine those trips with an interview. Prepare a list of questions, asking about all the features and focusing especially on the external circumstances surrounding their use of the features. Get them talking about specific times when they used the system for certain tasks and then keep following up so that you understand the details. Have them show you while they tell you about problems, so you're sure you understand the situation they're describing. (People often develop theories about why problems occur that may be inaccurate, so it's best to see them yourself.)

In our case, there were certain questions we could answer only through interviewing. One was about Hubbub's privacy implications, an important concern for a system that provides so much information about users' activity. We were especially interested to get reactions from the administrative assistants, who might feel overly exposed. All three of them told us that they were not concerned, and if anything, they were glad that people could see how hard they worked! We asked others whether they felt their manager was observing them, and the consensus was that people expected their managers to understand that they have many reasons to be working away from the computer. The managers in the group said they didn't make judgments about their employees based on Hubbub, although of course it's hard to know whether they subtly did without realizing it themselves. One manager did say he liked getting a global feel of activity in his group, and it felt good when there was lots of activity and a little disappointing when there was little, even though he knew why people might be away. A few people said they found the patterns of activity interesting, noting that some people seemed to work for long stretches at a time during business hours, whereas others seemed to be active on and off through the day and into the evening. We concluded that there's some potential for misinterpretation of behavior, but at least within this organization where trust is high, people seemed to take the information in context.

Based on these interviews and on general observations of use, we decided that we should allow people to block others' access to their activity information and location, but we no longer thought it was necessary to allow people to block a bub from sending a text or sound message, which had been on our Important list. The only hints of concern we detected were about observing activity and location; no one seemed to mind getting messages. Also, since Hubbub membership is reciprocal, people can prevent someone from sending them messages by removing that person from their list, which would take their own name off of that person's list. Interestingly, once we did implement the ability to block access to activity information and location, the logs showed no instances when it was used during the usage study. Still, since this population may not be typical, and since it's better to err on the side of protecting privacy, we left the feature in.[5]

Sometimes, we "interviewed" people by phone or in person by asking them to comment about a specific feature or issue. Each time you find a problem, you try to find the best solution but you don't know for sure

---

[5] Once we made Hubbub more widely available, we saw a smattering of cases when people blocked a bub's access to their location and/or activity.

whether it works until you try it out. After releasing new versions, contact people to ask them about a specific feature to see whether you have solved the problem (as long as you don't bother any one person too often). Here's a case where we used a "one-feature interview." In Chapter 8, we explained that it's important to let people know whether each message has been received so that people don't misinterpret pauses or failures to respond. Our solution was to show a message in the upper pane of the Message window only after the other person had received it (when the client had received an ACK from the recipient's client). On the Palm, this seemed to work well because it was natural to see delays with the wireless connection. But on a PC, it was disconcerting to get a delayed response (the delays when interacting with someone on a Palm were typically half a second or more). We came up with the following solution: When you send a message, it immediately appears in gray type in the message area so that you know it was sent, and then it turns blue when the other person receives it (see Figure 10.13). If you're interacting with someone on another PC, this happens so fast that you don't notice it, but if the other person is on a Palm, you get a good sense of the pace of the transport. **[Show Signs of Progress]** We implemented it and liked the result, but we were unsure whether to include it because we were exposing technical issues and we weren't sure whether people would understand the meaning of text changing from gray to blue. We figured we'd try it out, and if it confused people we'd try something else.

A

B

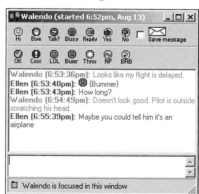

10.13

When you send a text message from the PC, the text appears immediately in the conversation area in gray type to let you know it was sent (A), and it turns blue once it is received by the other person (B). Although we had doubts about this design, we discovered in interviews that people instinctively understood its meaning. This feature was very effective in helping people coordinate their conversations even when one or both had a low-speed or intermittent connection.

Usage Study Guideline
Interviews allow you to get detailed information about people's attitudes and opinions of the system after they've used it for a while, which you may not be able to find out any other way. You can also do quick interviews on a single topic to find out how people are reacting to new features or feature redesigns.

Much to our surprise, the feature worked exactly as we'd hoped. After we released the feature, we contacted several people to find out their reaction to it. Nearly everyone we asked instinctively understood the colors, and some people said they loved it. They said that the gray felt "incomplete" somehow and that it was satisfying when it turned blue. People especially liked knowing right away if there was a problem with the connection. They might send a message just as someone disconnected or went out of coverage, and they knew the message was "in limbo" right away, so they stopped sending more messages and waited to see whether the message got through. As with many successful features, this one was helpful in other situations. Sometimes people who were using dial-up modems downloaded Web pages while having a Hubbub conversation. The extra network traffic had a visible effect on the speed of the Hubbub message transport, and people adjusted rather than wondering why the other person was so unresponsive. This approach was so successful that we wanted to adjust the Palm accordingly. We couldn't use color or italics because they were not supported.[6] We considered putting square brackets around the messages, but that would require redrawing the screen to remove the brackets when the message was received, which would slow down the system. (It seemed unlikely that anyone would send a message encased in square brackets.) In the end, we changed the label of the "Send" button to "Send…" until the message was displayed. It was only a subtle change, but we couldn't find a better solution, and delaying the message display seemed to be working sufficiently. Still, it's on our list of things to improve.

Participant Suggestions and Complaints

While you're running the study, make it easy for people to contact you if they're experiencing problems. The participants will appreciate the support and you'll get valuable information. You especially want to capture those little ideas that occur to people but then fade away if they are not written down. We mentioned that we created an e-mail address for the Hubbub team, and we made a link to it on the Web site.

---

[6] As we mentioned earlier, some Palms now support color, but at the time none did. Also, color models use up batteries much faster, so they are not appropriate for an "always on" application—at least not yet. We could also add our own italic font, but we haven't tried that yet.

Since Hubbub is designed for lightweight communication, we also put all three of us (Ellen, Alan, and Dipti) on everyone's bub list and told people to contact us for any reason. That seemed like enough, but it wasn't. Early in the study, one participant suggested that we add a menu item on the PC client to send feedback. In the next version, we included a Send Feedback item in the Help menu that opened a small e-mail window pre-addressed to us. This way, when people had an idea, they didn't have to remember the e-mail address or go to the Web page. **[Respect Mental Effort | Respect Physical Effort]** They just chose a menu item from within the application and typed. That feature is still in Hubbub and continues to be used. (A great side effect is that, since the e-mail is generated from inside Hubbub, we can include other diagnostic information, such as which version of Windows they're running—a suggestion that came from yet another user.) Here's a case where collecting ideas from users helped us get better at collecting ideas from users.

We made quite a few changes based on participants' suggestions. An early one came about when people were learning each other's Sound IDs. Right away, people told us they wanted to be able to play someone's Sound ID at any time to find out what it was and to learn it. Initially, the only time you heard a Sound ID was when a bub became active or sent you a message. So in the next release, we added a mechanism to play someone's Sound ID. As soon as that was released, people said they also wanted to be able to see the name of the song because it was sometimes hard to place the tune without seeing its name. We had been planning to provide that information in a bub Info pop-up on the PC, but we decided to display the song name in the footer any time you played a Sound ID, saving the user a couple of clicks. **[Treat Clicks as Sacred]** One participant told us that she liked seeing the time when a message arrived in the header of the Message window, but she also wanted to see the date. She said she had once been away from the office for two days and when she came back, she couldn't tell how long the messages had been there. This scenario might not happen that often, but it's a simple fix and doesn't overly clutter the screen, so we did it.

One important word of caution: Be careful when interpreting partic-ipants' suggestions. Often when people experience a problem, they tell you they want a feature that they think would solve that problem rather than telling you the problem. But they don't have all the information

Usage Study Guideline
Make it easy for participants to send you comments and suggestions. If they send you feature ideas, your job is to find out the problem they're trying to solve. Users can give you great insights into problems, but they are not designers. You are in a better position to figure out how to create a solution that fits with the rest of the design.

you have about the rest of the system, and they are not designers. They may propose a design that would be just as confusing to other people or would be costly to implement. When your users suggest features, your job is to find out what problem they're trying to solve. Find out when the problem occurs and what they're trying to accomplish with their solution. Many times, you'll come up with a different way to address it that is more consistent with the design. If you do, ask the person who reported the problem whether your solution will work for them. Maybe they forgot to mention another aspect of the problem that isn't addressed by your solution, so you may need to keep adjusting. People are usually happy to accept another solution, especially if you involve them in the process, so don't worry that they'll think you're unreceptive if you don't do just what they asked. The challenge is in working together to find a solution that meets the user's needs, is consistent with the rest of the design, and can be realistically implemented.

Here is an example of how we turned a number of feature requests into a different feature that we think addressed the underlying problems. In an interview, one administrative assistant told us that she once set up an appointment for her boss through Hubbub, but then she forgot to enter it into his calendar. She asked us if we could notice calendar appointments in Hubbub messages and add them to the calendar. We didn't think we could parse free-form text to detect calendar appointments, and we doubted people would insert calendar templates while in a conversation, but we noted the problem. Later, a couple of other people asked for a Save button on the Message window to save conversations to a file. We asked them when they had wanted this feature, and both said that they had wanted to save information in a message while the conversation was in progress, but then they closed the window before remembering to copy it down. It seemed as if they really needed a way to automatically save messages. Finally, another clever user suggested an interesting idea. He noticed that he couldn't always remember whether certain conversations had been in e-mail or in IM. He wanted to save his IM conversations with his e-mail, not in a separate file. So he suggested putting a button on the Message window to e-mail the conversation to yourself.

We put all of these suggestions together to come up with a feature. We liked the idea of saving messages with e-mail, since that's where people already keep track of previous communications. But if we put a Save as

E-mail button on the Message window, people would sometimes forget to use it until after they had closed the window. We wanted it to happen automatically but allow people to opt out. We realized that having messages automatically e-mailed might have helped the administrative assistant, who would have been reminded of the appointment when she saw the IM conversation in her e-mail. So we came up with the design shown in Figure 10.14A. If the check box is on, the contents of that window are e-mailed to you as soon as you close the window. **[Respect Mental Effort]** This way, as soon as someone says something you want to save, you can check the box and forget about it; you don't have to remember to save it at the end of the conversation. After you close that conversation window, its contents arrive in your e-mail inbox.

10.14

Based on user input, we added a feature to allow you to e-mail messages to yourself when you close a Message window. The check mark allows you to indicate that you want to save a conversation at any point so you don't have to remember to do it when the conversation is over (A). We made this feature a Preference, but we tried to make it easy to find and set by putting it in the Hubbub menu (B) rather than inside a Preferences window.

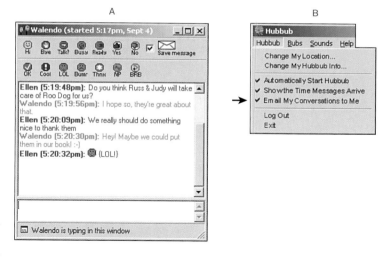

We figured that some people would want to save all of their conversations, but others, especially heavy users, would be annoyed if their e-mail inbox filled up with all of their conversations. Both scenarios seemed pretty likely and we couldn't think of a way to know who would want which, so we broke down and added a preference. **[Keep Preferences to a Minimum; Give Smart Defaults]** We set the default to On, which means that the check box on all Message windows will be checked, but you can uncheck one at any point in the conversation if you don't want it saved. Since few people look for Preferences when they are annoyed by a system's behavior, we didn't bury the option inside a Preferences window. We put it in the Hubbub menu so people would have a better chance of stumbling across it and realizing that they can change it (see Figure 10.14B). Once we released the new feature, people commented on the convenience of saving IMs with e-mail (sometimes in responses to us and sometimes in conversations with each other, which we saw in the logs), although we also saw conversations in which people complained that the e-mails were annoying. This seems to justify leaving it as a Preference. Our initial plans didn't include saving messages, but after considering the problems people were having and the features they actively missed, we decided to include a feature that distinguishes Hubbub from other IMs.

Here's another example of why you don't necessarily want to implement features just as your users request them. In an early version of Hubbub, a bug was causing new Message windows to pop up behind other windows instead of on top of them. People felt bad that they were missing messages and possibly insulting people by not responding. In the next iteration, we fixed the bug and made sure that windows popped to the top, but still people said that they sometimes missed Message, and indeed the logs still showed conversations with apologies. (Maya mentioned this problem in the conversation log shown in Figure 10.6.) We discovered that some users were leaving their Message windows open even after their conversations had ended. If the other person sent them another message an hour or so later, the window would not pop to the top because it already existed on their screen. One of our users asked us to pop the window to the top every time she got a message. If we had done that, people could not have multitasked while in a conversation—their cursor would be repeatedly pulled back to the Message window when they were trying to do something else. [Don't Impose] Instead, we decided to flash the window header and its representation in the Windows task bar if a message arrived while you had focus elsewhere. It wouldn't steal your focus but it would call your attention to it, even if you had the window closed. It would stop flashing as soon as you clicked in the window. [Make Common Tasks Visible | Respect Mental Effort] This seemed to work for most people. One user still sometimes missed messages because she mainly worked on a Unix machine and only glanced at her PC when she heard a message, which might be buried below another window. We decided that this was a relatively uncommon case and we didn't want to be even more insistent about forcing people's attention to the

Message windows. Since the logs were no longer showing other people apologizing for missing messages, we decided that our design had solved the problem for most users while keeping distractions down. (We have considered popping the window to the top if a certain amount of time has passed since the last message, but we would need to try it to know whether it usually has the right effect.)

Combining Data Sources

Sometimes diagnosing a problem and devising a good solution requires using a combination of clues from different sources. You can feel a little like a detective tracking down the clues to a crime!

Here's how we found one important problem as a result of troubleshooting requests and both formal and informal observations of use. We designed the sound buttons as icons with ToolTips providing the labels, which kept the window size nice and compact, as shown in Figure 10.15A. After a few weeks, one participant asked us how she could find the button labels. It turned out that ToolTips were not displayed on her system on any application that was not a part of Microsoft Office. This was a strange bug, and we couldn't find a solution right away, so we sent her a piece of paper showing the icon labels to tape to her monitor as a short-term fix. Then while watching someone use Hubbub, we noticed her trying to view the ToolTips when Hubbub was not the selected window. For some reason, Windows doesn't display ToolTips if the window isn't selected. Finally, Ellen happened to see someone in her office sending a Hubbub message. She wanted to send a sound message so she grabbed her mouse and started dragging it across all the icons to see each label, which took far too long. She gave up and typed the word instead. We realized that when someone is in a conversation, they don't have time to hunt for the message they want, and they can't easily learn the icons because the labels aren't visible. Labels would allow people to find the sound messages they wanted quickly and would avoid the problem of ToolTips not appearing. **[Make Common Tasks Visible | Respect Physical Effort]** This seems obvious now, but we didn't realize it up front because we were concerned about not hogging too much space on people's computer screens. We didn't notice the problem ourselves because we had learned the meaning of the icons. We added the labels, and even managed to make them fairly small, as shown in Figure 10.15B. (If we were to internationalize this interface, the buttons would probably get wider, but we know the extra space would be well spent.) After we changed the design, the logs showed an increase in the number of sound messages sent, so we had evidence that the change was effective.

10.15

In our initial design of the PC main window (A), we chose not to include labels on the sound message buttons to keep the window as small as possible. When we discovered that some people could not view ToolTips and that people couldn't find the button they wanted quickly enough, we added the labels (B). This increased the size of the window, but the extra space greatly increased the usefulness of the buttons.

A

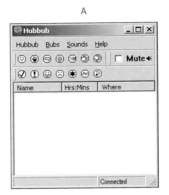

B

We used two types of data from the logs plus the surveys to iterate on the sound messages. We had started with 14 sound messages, which were based on our experience with instant messaging and chat conventions, but we assumed that we would need to change some after we learned which ones were used in practice. First we looked at the logs to see how frequently each sound message was used. We found that "Hi," "Bye," and "OK" were by far the most commonly used, and most of the rest were used regularly, but that "Eat?," "Five Minutes," and "??" were hardly ever used. Then we looked at the one-week surveys to see what messages people said they would like. The most common request was "Cool," and there were several suggestions with only one or two mentions. We also looked at the conversation logs, since we had noticed instances when someone said something like, "they should have a sound for 'No Problem.'" This was great evidence that they had looked for the sound but hadn't found it. We found several "requests" for either "No Problem" or "You're Welcome," which were also mentioned in the survey. We also noticed that people would often start a conversation with a "Hi" sound, and get a response such as, "hang on, I'm on the phone," or "someone's in my office." We thought it would be helpful to have a sound message to indicate that you couldn't interact right then. We came up with "Busy" to capture a range of situations. So we went back to the mixing board and came up with some new sounds and icons and added them to the next release. Figure 10.15B shows the final set of sounds. After we made the change, "Cool" and "No Problem" ranked in the middle in usage, although "Busy" wasn't as commonly used.

Changes Based on the Usage Study

Even though we've explained a number of examples in detail, these are just a few of the many adjustments we made to Hubbub during the usage study. As this sample indicates, we spent a lot of time refining the features we had already "finished." We also added new features that we had not anticipated, many of them resulting from careful analysis of multiple problems. With each release, we also added a small number of features we had already planned to implement, sometimes because they were obviously needed (for example, a way to create an account and add or remove bubs), but sometimes only after we confirmed that they were needed (a way to mute individual bubs, for instance). Figure 10.16 shows the list of features we changed during this phase. This time we made many more changes than we had during development and after we had started using it ourselves. We either modified or removed 39% of the items in the Functional Requirements, compared with 15% based on development issues and 11% based on our usage. Of the requirements left on the list, 24% of them were new items we had not anticipated when we started (compared with 2% and 0%, respectively). Clearly, the usage study played a significant role in improving Hubbub.

10.16

The changes we made after observing people using Hubbub. We made many more changes at this stage than we did during the implementation phase and after using it ourselves, and the changes were much more substantive. Most of them focused on refining a feature to make it smoother to use or adding features in response to needs that we had not anticipated. We also learned which features we could remove or safely postpone until later.

Changes After Observing Others

Changed

PC Client

Added text labels to sound message buttons
Made sure to pop window to the top when message arrived
When new message arrives when window already open, window header flashes and window entry in Task Bar flashes until user clicks in window

Palm Client

Changed icon for sound menu on Palm to a musical note
Can view all conversation partners' status (typing, focused, not focused) from Main screen
Header doesn't flash with activity updates if you're on a text entry screen
Handled new password on Palm when changed on Web site

Web Site

Put all administration and privacy features on the Web
Only included ability to block access to activity and location, not sending sound and text messages

Both Clients

Created the states typing, focus, and no focus, with an icon to go with each
Changed the icon to show which device the other person was on
Expanded location to 24 characters
Popped open a text window/created a text screen when a sound arrived, rather than just playing the sound

Added

PC Client

Show the name of a SID in the footer when you played it from the menu
Added ToolTips to explain meaning of time field, full name, meaning of icons
Added ability to play someone's Sound ID from a menu

Added keyboard shortcuts to sound messages
Added ability to tell when message arrives (gray to blue)
Header time stamp
Message time stamp (Preference)
Added Send Feedback window
Added e-mail messages to myself (Preference)
Added auto-start Hubbub (Preference)
Added prompt for location on startup (Preference)

Palm Client

Added send e-mail if bub is offline
Added icon to show status of connection
Changed "Send" button to "Send..." until the message was received

Web Site

Ability to log off Web site
Added ability to get back to download page once you're already logged on

Both Clients

Added ability to mute/unmute all bubs at once (three mute states on Palm)
Added message is re-sent if no ACK arrives
Update icon if person moved from one device to another
Resend messages sent to active client when next activity is from new client
If conversation partner went offline, text message appeared saying so after 1 minute

Removed

PC Client

Recent Messages window

Web Site

Ability to specify privacy settings when you add a bub
Per person, ability to specify whether you want to:
    Accept text messages (per person)
    Accept sound messages (per person)

Both Clients

Play sound when any bub goes idle
Ability to choose which device to send message to (if other person is on more than one)

Postponed

Palm Client

For other IMs not visible, ability to tell
> Whether they've sent a contribution to which you haven't responded
> Time stamp of when first message in conversation arrived

Both Clients

Ability to manually order bubs
Possibly, sound to indicate what device they came on/went off (device sound)
For each group, an indication of the group's average level of activity
Ability to compose new Sound IDs and Sound Instant Messages
Ability to hear what your new sound will sound like on a Palm and a PC
Ability to import new sounds into Hubbub
Ability to send new sound messages to others
Multi-way messaging
Ability to create groups
Ability to add/remove people to/from groups
Ability to see who is messaging with whom
For each group, an indication of the group's average level of activity
Sound when someone changes location

Deciding When You're Done

Usage Study Guideline
You're done with a usage study when you have gone through the list of Core and Important requirements and either checked off every item or explained why it is not needed. If people are able to use the system easily and smoothly to do a useful range of activities, you can ship. You will probably want to add or improve some features, but you can do that in the next release.

It's difficult in any development project to know when you're "done" and it's time to ship. Usually, there is pressure to ship by a certain date, so you may be done when that date comes. A usage study can make it easier to know when you're done, because you have direct evidence indicating whether your system is "good enough." You should be able to look at each feature in your Core and Important lists and either check it off or state with confidence why you don't need it now or at all. If people are able to use the system easily and smoothly to do a useful range of activities, you can ship. You may not have all the features you want, but you'll know you're offering the features people want most. If your technology is successful in the market (and the ease with which people can use it plays a role in that), you'll have an opportunity to improve the product and incorporate yet more feedback from real customers in the next release. The iterative process continues.

The Effect of Iterative Design

As you've seen, the iterative design process had a major impact on Hubbub—both on the features it included and on its design. If we look at the version we released and consider how many items in the Functional Requirements changed at any point during the process, we find that 57% were modified or removed and 19% were postponed; only 24% of the items in the Functional Requirements were implemented as originally designed. Of the features that appeared in the first release, 26% were new items that we had not originally planned to include. Figure 10.17 shows the original prioritized Functional Requirements for Hubbub modified to indicate which items we changed, added, removed, and postponed at any stage in the process. As you can see, the first release included all Core functionality, most of the Important functionality, and very few of the Nice to Have items. The vast majority of requirements changed significantly in their design. We added quite a few items, mostly in the Important and Nice to Have categories. (We categorized these items by judging how we would have classified them had we included them in the original list.) We removed several requirements from both the Important and Nice to Have lists, and we postponed most of the Nice to Have items that we didn't remove outright.

10.17

The Functional Requirements modified to show how Hubbub changed during the Iterative Design and Development process. The final product included all of the Core requirements and most of the Important ones, but few of the Nice to Have items made it in. Instead, we added quite a few items based on evidence from the usage study. The design of the vast majority of the requirements changed during the process.

Changes to Hubbub Functional Requirements

Functionality that was included in the final version essentially as designed
Functionality that was included but that changed significantly in its design
New functionality
~~Removed functionality~~
Postponed functionality

Core Functionality

Can't meaningfully start using application without:

Bub list
Indication of whether each bub is active, idle, or offline
Indication of how long each bub has been active or idle
Sound ID for each bub
Sounds to indicate when someone starts using computer (active sound) ~~and goes idle (idle sound)~~
Visual indication of who went active/idle (to learn meaning of sounds)
Ability to play and see the name of anyone's Sound ID at any time
Ability to send and receive sound messages
Visual indication of meaning of incoming sounds and who sent them
Ability to Mute All
Ability to send and receive text messages
Visual indication of incoming text messages and who sent them
Sound to announce arrival ~~(and maybe sending)~~ of each text contribution
Ability to run Hubbub on a wireless device and a PC
Ability to stay logged in from multiple clients at once
Messages automatically "find you" as you move from device to device

Important Functionality

Can't ship without:

Indication of which device each bub is on or was last on
Indication of each bub's location
For active bubs, indication of level of activity:
    Current level
    ~~Average over some period~~

Sounds to indicate when someone starts or exits Hubbub (login sound, logoff sound)

Ability to tell if bub's device is muted

Ability to mute each bub's activity sounds

Log of last *N* incoming sound messages (*Removed on the PC client*)

Ability to visually differentiate each person's text

Indication of bub's window focus and typing activity during conversations

Indication of bub's device while in a conversation

Ability for sender of messages to tell when the other person receives them

Ability for recipient of messages to tell when they arrived

Indication if other person's goes offline while in a conversation

Ability to have multiple IMs at once

Ability to tell status of connection on Palm

Ability to choose which device to send message to (if bub is on more than one)

Ability to download and install the application

Ability to register for an account

Ability to choose a Hubbub name and password

Ability to change your Hubbub name

Ability to change your password

Ability to choose a sound to represent you (Sound ID)

Ability to change your Sound ID

Ability to label the device

Ability to change device label

Auto-login when you log on/turn on device

Manual logon/off

Ability to add bubs (requires permission)

Ability to remove bubs

Ability to grant/deny permission to add

Ability to log off administration Web site

Ability to download application multiple times with one registration

Reciprocal bub membership

Ability to specify privacy settings when you add a bub

Per person (and across clients), specify whether you want to:

    Provide active/idle info (per bub)

    Provide location info (per bub)

    Accept text messages (per bub)

    Accept sound messages (per bub)

    Provide info about whom you're messaging with

Online help

Ability to send in feedback and suggestions about Hubbub

Log of user actions (for usage study)

Nice to Have Functionality

Great feature ideas that you can ship without. Evidence from real use can tell you whether to include them:

Ability to save messages
Preference to start up automatically
Prompt for location on start up (for laptops)
E-mail messages if bub is offline
Preference for recipient to see the time each message arrives
Possibly, sound to indicate what device each bub became active on (device sound)
Ability to manually order bubs within list
~~Sound to indicate when someone moves into or out of a "special zip code"~~
~~Sound to indicate when someone gets on/off a call~~
Ability to compose new Sound IDs
Ability to compose new Sound Instant Messages
Ability to test new sounds on Palm and PC
Ability to import new sounds message into Hubbub
Ability to send new sound messages to bubs
For other IMs not visible on Palm, ability to tell
    Window focus and typing status of bub
    Whether they've sent a contribution to which you haven't responded
Time stamp of first message in conversation
~~Ability to see who is messaging with whom~~
Multi-way messaging
Ability to create groups
Ability to add/remove people to/from groups
Indication of each group's average level of activity
Tutorial for learning sounds

To get a visual sense of how much Hubbub changed, take a look at Figures 10.18–10.22, which show the original design mock-up of each of the main Hubbub screens compared with a snapshot of the design of the first release.

10.18

Before and After pictures of the Hubbub Main screen on the PC. The biggest changes included adding labels to the sound buttons, changing which sound messages were provided, reducing the amount of color, extending the location field, removing the groups feature, removing the Self pane, adding more information in the footer, and moving all of the account setup and administration features to the Web.

Before

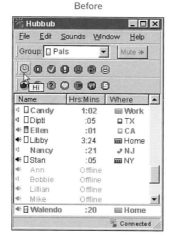

After

10.19

Before and After pictures of the Hubbub Message screen on the PC. The biggest changes included adding labels to the sound buttons, playing the sound messages when they are sent in addition to when they are received, revising the design of the footer status messages, showing which device the other person is using, adding the ability to e-mail messages to yourself, adding a timestamp to messages, and changing the text from gray to blue when the message is received.

Before

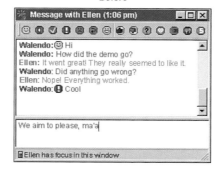

After

Before   After

10.20

Before and After pictures of the Hubbub Main screen on the Palm. The biggest changes included extending the location field, adding the ability to mute all activity sounds in one click, showing the status of the connection, removing the groups feature, making the activity meter wider and the device icons a uniform width, and moving all of the account setup and administration features to the Web.

Before   After

10.21

Before and After pictures of the Hubbub Bub screen on the Palm. The biggest changes included adding a field to modify your location, changing which sound messages are provided, and allowing users to e-mail a bub who is offline.

Before   After

10.22

Before and After pictures of the Hubbub Message screen on the Palm. The biggest changes included providing information about the other person's activity and device next to their name, playing the sound messages when they are sent in addition to when they are received, preventing activity messages from flashing (and stealing focus) when you are on this screen, and changing the icon for the Sounds menu.

Now that we've seen Hubbub in use, we cringe at the thought of shipping it looking and behaving as originally designed, even though at the time we thought the design was pretty good. Our iterative user-centered design process allowed us to catch many problems and refine many features that would have made Hubbub clunky to use. Without it, we would have had to make these changes in the next release, after people had already had bad experiences with the system and while the pressure was on to add new features rather than fix existing ones. Still, even with all this design iteration, there are plenty of features we would love to add and too many features that still are not right.[7] We are still in search of graceful and practical solutions for some problems; others are just a matter of doing the work.

Usage Study Guideline
Usage studies do not have to extend the development cycle; instead, they allow you to do fewer features well, with confidence that you have included the features people really use. They do require more time and energy from the designer and a usage study tester, but that effort keeps the rest of the team focused on the tasks that matter most to users.

We hope that we have demonstrated how powerful usage studies can be in allowing you to vastly improve the quality of your product. Including a usage study does not extend the development cycle—it reallocates the time so that you spend it building and improving features people really use instead of building features that you initially thought were important and then moving on. You ship with fewer features, but you know that you have the right ones. (The Hubbub study took only about five months, which is about how long it would have taken to implement the features originally planned.) Yes, usage studies do take time and effort from a dedicated usage tester, and the designer must stay with the project through the end, but their efforts ensure that the rest of the team spends its time and effort wisely. The engineers continue to implement features as usual, but much more of their code is written to refine existing features than to add new ones. Use the usage study as your strategic guide. Let it tell you which features are needed; don't add features just because they were included on your original list when you had less information. Your customers will be happy to have fewer features that are easier to use, as long as they are the ones they need. After you ship, you'll be in a position to start working on the next tier of features and improvements, rather than using the next release to fix the problems discovered after your first release.

[7] No doubt, readers of this book who download Hubbub will find problems; we welcome feedback about them.

CHAPTER 11
Conclusion

We've described in great detail our approach to user-centered design, at least as we applied it while building Hubbub. You may be wondering how realistic it is for you to do user-centered design. Your situation and your technology are no doubt different from those of our small team at AT&T that built an end-user communication system. How much of this approach can you apply to your process? We can't know your situation, but we do know that we have been able to apply user-centered design to a variety of projects and we've seen it done by others in quite different situations.

The three most important components of the user-centered design process are

1. Understanding why and how people currently carry out the task your technology will support

2. Designing the user interface first and building the architecture to support it

3. Studying the technology in use during development (preferably by conducting a usage study) and repeatedly iterating the system based on the feedback

Doing all three greatly increases your chances of building something that behaves like a butler. Even if you can't do all three thoroughly, it's hard to imagine a development project that can't accommodate at least two of these steps. If yours doesn't, then you may have to admit that you're abandoning the goal of creating cooperative technology.

In the next two sections, we briefly summarize two very different projects that we worked on that employed user-centered design concepts to varying degrees. Like the Hubbub project, these projects might not have all the same characteristics as yours, but you'll see how the process can vary depending on the type of technology, the team, and the circumstances. Perhaps you'll get some ideas that you can apply to your situation.

Example 1: Forum

While at Sun, Ellen worked with a small team of engineers to build an application for giving live video-based presentations to audiences who watched from their computers over the network. The application was called Forum and it ran on Sun workstations over a multicast network. We carried out all three major components of the user-centered design process, and the usage study was especially powerful in shaping the design of the technology. This project was conducted by a small team with two main engineers and help from a third, a UI designer, and a part-time graphic designer, and it took about a year. We describe this example mainly because we did a systematic task analysis and because the usage study was unusual.

Understanding the Task

To understand how to support presentations, the team attended several talks and observed speakers and audiences. Team members interviewed people known to be good speakers, and asked a variety of people what they look for when they attend a presentation. Based on that, we came up with a list of tasks and a set of requirements. One of the most important things we learned was that we should focus on allowing people to interact with the speaker and with other audience members. We also realized that it was important to enable speakers to get ongoing feedback from the audience, although we weren't sure how to do that with a distributed audience.

Designing the UI

Ellen worked with the graphic designer to design the user interface, spending about a month while the engineers finished up their previous project. Then the engineers designed an architecture to support the UI. In this case, we designed the interface in a Unix-based GUI builder available at the time called DevGuide, which allowed designers to lay out an interface using real UI widgets and even build in some simple behaviors. This interface tool was wonderful because it did not require the designer to understand programming, and yet it produced working UI code. Once coding began, the engineers wrote some scripts to postprocess the code produced by the tool to match their coding conventions. This tool enabled Ellen to make changes to the design throughout the process. It was especially helpful that she could make layout adjustments herself rather than bothering the engineers, who had more substantive issues to worry about.

Running a Usage Study

We conducted an unusual usage study. Since Forum was designed for presentations, we had to try it out by giving real talks. Once we had the Core features (namely transmitting video and audio from the speaker to the audience), we started by having our manager talk to the group through Forum while we watched from our desktops. It was primitive, but it was exciting to see something working. Once we fixed the major bugs and got it running reliably, we gave another talk, this one about a real topic and to a slightly expanded audience of close colleagues. As we got a few more features working, we established a weekly talk series. We started by inviting colleagues to give real presentations about their work or even their hobbies and we gradually invited a larger audience. Everyone who signed up for the talks knew that they were testing an application, but they signed up only if they were interested in the topic. During each talk, we videotaped the speaker plus one or two willing audience members watching the talk in their office. We interviewed each speaker after the talk, sent out periodic surveys to audience members, and had many hallway conversations with people who had used it. Ellen went through the tapes and surveys, and every week or so the team got together to go over findings and to look at video highlights of people using a particular feature or having trouble with a task. Then we brainstormed solutions to try in future presentations. This process continued for about six months and culminated in a presentation by our company's CEO to most of the employees in the engineering and marketing departments; more than 600 people scattered around the campus attended this presentation.

As with Hubbub, Forum changed dramatically based on the usage study. We were not sure how to get ongoing feedback from the audience, so we started by creating a mechanism that would chart the number of audience members pressing a Feedback button, shown in Figure 11.1. The chart moves from left to right, tracking the number of people pressing the button over time. We figured that speakers could ask audience members to press the Feedback button if they were confused, bored, and so on, and monitor the chart to adjust the talk. In practice, though, speakers used this feature to take polls. They asked questions like, "How many of you are familiar with this technology?" and watched to see how high the line went, and then asked, "How many of you are not familiar with the technology?" They would then compare the height of the two peaks, assuming the first one had not moved off the chart. Given this, we decided to change the Feedback mechanism to a two-choice poll mechanism (see Figure 11.1). Once that was in, speakers used it frequently and audiences rated it as one of the most useful features. Over time, speakers wanted to offer more than just two options, so we made it possible to configure the poll to offer multiple choices.

11.1

The first version of Forum had a generic Feedback button that generated a line graph showing the number of people pressing the button over time (upper left). Once we observed Forum in use, we found that people used it mainly to take polls, so we redesigned it as a Poll meter (lower right).

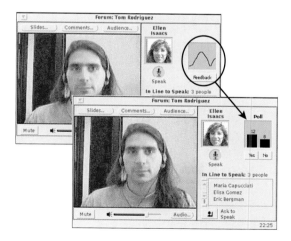

The usage study also showed that we were just plain wrong about what would be easy to use. Forum allowed users to ask voice questions (if they had a microphone), but we had to use a press-to-speak model to avoid audio echo problems. We thought about having a button on the interface to hold down with the mouse while speaking, but we believed this was too physically difficult. Instead, we decided to have users hold down the space bar on the keyboard while speaking, a much easier behavior to sustain. The problem was that no one could figure it out. Even though we put in big red letters "Press the Space Bar" on the interface when it was someone's turn to talk, people just didn't see it. When you're about to ask a question in front of a lot of people, your attention is not focused on the interface but instead on how to phrase your question. Although Alan was not a part of the Forum team, he was working at Sun at the time, and he remembers attending some of these talks. His strongest memory of this experience was hearing people shouting from their offices, "Press the space bar!" when someone in his hallway was trying to ask a question. We changed the design to include a big round button on the interface with a microphone on it; when held down, the microphone color changed to show that the user's voice was being picked up (shown in Figure 11.1). This design worked very well. No longer did the speaker have to explain how to ask a question while the embarrassed audience member fumbled with the interface. We asked those who had asked questions if they minded holding down the mouse button, and most said it wasn't a problem. (Of course it might be for those who have difficulty using a mouse, so we kept the space bar mechanism for those users.) Despite our earlier conviction, this design was clearly better.

We also discovered that we could scrap plans to include certain features. We initially offered speakers some basic support for annotating their slides (the ability to draw or type text over the slide in either of two colors and to clear the annotations, for example). We planned to offer a more complete set of drawing tools (ability to make shapes, choose more colors, erase, and so on), but it turned out that the basic support was plenty. Again, when giving a talk, speakers can't focus on fussing with annotations; they mainly want to underline or circle an item and occasionally add some text. Every now and then, they might clear the screen, but they didn't need to selectively erase. We saved a lot of time by dropping those advanced features.

This example is similar to the location feature in Hubbub. We had a strong opinion up front that people would not use the location field because it wasn't used much in other similar applications. But by watching real use, it became clear that we had been wrong. People used it and wanted more room to post information about their status. It is useful to remember these examples while in the design stage. As much as you may think you know your users and how they do their tasks, you will probably get a few things dead wrong—you just don't know which ones until you try it out.

Example 2: Shopping Web Site

In another case, Ellen was working on a shopping Web site for a Web portal. The purpose of the site was to provide a single place where people could search for products sold by a wide range of merchants. The project included more than 40 people across two organizations, including engineers, UI and graphic designers, product managers, a testing team, project managers, business development and sales representatives, and managers. It lasted about nine months. We include this example because it involved a much larger team with more clearly defined roles (which meant we had to focus as much on communicating the design to the team as on designing it), and because we did several rounds of usability testing rather than a usage study.

Understanding the Task

At the time, shopping on the Web was a new phenomenon, so we had only preliminary information about people's online shopping behavior. On the other hand, we had reams of data about how people searched on the Web in general, and some of the team members had years of experience in the merchandising field so they knew how people shopped in the real world. People on the team were encouraged to buy items from other Web sites so that we could get firsthand experience with what worked and what didn't. We also spoke with friends and colleagues about their online buying experiences, and we read some interesting articles about designing stores for comfortable shopping experiences and early reports on trust in e-commerce. Our process was informal, but we managed to accumulate a lot of good information quickly. Based on this and other information, the senior product manager wrote up a Functional Requirements Document.

Designing the UI

Once again, we designed the UI up front based on the Functional Requirements Document and our understanding of user behavior. First we worked out the structure of the site and how the user would flow from page to page when carrying out different tasks. Then we did detailed HTML mockups for each page, which we iterated as we got feedback from the rest of the team. Since this was a large project, we focused especially on communicating the design so that people in different parts of the organization would understand what we wanted to build and so that they could point out flaws as early as possible. We bought a large poster board and laid out the structure of the site, first using yellow stickies with crude representations of each page and later replacing them with scaled-down versions of the high-fidelity mockups. People were amused as we carried that board around from meeting to meeting, presenting it as often as possible, but it allowed us to collect enough input until the design solidified. Then we wrote up a UI Spec that described those behaviors that were not obvious from the mockups, and made it available for review by the engineering and testing team.

Doing Usability Testing

With this project, we needed to observe users long before we had a system for purchasing real items. Since this is the type of product that people use every now and then, usually in one sitting, usability testing was appropriate. We wanted the data to be as realistic as possible, but we were dependent on merchants to provide us with their inventory data, which would not become available until late in the process. So we worked with the business team to find a few merchants who signed on early and were willing to give us a sample of their data, even if it wasn't current. We needed enough real data to populate the pages in at least one product category so that the task of searching for items would be realistic for our test users. We found an electronics merchant willing to provide us with a large data set, so we built that portion of the site. Just having that data raised many issues about the information merchants would provide and its format, and made us realize we would have to work with them to get more information that would be meaningful to users.

Then we brought people into a lab (a room with a computer and a camera) and asked them to search for various types of electronic equipment, encouraging them to search for products they had a real interest in if possible. It wasn't as realistic as we would have liked, but we tried to make up for this by doing three rounds of testing. In the first round, the mechanism for sending the user to the merchant to make the purchase had not been implemented yet, so we focused just on searching for products. We found plenty of problems to address, including the organization of the product categories, the flow from search results pages to the individual product listings, and even the visibility of the links on the background color we had chosen. We came up with solutions and then did another round of testing to see how well our fixes worked and to test new functionality, including the process of sending people to the merchants' sites to make purchases. We found that people did not understand that they could use the site to search for products but not to buy them, so we made several changes to communicate this concept, which we tested in the next round. In the end, we had smoothed out many of the site's glitches.

These examples illustrate two more ways that we applied our approach to user-centered design. However, we have not had experience applying our approach to hardware design, for example, or to enterprisewide workflow systems, factory-floor systems, or many other types of technology. We see no reason why this process would not work, but we don't know what would need to be adjusted. If you use this approach in your project, whatever it might be, we invite you to send us e-mail telling us how it turned out. Tell us what worked, what didn't, and how you adjusted to overcome obstacles. We'd like to share this information on our Web site as we learn more (www.uidesigns.com).

Taking a Step Back

We have spent most of this book focusing on the details of the user-centered design process, working through many examples in the hopes that they would make the ideas concrete. Now it's time to step back and point out the major themes we have tried to demonstrate along the way.

1. **Technology should behave like a butler.** Technology should be designed with the idea that its goal is to support people in their activities. It has a relationship with its users, and that relationship is very much like a butler's relationship with his employer: He is there to make the employer's life easier. Butlers should be helpful and pleasant, following basic rules of politeness and common sense; they should never get in the way or impose. When designing and evaluating your technology, keep asking yourself, "How would a butler handle this?" and use that as your guide.

2. **Creating cooperative technology is not easy.** It takes a lot of effort to build cooperative technology and involves a real adjustment to the development process. It's not something you can achieve simply by deciding your system should be easy to use (or by having management decide for you). Then

again, developing technology so that it works reliably is also hard, and yet people do it (or try to do it) all the time. It isn't even especially easy for humans to cooperate with each other, even though we get to adjust our behavior to each other's in real time. So the challenge of designing technology to anticipate and accommodate users' behavior as they interact with a complex system is considerable. Give yourself time to adopt a user-centered design mentality and to learn the techniques. Each time you go through the design process, you get better, and every bit helps. We hope this book has made the goal of producing cooperative technology seem within reach.

3. **Creating cooperative technology is a highly iterative process.** No matter how much you prepare, your initial design will be a rough draft. It will change as you gather more information about the technical issues and about users' reactions to the system. Even if you have years of design experience, it's impossible to make every detail of the design smooth and intuitive to use. In every project we've done, we have been dead wrong about one or two features, and we've been surprised by a host of others that required several rounds of adjustments to get right. Even when we were "done," there were still ways we could improve the system to make it more cooperative and more polite.

   Having said that, software is still fairly brittle and takes a lot of effort to change once the system architecture has been set. So it's very important to start with a solid underlying design structure before implementation begins. In all the projects we've been involved with, we've rarely seen the underlying architecture change dramatically during development. Usually there is too much time pressure to stop everything and rework the internals. We have seen systems completely revised after a release when the first approach was so flawed that it prevented customers from doing their tasks—a demoralizing outcome after so much work. This is where experience helps. The more you design, the more likely it is that you'll get the design architecture close on the first attempt—provided you later observe people using your designs. Without that observation, you'll keep making the same mistakes.

4. **Creating cooperative technology requires balancing many trade-offs.** One of the biggest challenges of designing cooperative technology is in deciding how to trade off many competing goals. Laying out a user interface requires balancing many of the design goals described in the first section of the book. The design principles are not a step-by-step recipe; they convey

the goal, and you have to decide how to achieve them and sometimes how to balance them against each other. While developing the application, you have to balance many constraints imposed by the device, its OS, the network, and so on against your desire to provide a good user experience. Many times, you can adjust the user interface to work around engineering constraints and still achieve the same goal. As you get feedback from users, you again have to balance their needs against the cost of different solutions. We hope this book has given an idea of how to make these tradeoffs while still building cooperative technology.

5. **Creating cooperative technology requires cooperation among team members.** We have found that most conflict between designers and engineers does not stem from conflicting goals, but rather boils down to misunderstanding or not appreciating the other's constraints. We've tried to demonstrate how it pays to spend a little time explaining the effect you're each trying to achieve and the problems you're each trying to avoid. If you do, usually you can work together to find a solution you can both live with. Designers need to take the time to develop a basic understanding of the system's architecture and related technical issues so they can communicate more effectively with engineers. Engineers need to trust that user interface designers understand users' behavior better than they do even though they happen to be users too. And when you can't agree, try to accommodate the other on issues they consider critical—if you do so, they will be more inclined to accept your position when you feel strongly about a decision. And if you later observe the system in use, you'll learn whose judgment to trust in which situations the next time. Also, pick your battles. Designers shouldn't consistently push for ideal solutions that take a long time when there are workable solutions that take less time. Engineers shouldn't complain about implementing the refinements that make features easy to use—if you think that a feature is not worth the work, argue against the entire feature, not against finishing one you've partially built.

6. **Creating cooperative technology requires observing people in action.** It is impossible to design cooperative technology without observing people and understanding how they go about their tasks, before and after they use your technology. The first step is to observe people before you build your system so you can understand their goals, how they carry out their tasks, and how they think about their activities—and then design your technology around that. Once you have

something working, watch people again as they use it, starting as early as possible. It has become common practice to do usability testing to get user feedback, which is a huge improvement over the days when technology was shipped without any user input. If you intend for people to use your system repeatedly over a period of time, we highly recommend doing a usage study so you can learn how it will be used in practice under realistic conditions. It takes effort and an adjustment to the development process, but the gains are phenomenal. You can afford to do fewer features because you learn which ones people really use. And you can focus your energy on making those features easy and pleasant to use. Your product will stand out among those jam-packed with features that are frustrating to use and hard to find.

Above all else, the most important thing you need to carry out user-centered design is a willingness by the team to adjust its process to focus on activities critical to improving the user experience. Far more than time pressure or business constraints, the biggest obstacle we've seen to user-centered design is resistance by key team members to making the user experience a primary concern instead of an afterthought. If you decide it is important, you will find a way to work together to make sure that you understand your users, to build the architecture to support your well-defined user interface, and to iterate the design as you observe people using your technology to do their tasks. And if you can do that, you can design technology that behaves like a butler, not like a brute.

APPENDIXES

A
Guidelines

Respect Physical Effort

Design Guideline: Agonize over every click you ask of your user. Every click you remove improves the feature, saves your user time and effort, and makes your technology more pleasant to use. Be especially sparing with "complex clicks," such as menus, drag-and-drop, scrolling, and keyboard-mouse combinations.

Design Guideline: If the effort required to implement a feature is significantly lower than the cumulative effort saved by your customers, build it. Apply extra implementation effort to smoothing out flow breaks in features that many customers encounter frequently.

Design Guideline: If you have an Undo feature, there is no need to break the users' flow to ask them whether they really want the program to do what they just asked it to do.

Design Guideline: Engineers are trained to think of edge cases, while interaction designers think of common cases. When designing an interface, make the features that most people encounter most of the time as smooth to use as possible, even if it means requiring more effort for infrequent tasks. It is much better to bother few people rarely with a big effort than to bother most people frequently with a medium effort.

Design Guideline: Sometimes to reduce clicks, you have to revise related features to make those clicks unnecessary. Determine the underlying need for a click and be creative about removing the click while supporting the need.

Design Guideline: Remember everything users do to adjust the application. The next time they come back, it should be just as they left it. This includes moving or resizing windows, choosing tabs, scrolling, moving toolbars, sorting data, reordering items, and so on.

Design Guideline: It is surprisingly common for people to take the same action many times in a short time frame. When designing a task, consider what it would be like to carry it out several times in a row. What might seem okay to do once might start to feel burdensome if you had to do it repeatedly.

Design Guideline: If you ask people to give you information, remember it. If they update their information, remember it. If you ask them to fill out forms that include information they've previously given you, fill in those fields with the information you have.

Design Guideline: Avoid asking the user to shift hand position. If you have more than one input device, make it possible to do each task without switching between input mechanisms.

Respect Mental Effort

Design Guideline: Agonize over every visual element on the screen. The more there are, the fewer that get noticed. Make sure every visual element on the main screen is worthy of prime real estate. Even hidden elements must pull their weight because each one adds complexity.

Design Guideline: Determine the most common user tasks and make sure they are visible and easily accessible. Hide less common tasks that clutter the screen and make it hard to find the common tasks.

Design Guideline: Always acknowledge the user's request and, if you can't comply immediately, let them know what you're up to and how much longer it will take.

Design Guideline: If a command can't be carried out quickly, allow users to interrupt.

Design Guideline: Sounds are effective for letting people know when something has occurred or that a task is in progress. It is good to combine sounds with visual cues to reinforce the information and to support those with visual or hearing impairments.

Design Guideline: Treat "We'll make it a Preference" as a copout. The default behavior *is* the application's behavior, since few people ever modify Preferences that affect the *behavior* of the application. Use Preferences mainly to allow people to customize the application's *appearance*.

Design Guideline: Use platform conventions. Violating a convention confuses people about when the convention applies, so they stop using it across all applications, including yours.

Design Guideline: Look for widgetless features—features that do just what you need when you need it, without any visible representation on the screen. But beware of becoming *too* helpful. It's worse to offer help that people don't want than it is to not offer a pleasant surprise.

Be Helpful

Design Guideline: If you have expectations of the user, let them know up front rather than surprising them later. Indicate which information is required, what format you're expecting, and so on. Try to prevent errors wherever possible.

Design Guideline: If you have a multistep process, give users relevant information about the procedure before they start.

Design Guideline: Beware pop-ups with a single option (usually an OK button), especially those the user did not request. If there's a problem, handle it yourself or offer some help—don't just inform people. If you want to provide status information, don't use a single-option pop-up unless it's urgent; instead, put a message in the status area.

Design Guideline: Don't bother the user with problems you can solve yourself. If you can figure out the problem well enough to tell the user how to solve it, try to solve it yourself.

Design Guideline: If you find yourself wanting to ask the user what they meant (that is, if you're tempted to put up options before you complete the task), redesign the feature to provide an unambiguous command. Decide what most people want most of the time, and let them do that with few clicks. Then let the few choose a different command if they want something else.

Design Guideline: Develop a set of conventions and use them throughout the application. You've succeeded if your users can predict how to use a new feature based on other features' behavior.

Design Guideline: Don't offer options that are not available. Instead of surprising people with a "That's not available" message, gray out the option or don't present it. Don't mislead people.

Design Guideline: Ask for information only if and when you will use it (and then remember it). Never collect and then ignore sensitive information.

Design Guideline: Use everyday language. Don't assume people know the jargon of your industry or the terminology specific to your application.

Design Guideline: If something goes wrong, assume it's your design or implementation error and take responsibility. Write your error messages with humility, not blame.

Design Guideline: If you give options or ask questions, explain the consequences of the choices.

Design Guideline: Avoid at all costs blocking pop-ups that prevent people from using the rest of the application before handling a dialog box or responding to an error message. Often people need to look at something else in the application to make their choice. Even if you can't imagine why they would need to look elsewhere, don't prevent them from doing so.

Design Guideline: Avoid labeling buttons with generic terms such as "Yes," "No," or "OK," which force people to read the text carefully every time. Instead, label them with the action that will take place, such as "Search," "Add," or "Print."

Design Guideline: Do a sanity check on all the language in your application. Get someone else to look over all the text and tell you when you're not making sense.

Requirements Gathering

Requirements Guideline: When conceiving of a new technology, it is better to build something that supports an observed unmet need than it is to build something because you can and then hope people have the need it fills.

Requirements Guideline: To understand the requirements for your technology, observe people doing the activity you want to support and talk with them about their experiences. Stay open to what you see; don't simply look for confirmation of your initial ideas.

Requirements Guideline: Find out whether similar products exist. If they do, become familiar with them and how people use them. Try to understand how people think about the activity and what tasks they do to carry out their goals. Look for tasks that work well and areas that could be improved. Where possible, read reports about the underlying need for the technology and how people are using existing technology that supports it.

Requirements Guideline: When considering product requirements, focus on users' tasks, not just the features you want to provide. Consider developing use scenarios that characterize users' tasks, as well as personas that describe the prototypical people you expect to use the product.

Requirements Guideline: The Functional Requirements Document lists the functions the system should perform. It should be generated primarily from the tasks you want users to be able to accomplish with the system. Some tasks will be supported by multiple functions, and some functions may support multiple tasks, so keep track of which functions support which tasks.

Requirements Guideline: The Functional Requirements Document should list items in terms of requirements, independent of how they are designed or implemented. This allows the designer and the engineer the freedom to fulfill those requirements in the best way possible given other design and engineering constraints.

Requirements Guideline: The requirements will change during the development process as you learn more about implementation constraints and as you observe people using the system. You will discover that some requirements are not as important as you thought, others are more important, and some are too costly to provide given their value.

Requirements Guideline: Divide your requirements into priority categories such as Core, Important, and Nice to Have, and get agreement on those priorities from the entire team. Be conservative as you assign categories. You should have strong evidence for each feature's necessity, so when in doubt, choose the lower priority. If the feature is really needed, you will find out during the usage study or usability testing.

Requirements Guideline: The Core requirements are the minimum features needed to use the system. This category should include the features with which users can start to try out the most basic aspects of the system, not the full set of useful features. The fewer items you put in the Core list, the more your development will be driven by real usage data rather than your perceptions of what users need or how they behave.

Requirements Guideline: The Important requirements category includes the minimal set of features needed to ship the application. Keep this list as small as possible so you have time to polish each feature, and so you can add items that usage feedback indicates are needed. The Important list will change during development, but it is helpful for the team to agree up front on which features are considered necessary to ship.

Requirements Guideline: The Nice to Have requirements should include all the great ideas that could make the technology more interesting but are not required to ship. Most of them will not be included in the first release, but they may become important later as you get data from users.

Requirements Guideline: Users ask for features the way kids ask for candy. Don't be tempted to add too many requirements to your higher priority categories.

Design Guideline: To develop cooperative technology, you must design the user interface first and then design the architecture to support that user experience. If the engineers don't know how the system should behave up front, they unwittingly make design decisions that preclude satisfying basic user needs. If they have UI information up front, they can balance those constraints against all the other engineering constraints.

Scheduling Guideline: Don't try to estimate schedules based on the Functional Requirements. Until you know the details of the design and architecture, these estimates will be wildly optimistic. If you then commit to deadlines based on those estimates, you set yourself up to rush through the features and omit the work needed to make them easy to use. It will take only a little while longer to design the UI and architecture, so wait until you have that information.

Design Guideline: When designing a UI, focus mainly on providing the best possible user experience, forgetting all but the most basic platform constraints. Be willing to explore ideas that may be hard to implement; you may come up with great ideas that can be implemented another way. At this stage, your goal is to figure out how to cooperate with the user. Later, you can adjust the design to accommodate engineering issues.

UI Structure

Design Guideline: It's very important to write a User Interface Spec that includes mockups of how the system should look as well as a written description of how it should behave. The UI Spec should be easy for the team to use. The more accessible it is, the more likely it is that the team will build the system as it was designed.

Design Guideline: Keep the UI Spec updated as the design changes so that everyone on the team knows how each feature is supposed to behave. If used well, the UI Spec can help the team stay coordinated. It not only helps the engineers know what to build, but also helps the business team communicate the concept to interested parties, the testing team find features not implemented as designed, and the documentation team get started on manuals.

Design Guideline: To determine the priorities of the tasks for the user interface, divide the tasks into those done (a) frequently by many, (b) frequently by few, (c) occasionally by many, and (d) occasionally by few. These categories will not only tell you which features you should concentrate on making smooth and easy to accomplish, but will also suggest where they should be placed in the interface and how they should be designed.

Design Guideline: Tasks done frequently should require fewer clicks than those done occasionally; tasks done by many people should be easier to find than those done by few. Therefore, Frequent by Many tasks should be visible and take few clicks; Frequent by Few tasks should take few clicks but may be a little harder to find; Occasional by Many tasks should be easy to find but may take more clicks; and Occasional by Few tasks should be hidden and may take more clicks.

Design Guideline: You can "reverse design" an application to figure out which tasks were placed in which Frequency by Commonality category. Make sure your design reflects the priorities you set out to achieve.

Design Guideline: The main screen is the place to put Frequent by Many tasks, and to offer at least the first step in Occasional by Many tasks. Frequent by Few tasks can be placed on another screen, but they should be easy to access, perhaps with shortcuts. Occasional by Few tasks should not be on the main screen.

Design Guideline: In your first design pass, try to include all features, including Nice to Have ones, so that you can make sure your design will accommodate a range of features. Then pull out the Nice to Have features to make sure the design still works without them.

Design Guideline: Create a Task Flow Diagram that shows the set of screens and the user's path through the screens for each task. As with engineering architectures, try to make the design architecture as clean and simple as possible.

UI Layout

Design Guideline: Try to use visual cues that are easy to interpret without conscious thought. For example, bold and larger type convey more importance, motion conveys activity, fading an item out conveys that it went away or was deleted.

Design Guideline: Try to use different types of visual cues (font, color, position, borders, text, icons, and so on) so that you don't overload one type with too much information.

Design Guideline: Use icons alone if people can understand their meaning without a label or if the information represented is not critical and doesn't have to be interpreted immediately. If people need to interpret an icon quickly, combine it with a label. If you plan to internationalize the interface, keep in mind that labels will probably get longer in other languages, and you may have to modify icons if there are culture-specific references.

Design Guideline: Information is easier to comprehend if it's laid out in rows and columns. A grid structure helps organize the information, and it helps people to focus on certain pieces of information while ignoring others.

Design Guideline: Try to keep menus and menu items to a minimum. As common as they are, people often don't hunt around in them for features.

Design Guideline: When using color, try to make color redundant with some other cue (such as size, position, or font). Some people have trouble distinguishing certain colors, so make sure they can still use all the important features of your application.

Design Guideline: On desktop computers, use footers to provide dynamic status information. Footers are useful because people don't notice them when all is well, but they often find them when something is wrong and/or they're looking for an explanation of what's happening or has just happened.

Design Guideline: After laying out the UI, walk through each of the tasks using the mock-ups. Look for tasks with too many clicks, no visible cues, awkward flow, and so on. Walk through the clean version of each task, and then think of common nonstandard scenarios and things that might go wrong. As you find problems, adjust the design and walk through the tasks again. This technique can help you find problems very early, when it's fast and cheap to fix them.

Architecture

Engineering Guideline: When designing an architecture, start with the behavior specified in the UI Spec and build the system to support it.

Engineering Guideline: If there are technical reasons not to support the UI as specified, find out which behavior is critical to the user experience and then adjust the architecture and UI to support it. You may need to adjust the way that the UI deals with noncritical behaviors to handle the technical constraints.

Engineering Guideline: Consider UI requirements along with system constraints when making technical decisions.

Engineering Guideline: Remember to check the UI Spec often so that you don't base your technical decisions on implicit engineering assumptions about how a feature should behave. Understand the specified behavior first and then design the system to support it.

Project Management

Project Management Guideline: Implement features in priority order, building Core features first, so you can try out the system with users as soon as possible. Prioritizing will help you avoid working on features that turn out not to be needed, giving you more time to work on those that are.

Project Management Guideline: Estimate the schedule based on detailed descriptions of each feature. Have each person estimate the time it will take to complete their components, and then double their estimates to account for inevitable inaccuracies.

Project Management Guideline: The final schedule estimate should be triple the cumulative estimate for all the tasks. Double the estimate to account for estimate inaccuracies, and then add the same amount again for making ease-of-use adjustments.

Project Management Guideline: Treat ease-of-use improvements as features in the Feature List or as ease-of-use bugs in the bug database. Either way, you should plan time to fix them before moving on to new features, just as you should fix functionality bugs before moving on. Doing so ensures that whatever you ship will behave cooperatively, even if it has fewer features than its competitors.

Designer-Engineer Collaboration

Collaboration Guideline: When rare but possible cases arise, remember that you don't have to design for those scenarios, you just need to handle them gracefully.

Collaboration Guideline: When conflicts emerge between design and engineering goals, get concrete and specific about your concerns. Try to clarify the crux of the engineering concern and the key elements of the user experience. Don't assume you're imagining the same constraints on the feature. And don't assume the feature has to be implemented literally as first designed. Instead, work together to find an alternative design that is acceptable from both perspectives.

Collaboration Guideline: Designers should take time to learn the basics of the technical issues affecting their system so that they can understand the engineering constraints and communicate user needs more effectively. Engineers should assume that the designer knows more about user behavior than they do, even though they are users too.

Collaboration Guideline: If the effort required to implement a feature outweighs the value it provides the user, redesign it so that it's easier to implement or don't offer it.

Collaboration Guideline: Time spent on one feature is time not spent on another. Spend your time on the features that you're confident will add the most value for users.

Collaboration Guideline: If you're not sure of the value of a feature, build a simple version of it and find out from usage testing whether a more complex version is needed.

Collaboration Guideline: People like to work on things they believe will be used. Once you have real usage data indicating that a feature is needed, it's much easier to reach agreement that the effort is justified.

Collaboration Guideline: Sometimes it's worth providing an acceptable if not ideal user experience to keep the project moving and to meet deadlines.

Collaboration Guideline: Sometimes you just have to do boring work to make features operate smoothly. Get it over with before moving on to the next feature rather than putting it off until the end.

Collaboration Guideline: When a UI issue arises that isn't covered in the UI Spec, work together to come up with a solution. Engineers shouldn't just do whatever's easiest, and designers should be receptive to engineers' suggestions.

Collaboration Guideline: If you want to change a design after implementation has begun, you should be reasonably sure that the usability improvement is worth the additional estimated effort. If not, wait until you have evidence from usage data that the change is necessary. (If you decide it's worth it, it helps to bribe engineers with food and drinks.)

Collaboration Guideline: Designers and engineers should check in with each other frequently. Doing so will allow you to work around implementation issues as they arise while avoiding ease-of-use problems.

Collaboration Guideline: The user experience encompasses more than just the UI widgets and how they behave. Technical concerns such as performance, stability, and resource usage affect the user if they are not managed well. Try to handle them in a way that is invisible to the user.

Development

Development Guideline: When using your own technology, notice when your flow is broken, even for a split second. Pop out of your task to figure out what caused the break and write it down before moving on. You might have to accumulate several related problems before you can figure out how to improve the design.

Development Guideline: If you find ease-of-use problems that are complicated to fix properly, don't just file a bug report and move on. Find a way to adjust the UI that is relatively easy to implement, in case you never find a better solution or the time to fix the problem.

Development Guideline: Using your own technology can help you find problems, but it will not tell you whether your customer will find the technology easy to use. You simply know too much about the design to tell whether others will understand it.

Usage Studies

Usage Study Guideline: It is critical to start usage studies *very early,* when you have just enough functionality working to make it possible to do a basic set of meaningful tasks. Give people the system to use for just those tasks in their real settings, and then continue to build the rest of the system, incorporating feedback as you go. Each new "release" should include many revisions of existing features and a few new features until you stop adding new features and have polished all the existing ones.

Usage Study Guideline: Usability testing is more effective for studying technology people use on an occasional basis for tasks they complete in one session. Usage studies are more effective for studying technology that people use on a regular basis to complete tasks that take time and that evolve over time.

Usage Study Guideline: The usage tester must be (a) trained in observational techniques, (b) open-minded and eager to find problems rather than trying to defend the system, and ideally, (c) deeply knowledgeable about the system so they can decipher the underlying causes of problems.

Usage Study Guideline: Take care to protect study participants' privacy. Make sure that they understand what data you will collect and how the information will be used before agreeing to participate. If you later want to use the data for another purpose, go back and get their consent.

Usage Study Guideline: Before giving out the technology, include a mechanism to log all important user actions. This information is critical for learning which features people use, how often, and in what ways. There is no other good way to collect this information accurately.

Usage Study Guideline: Log information is ideal for learning how frequently people use certain features and in what combination. It also reveals scenarios of use that you may not have imagined, and it can help you decide to remove features or not expand on them if they are rarely being used.

Usage Study Guideline: Formal observations allow you to understand the context in which people use the technology, giving you a rich understanding of how people use the system for real tasks. They are especially helpful for finding subtle ways in which the design causes important usage problems.

Usage Study Guideline: Try to chat with participants and observe their use informally, if possible. You may uncover problems, suggestions, or interesting new uses. It's helpful to check in with people informally to follow up on data from other sources, such as logs or surveys.

Usage Study Guideline: Surveys can give you a systematic overview of participants' opinions of each feature, as well as their complaints and suggestions. It's good to follow up surveys with other information-gathering techniques to get a deeper understanding of any issues.

Usage Study Guideline: Interviews allow you to get detailed information about people's attitudes and opinions of the system after they've used it for a while, which you may not be able to find out any other way. You can also do quick interviews on a single topic to find out how people are reacting to new features or feature redesigns.

Usage Study Guideline: Make it easy for participants to send you comments and suggestions. If they send you feature ideas, your job is to find out the problem they're trying to solve. Users can give you great insights into problems, but they are not designers. You are in a better position to figure out how to create a solution that fits with the rest of the design.

Usage Study Guideline: You're done with a usage study when you have gone through the list of Core and Important requirements and either checked off every item or explained why it is not needed. If people are able to use the system easily and smoothly to do a useful range of activities, you can ship. You will probably want to add or improve some features, but you can do that in the next release.

Usage Study Guideline: Usage studies do not have to extend the development cycle; instead, they allow you to do fewer features well, with confidence that you have included the features people really use. They do require more time and energy from the designer and a usage study tester, but that effort keeps the rest of the team focused on the tasks that matter most to users.

B

Recommended Readings

You can't possibly cover everything about user interface design in one book, and if you did, no one would read it. Here are some books and articles we recommend that go into more detail about different aspects of design and engineering. Our bias is toward readable, practical books rather than comprehensive textbooks that teach the ideal goal. There are other books we wish we had read by now, and more are always being written. We'll keep trying to keep up, and as we find new books to recommend, we'll update our Web site (www.uidesigns.com).

The Problem

Norman, Donald A. *The Design of Everyday Things.* Doubleday & Company, 1990.

Over ten years old, this book still is an excellent summary of why technology is hard to use and how it could be better. It is chock-full of good examples. We recommend it as a good overview of the problem.

Cooper, Alan. *The Inmates Are Running the Asylum: Why High-Tech Products Drive Us Crazy and How to Restore the Sanity.* Sams Publishing, 1999.

The first half of this book makes a good case for building cooperative software and the second half describes techniques for doing so, including some excellent examples. The attitude toward engineers is a little too harsh for our tastes, however.

Usability

Nielsen, Jakob. *Usability Engineering.* Morgan Kaufmann, 1993.

This book has a very nice overview of usability principles and the user-centered design process, incorporating many findings from studies and anecdotes from real experiences. It has a very good summary of design principles, which Nielsen calls Usability Heuristics, and summarizes usability testing well. The book also describes heuristic evaluations and their effectiveness.

Understanding Users' Needs

Hackos, JoAnn T. & Redish, Janice C. *User and Task Analysis for Interface Design.* John Wiley & Sons, 1998.

This is a complete and interesting book explaining the importance of understanding users, how to conduct site visits, and how to analyze and use that information to design an interface. The authors include many short but useful examples from their real experiences. The book is a bit long, but it's written in a very readable style.

Beyer, Hugh & Holtzblatt, Karen. *Contextual Design: Defining Customer-Centered Systems.* Morgan Kaufmann, 1997.

This book provides a nicely written case for observing customers in context with a detailed description of how to do so. The book describes how to get from observations of users' behavior to a UI structure that supports their tasks. We like the authors' sensibilities about interpreting human behavior and the design process.

Kelley, Tom. *The Art of Innovation: Lessons in Creativity from Ideo, America's Leading Design Firm.* Doubleday, 2001.

In this book, Kelley gives his inspiring description of how Ideo fosters the creative process. The book explains how they get their ideas for technology solutions—mainly by observing people in action, accumulating a bag of design tricks, and arranging their organization to keep people's creative juices flowing.

Desktop Software Design

Johnson, Jeff. *GUI Bloopers: Don'ts and Do's for Software Developers and Web Designers.* Morgan Kaufmann, 2000.

This book has an impressive collection of specific do's and don'ts on a broad range of user interface issues. It focuses mainly on desktop software but it has a chapter on Web design, and many of the concepts apply across multiple platforms. If you have a question about how to handle a UI issue, it's hard to imagine not finding some relevant advice in this book.

Spolsky, Joel. *User Interface Design for Programmers.* APress L. P., 2001.

This is a short rant about user interface design from an engineer's perspective, focusing mainly on desktop software. Spolsky is very perceptive, and many of his points are dead on (that is, we agree with him). We found the style entertaining, but others might find it over-the-top.

Web Design

Krug, Steve. *Don't Make Me Think: A Common Sense Approach to Web Usability.* New Riders Publishing, 2000.

This is a short, insightful, and highly readable book about Web design. Some of the design principles also apply to other technologies (as does the "Don't make me think" rule). This book is fun to read and covers the bulk of what you need to know to create competent Web pages. It also includes a section on the basics of running a usability test.

Nielsen, Jakob. *Designing Web Usability: The Practice of Simplicity.* New Riders Publishing, 1999.

In this book, Nielsen offers his opinionated, richly detailed description of good and bad practices when designing Web sites, with hundreds of examples. The book focuses mainly on page design and site design, and not as much on supporting users' tasks as they move through a site.

Design for Devices

Bergman, Eric. *Information Appliances and Beyond: Interaction Design for Consumer Products*. Morgan Kaufmann, 2000.

This is a collection of articles from UI practitioners about their experiences designing various consumer products, including cell phones, PDAs, car navigation systems, toys, and games. We especially recommend Bergman's interview with Rob Haitani of Palm.

Graphic/Visual Design

Mullet, Kevin & Sano, Darrell. *Designing Visual Interfaces: Communication Oriented Techniques*. Sun Microsystems, Incorporated, and Prentice Hall PTR, 1994.

This excellent book shows how graphic design for user interfaces is about communicating visually. It includes many examples of "before and after" designs so you can see what's better about a good design and learn how to improve a bad design. The explanations are clear and easy to follow.

Development Process

McConnell, Steve. *Rapid Development: Taming Wild Software Schedules*. Microsoft Press, 1996.

This is a top-notch book on software development that many people consider required reading for software managers or project leads. We especially like the list of 36 "classic mistakes" at the beginning of the book. Unfortunately, the book has little to say about building in a good user experience, but we recommend it on its own terms.

Maguire, Steve. *Debugging the Development Process: Practical Strategies for Staying Focused, Hitting Ship Dates, and Building Solid Teams*. Microsoft Press, 1998.

This book has another excellent account of good software engineering practices. It's relatively short and easy reading and is filled with good advice. Again, though, the role of user interface design is woefully ignored.

Networking

> Stevens, Richard W. *Unix Network Programming, Networking APIs: Sockets and XTI*. Prentice Hall, 1998.

If you want to understand network programming with sockets and dig into the details of TCP and UDP, this is the book. It covers the APIs and then shows you what happens under the hood. Don't hesitate to pick up any of Stevens's books.

Usability Testing

> Dumas, Joseph S. & Redish, Janice C. *A Practical Guide to Usability Testing*. Intellect Books, 1999.

The title of this book is right on—it is a practical, no-nonsense guide to usability testing, defined broadly to include many forms of evaluating usability. Engineers might especially like this book because it bases many of its claims on research findings and explains how the authors reached their conclusions.

> Rubin, Jeffrey. *Handbook of Usability Testing: How to Plan, Design, and Conduct Effective Tests*. John Wiley & Sons, 1994.

This is a detailed description of all facets of conducting a usability test in an easy-to-read style. Rubin does a nice job of explaining the advantages and disadvantages of different techniques.

Also see the section on usability testing in Steve Krug's *Don't Make Me Think* (see the "Web Design" section in this appendix), and Jakob Nielsen's description in *Usability Engineering* (see the "Usability" section).

Usage Studies

Not much is written about the type of usage testing we recommend. Here are some articles about usage studies we conducted on other systems and how they affected the design.

Isaacs, E., Morris, T., and Rodriguez, T.K., 1994, "A Forum for Supporting Interactive Presentations to Distributed Audiences," *Proceedings of the Conference on Computer-Supported Cooperative Work*. ACM Press, 405-416. Available from http:/www.uidesigns.com/bothsides/refs/forum/.

This paper describes a usage study of Forum, the video-to-the-desktop presentation tool described briefly in Chapter 11. During the study, we conducted 26 talks with the system, each time studying how it was used and iterating the design based on that feedback.

Tang, J.C., Isaacs, E., and Rua, M., 1994, "Supporting Distributed Groups with a Montage of Lightweight Images," *Proceedings of the Conference on Computer-Supported Cooperative Work*. ACM Press, 23-34. Available from http://www.uidesigns.com/bothsides/refs/montage/.

This paper describes a usage study of Montage, a desktop video conference system designed for lightweight interaction. During the study, we gave the system to a team of 10 people and studied their use of the system over a span of three months.

Other

Penman, Sharon Kay. *The Sunne in Splendour*. Ballantine Books, 1990.

This historical novel is about 15th-century England and it has nothing to do with designing technology, but it's one of our all-time favorite books. We also loved her Wales trilogy.

Index

V – Z